Samuel Beckett and Experimental Psychology

Historicizing Modernism

Series Editors

Matthew Feldman, Professorial Fellow, Norwegian Study Centre, University of York; and Erik Tonning, Professor of British Literature and Culture, University of Bergen, Norway

Assistant Editor: David Tucker, Associate Lecturer, Goldsmiths College, University of London, UK

Editorial Board

Professor Chris Ackerley, Department of English, University of Otago, New Zealand; Professor Ron Bush, St. John's College, University of Oxford, UK; Dr Finn Fordham, Department of English, Royal Holloway, UK; Professor Steven Matthews, Department of English, University of Reading, UK; Dr Mark Nixon, Department of English, University of Reading, UK; Professor Shane Weller, Reader in Comparative Literature, University of Kent, UK; and Professor Janet Wilson, University of Northampton, UK.

Historicizing Modernism challenges traditional literary interpretations by taking an empirical approach to modernist writing: a direct response to new documentary sources made available over the last decade.

Informed by archival research, and working beyond the usual European/American avant-garde 1900-45 parameters, this series reassesses established readings of modernist writers by developing fresh views of intellectual contexts and working methods.

Series Titles:

Arun Kolatkar and Literary Modernism in India, Laetitia Zecchini
British Literature and Classical Music, David Deutsch
Broadcasting in the Modernist Era, Matthew Feldman, Henry Mead and Erik Tonning
Charles Henri Ford, Alexander Howard
Chicago and the Making of American Modernism, Michelle E. Moore
Ezra Pound's Adams Cantos, David Ten Eyck
Ezra Pound's Eriugena, Mark Byron
Great War Modernisms and The New Age Magazine, Paul Jackson
James Joyce and Absolute Music, Michelle Witen
James Joyce and Catholicism, Chrissie van Mierlo
John Kasper and Ezra Pound, Alec Marsh

Katherine Mansfield and Literary Modernism, Edited by Janet Wilson, Gerri Kimber and Susan Reid
Late Modernism and the English Intelligencer, Alex Latter
The Life and Work of Thomas MacGreevy, Susan Schreibman
Literary Impressionism, Rebecca Bowler
Modern Manuscripts, Dirk Van Hulle
Modernism at the Microphone, Melissa Dinsman
Modernist Lives, Claire Battershill
The Politics of 1930s British Literature, Natasha Periyan
Reading Mina Loy's Autobiographies, Sandeep Parmar
Reframing Yeats, Charles Ivan Armstrong
Samuel Beckett and Arnold Geulincx, David Tucker
Samuel Beckett and the Bible, Iain Bailey
Samuel Beckett and Cinema, Anthony Paraskeva
Samuel Beckett's 'More Pricks than Kicks', John Pilling
T. E. Hulme and the Ideological Politics of Early Modernism, Henry Mead
Virginia Woolf's Late Cultural Criticism, Alice Wood
Christian Modernism in an Age of Totalitarianism, Jonas Kurlberg

Upcoming titles
Samuel Beckett and Science, Chris Ackerley
Samuel Beckett's German Diaries 1936-1937, Mark Nixon

Samuel Beckett and Experimental Psychology

Perception, Attention, Imagery

Joshua Powell

BLOOMSBURY ACADEMIC
LONDON • NEW YORK • OXFORD • NEW DELHI • SYDNEY

BLOOMSBURY ACADEMIC
Bloomsbury Publishing Plc
50 Bedford Square, London, WC1B 3DP, UK
1385 Broadway, New York, NY 10018, USA

BLOOMSBURY, BLOOMSBURY ACADEMIC and the Diana logo are trademarks
of Bloomsbury Publishing Plc

First published in Great Britain 2020

Copyright © Joshua Powell, 2020

Joshua Powell has asserted his right under the Copyright, Designs and
Patents Act, 1988, to be identified as Author of this work.

For legal purposes the Acknowledgements on p. viii constitute an extension
of this copyright page.

Cover design: Eleanor Rose and Jade Barnett

All rights reserved. No part of this publication may be reproduced or transmitted in any form
or by any means, electronic or mechanical, including photocopying, recording, or any information
storage or retrieval system, without prior permission in writing from the publishers.

Bloomsbury Publishing Plc does not have any control over, or responsibility for, any
third-party websites referred to or in this book. All internet addresses given in this book were
correct at the time of going to press. The author and publisher regret any inconvenience
caused if addresses have changed or sites have ceased to exist, but can accept no responsibility
for any such changes.

A catalogue record for this book is available from the British Library.

Library of Congress Cataloging-in-Publication Data
Names: Powell, Joshua, author.
Title: Samuel Beckett and Experimental Psychology: Perception, Attention, Imagery / Joshua Powell.
Description: London; New York: Bloomsbury Academic, 2020. | Series: Historicizing modernism |
Includes bibliographical references and index.
Identifiers: LCCN 2019039806 (print) | LCCN 2019039807 (ebook) | ISBN 9781350091726 (hardback) |
ISBN 9781350091733 (ebook) | ISBN 9781350091740 (epub)
Subjects: LCSH: Beckett, Samuel, 1906–1989–Knowledge–Psychology. | Beckett, Samuel, 1906–1989–
Aesthetics. | Psychology in literature. | Mind and body in literature. | Perception in literature. |
Imagery (Psychology) in literature. | Psychology and literature–History–20th century.
Classification: LCC PR6003.E282 Z78836 2020 (print) | LCC PR6003.E282 (ebook) |
DDC 848/.91409–dc23
LC record available at https://lccn.loc.gov/2019039806
LC ebook record available at https://lccn.loc.gov/2019039807

ISBN: HB: 978-1-3500-9172-6
ePDF: 978-1-3500-9173-3
eBook: 978-1-3500-9174-0

Series: Historicizing Modernism

Typeset by Deanta Global Publishing Services, Chennai, India

To find out more about our authors and books visit www.bloomsbury.com and
sign up for our newsletters.

Contents

Acknowledgements		viii
Series editor's preface		ix
Introduction: Literary experiments and the work of Samuel Beckett		1
1	Experimental transitions	21
2	Attention and speech perception in *Not I*	45
3	Face reading and attentional management in *That Time*	73
4	Inattention in *Footfalls*	99
5	Beckett and the mental image	127
6	Percept and image in *Nohow On*	151
Conclusion: Experimental Beckett		179
Notes		183
Bibliography		192
Index		205

Acknowledgements

More people than I can name have offered help and encouragement during the time in which this book has been written. I will try to name as many as I can, but I will inevitably omit some who have contributed significantly to this work. Apologies go to them.

This project was made appreciably more exciting and far-reaching by Laura Salisbury, whose PhD supervision encouraged and challenged my thinking. I am indebted to Stephen Monsell, my secondary supervisor, for his insights into the discipline of experimental psychology, as well as his fresh perspectives on my work. Thanks go to my PhD examiners, Ulrika Maude and John Bolin, who encouraged me to turn my PhD thesis into a book and offered invaluable advice on this process. And to Matthew Feldman and everyone at Bloomsbury Academic for helping to bring the book to the point of publication.

At the University of Exeter, Vike Martina Plock and Chris Campbell gave some thoughtful advice which helped me define the scope of the project more clearly, so many thanks go to them. I would like to thank Mark Nixon, Karin Lesnik-Oberstein, David Brauner and Conor Carville of the University of Reading, whose teaching at undergraduate and MA inspired many of the ideas that I have tried to develop in this monograph. A number of my colleagues at Cardiff University offered invaluable help and guidance when I was in the process of completing the manuscript. In particular, I would like to thank Alix Beeston, Josh Robinson, Josie Cray and Marine Furet, all of whom made comments that changed Chapter 1 for the better.

Many thanks also go to Hannah Little for inspiration, companionship and proofreading. And, last but definitely not least, my parents for their incredible support, and for encouraging me to pursue the things that I find most fulfilling.

A note on permissions: parts of Chapter 2 have previously appeared in the *Journal of Beckett Studies* 26 (2) and parts of Chapter 3 have previously appeared in *Critical Survey* 27 (1) and *Samuel Beckett Today Aujourd'hui* 30 (2).

The third-party copyrighted material displayed in the pages of this book is done so on the basis of fair dealing for the purposes of criticism and review.

Series editor's preface

This book series is devoted to the analysis of late-nineteenth-to twentieth-century literary modernism within its historical contexts. *Historicizing Modernism* therefore stresses empirical accuracy and the value of primary sources (such as letters, diaries, notes, drafts, marginalia or other archival materials) in developing monographs and edited collections on modernist literature. This may take a number of forms, such as manuscript study and genetic criticism, documenting interrelated historical contexts and ideas, and exploring biographical information. To date, no book series has fully laid claim to this interdisciplinary, source-based territory for modern literature. While the series addresses itself to a range of key authors, it also highlights the importance of non-canonical writers with a view to establishing broader intellectual genealogies of modernism. Furthermore, while the series is weighted towards the English-speaking world, studies of non-Anglophone modernists whose writings are open to fresh historical exploration are also included.

A key aim of the series is to reach beyond the familiar rhetoric of intellectual and artistic 'autonomy' employed by many modernists and their critical commentators. Such rhetorical moves can and should themselves be historically situated and reintegrated into the complex continuum of individual literary practices. It is our intent that the series' emphasis upon the contested self-definitions of modernist writers, thinkers and critics may, in turn, prompt various reconsiderations of the boundaries delimiting the concept 'modernism' itself. Indeed, the concept of 'historicizing' is itself debated across its volumes, and the series by no means discourages more theoretically informed approaches. On the contrary, the editors hope that the historical specificity encouraged by *Historicizing Modernism* may inspire a range of fundamental critiques along the way.

Matthew Feldman
Erik Tonning

Introduction: Literary experiments and the work of Samuel Beckett

In the *Routledge Companion to Experimental Literature*, the literary experiment is defined as largely separate from the scientific experiment. The editors suggest that in the volume 'the modifier *experimental* is used more or less interchangeably with *avant-garde* and sometimes *innovative*' (Bray, Gibbons and McHale 2012: 1, emphasis in original). The difference in these modifiers, for the editors, is a matter of connotations. The term 'avant-garde' has been 'allied with political radicalism', whereas 'experimental has scientific connotations' (1–2). The authors argue that 'the language of *experiment* is a relative novelty in literary discourse', suggesting that the term was first adopted as a descriptor of literary innovation at the end of the nineteenth century, but was embraced more fully in the early twentieth (2, emphasis in original). It is due to the use of the term in this period, they argue, that 'we continue to regard unconventional, cutting-edge literature as "experimental"' (2). From this perspective, literary experiments were going on long before the 'experimental' tag was applied to them; a new modifier was merely applied to an old process. The editors cite the eighteenth-century novel as a literary innovation that, in hindsight, 'we would surely be disposed to call "experimental"', though the term was not available at the time (2). The reason for this new modifier, the editors speculate, was cultural. It was a reaction to the growth of science: 'To call literature *experimental* is in some sense to aspire to compete with science, challenging science's privileged status in modernity and reclaiming some of the prestige ceded by literature to science since the nineteenth century' (2, emphasis in original). The identification between literary and scientific experiments, the editors suppose, works on a basis of analogy. The modifier demonstrates how literature, like science, can fit into a narrative of cultural progress: 'Experiment promises to extend the boundaries of knowledge, or in this case, of artistic practice. Strongly associated with modernity, it implies rejection of hide-bound traditions, values and forms' (2). The analogy, then, goes something like this: where the experimental scientist extends the boundaries of knowledge, the experimental writer extends the boundaries of artistic practice.

Both, in this sense, can overthrow the old and embrace the new. What remains questionable, however, is whether this analogy offers any real insight into how challenging literature is written and received.

One problem many have with the term 'experimental' is its older connotations of artistic failure. Here we might look to a comment made by John Ruskin, in 1857, in which the term is used to describe the necessary failures in the work of a developing artist: 'It stands to reason that a young man's work cannot be perfect. It *must* be more or less ignorant; it must be more or less feeble; it is likely that it may be more or less experimental, and if experimental, here and there mistaken' (Ruskin 1868: 35, emphasis in original). In Ruskin's sense, an experimental work is one that is not quite the finished article. There is the suggestion that experimentation will inevitably produce flawed art, but these flaws must be tolerated by the public if a young artist is to mature. This early sense of the descriptor continues to colour the idea of experimental literature into the late twentieth century and beyond. The editors of the *Routledge Companion* cite the writer B. S. Johnson's objection to the term: 'I object to the term *experimental* being applied to my own work. Certainly, I make experiments, but the unsuccessful ones are quietly hidden away and what I choose to publish is in my own terms successful' (1973: 19, emphasis in original). In Ruskin and Johnson's sense we get a slightly different analogy. Here, experimentation (artistic, literary or scientific) is the trialling process that comes before the finished product. It is a process that is necessary to – but should not be confused with – artistic achievement, or to the acquisition of scientific knowledge. Thus, the concept of aesthetic experimentation is caught between two analogies. In one sense, to call a work experimental is to say that it extends the boundaries of artistic practice and is thereby valuable in and of itself. In another, to call a work experimental is to say that it is only valuable insofar as it later leads to a successful finished work. The editors of the *Routledge Companion* find that, in the latter sense, 'experimental' has become a 'term of dismissal and condescension' (Bray, Gibbons and McHale 2012: 3). Their volume aims to 'rescue' the term from this context by emphasizing the sense in which the literary experiment is unconventional and cutting edge (3). In the sense that they use it, literary experiments name the process 'of change and renewal' by which literature reinvents itself (1). The terms 'avant-garde', 'experimental' and 'innovative' are amalgamated into the single term 'experimental'. This term, it is hoped, will be instilled with 'connotations of edginess, renovation and aesthetic adventure' (3). In this context, experimental literature can be 'irreducibly diverse' (1). A literary experiment merely has to ask the ontological questions that mainstream literature is 'dedicated to repressing':

'What is literature and what could it be? What are its functions its limitations its possibilities' (1)?

This study will set itself up in opposition to this broad definition of experimental literature. Some very interesting insights may come from the amalgamation of the terms 'avant-garde', 'innovative' and 'experimental' within a broad volume such as the *Routledge Companion*. But I think it is important that the terms do not lose their particularity. The editors point out that 'aesthetic avant-gardism continues to be allied with political radicalism in a number of twentieth- and twenty-first-century artistic and literary movements' (1–2). If these movements are allied more with 'political radicalism' than with scientific experimentation, why label them 'experimental' and not 'avant-garde'? Similarly, it will be my contention that twentieth-century literature had a relationship with scientific experimentation that went beyond the contest for cultural privilege. Rather than the all-encompassing version of experimental literature put forward in the *Routledge Companion*, I will identify a more limited tradition of literary experimentation. The editors of the *Routledge Companion* make a distinction between the scientific experiment's promise to 'extend the boundaries of knowledge' and the literary experiment's promise to extend the boundaries of 'artistic practice'. This study will scrutinize this distinction and will suggest that the experimentation of a literary work lies not only in its capacity to extend the boundaries of artistic practice but also in its potential to produce knowledge. The literary experiment, as I frame it here, should conduct a sustained investigation of a phenomenon or topic in a way that enhances our understandings of it. A literary experiment, by this account, not only could change our understanding of what literature is and does but might also change the way we think about a range of other topics from perception to moral and political agency.

This conception of the literary experiment is not altogether new. The editors of the *Routledge Companion* cite Émile Zola's essay 'The Experimental Novel' (1880) as the point at which 'the model of the scientific experiment becomes available to describe literary innovation' (2). Zola certainly used the term 'experimental' to describe literature. However, it is misleading to suggest that his use of the term is merely describing literary innovation. For Zola, the literary experiment did not just aim to extend the boundaries of artistic practice; it aimed to produce knowledge. Zola's fundamental concern was with the distinction between observation and experiment. He did not like the notion that the naturalist novel was a product of pure observation – that it was 'satisfied with photographing' (Zola 1893: 9). Instead, he argued that the naturalist novelist performed experiments. The process of the novelist, for Zola, consists firstly in observing 'facts in nature' (9). What comes next, however, is a process of experimentation: taking the observed facts and 'acting upon them by the modification of circumstances and surroundings without deviation from the laws of nature' (9). Thus, anyone might observe the day-to-day behaviour of a friend, but the novelist's experiment would be in imaginatively changing this friend's circumstances and surroundings in order to see what happens. If this process is carried out, for Zola, the novelist has produced knowledge: 'Finally, you possess knowledge of the man, scientific knowledge of him in both his individual and social relations' (9). For Zola, then, the naturalist novel is not just comparable to the scientific experiment; it is itself a branch of experimental science. This was, I think, a new idea in literature, but as early as 1836 the landscape painter John Constable had asked why painting 'may not be considered as a branch of natural philosophy, of which pictures are but the experiments' (qtd. in Thornes 1999: 51). In the nineteenth century, writers and artists were not just drawing loose analogies between artistic and scientific experimentation on the grounds of a common interest in innovation. Rather, they were questioning the distinction between the two.

Now, I find it hard to accept that the versions of artistic creativity described by Zola and Constable are acts of scientific experimentation exactly. Zola's experimental novelist, for example, imagines how individuals would react given the modification of their 'circumstances and surroundings'. What an individual does in these modified circumstances is merely what the novelist thinks would happen – not what happens in practice. It is hard to see how Zola's experimental novelist can get beyond the prediction stage. Moreover, there is still a defensible argument to suggest that the analogy between artistic practice and scientific experimentation was produced by the artists themselves with a view to claiming some of the prestige that science has acquired through the course of modernity. Nevertheless, in the sense that Zola and Constable use it, 'experimental' is not interchangeable with 'innovative' and nor does its use imply that the work described is not quite the finished product. Instead it implies the capacity to produce knowledge.

Literature and experimental psychology

The late nineteenth century also saw a development in experimental science that is crucial for the idea of a literary experiment: the emergence of experimental psychology. This development was of such importance because with it science began to study the topics that had long been of concern to literary writers. Scientists began to look for means by which to investigate how the human experiences and performs in the world. Furthermore, there came a surge of interest in the linguistic processes that make the production and reception of literature possible. Tim Armstrong writes: 'Psychological experimenters considered the possibility of forcing conscious process in writing to its limits. Moments of linguistic breakdown or systematic overload and the linguistic pathologies which mark the limits of language production became crucial' (1998: 194). This new type of scientific experimentation brought with it a great potential for overlap with literary writing. Not only did early psychologists draw on works of literature when developing their theories, but the production and reception of literary works became a topic of psychological study. The experimental psychologist June E. Downey, for example, published books on 'imaginal reactions to poetry' (1911) and the 'psychology of literature' (1929). This influence worked both ways. Literary writers had long been covering the scientific experiment thematically – Swift's *Gulliver's Travels* (1725) being particularly good proof of this. But at this point the practice of psychology began to influence the way in which literature was written. Various critics have recognized this trend. Judith Ryan has argued that the years 1880–1940 saw the development of a 'certain kind of modernist literature which responded creatively to the new psychologies of the time' (1991: 4–5). This literature, Ryan continues, is never a mere container for empiricist thought. Rather, it engages with psychological empiricism through 'formal innovations' (4). The very fabric of the literary text is seen to be influenced by the methods of experimental psychology.

Ryan finds a particularly strong example of this trend in the modernist writer Gertrude Stein. Stein spent a portion of her early life working at the Harvard Psychological Laboratory. Here she was under the tutelage of some of the key figures in early experimental psychology, namely Hugo Münsterberg and William James. Her time in the lab manifests in some experiments – partly carried out with partner Leon Solomons – on 'human automatism'. These experiments (the findings of which were published in early volumes of the *Psychological Review*) were what we might now call tests of selective and divided attention.[1] By this I mean that Stein and Solomons attempted to find out whether a subject could perform one task automatically while their attention was 'occupied as fully as possible' by another (Solomons and Stein 1896: 497).[2] For example, in one experiment the subject is asked to listen for and write down certain dictated words while attention is 'occupied as fully as possible in reading' a novel (497). At first, it is observed, the subject is too 'painfully conscious' of the writing task to comprehend what he is reading. Through training, though, the subject acquires a facility for 'rapidly shifting attention from reading to writing and back' (497). This is said to involve 'the formation of a motor impulse' and a 'feeling of effort' (497). But, as the task goes on, both the motor impulse and the feeling of effort are described to go away and, for Solomons at least, the act of writing becomes 'real automatism' (497). This usually occurs at points when the novel becomes particularly engrossing: 'Every once in a while the story grows interesting and we return to ourselves with a start to find that we have been going on writing just the same' (499–500). It is concluded that, under certain conditions, writing can be produced automatically. It should be stressed that these conclusions were largely those of Solomons. Stein's role in the first set of experiments was mainly that of an assistant. She was, it seems, more sceptical about the notion of automatic writing. Stein would, a few years later, carry out some experiments on her own which are described in the article 'Cultivated Human Automatism' (1898). In these experiments 'automatic writing' has a more limited definition. It does not consist in the production of words and sentences. Instead a planchette is used for the production of 'circles, the figure eight, a long curve or an m-figure' (Stein 1898: 296). In her experiments, Stein's definition of automatic writing was more akin to automatic movement. Indeed, as Steven Meyer points out, Stein more or less consistently held the view that 'if movements were automatic they would not produce writing and if, on the other hand, they did produce writing they were not automatic' (2001: 226). The experiments Stein produced, though, raise some crucial questions. To what extent, they ask, do the practices of reading and writing occupy attention? And, how far are these practices distinct from other types of bodily movement and expression?

There are numerous ways in which Stein's encounters with scientific method might be interpreted to have informed her later literary practice. An illuminating, if slightly blunt interpretation was made by the prominent behaviourist psychologist B. F. Skinner. In an article for *The Atlantic Monthly*, Skinner suggested that in her work *Tender Buttons* (1914) Stein merely reproduced the 'automatic' writing of her earlier psychological experiments (1934: 55). Skinner notes that Stein described the writing she produced in the lab as 'ordinarily unintelligible' (55). From this he asserts that Stein 'could not have failed to notice' the resemblances between this writing and the 'unintelligible product' that is *Tender Buttons* (55). Puzzling Skinner, though, is the question of why Stein would choose to publish this product 'as a serious artistic experiment' (55). Skinner's article gives a sense of the potential for convergence between literary and scientific experimentation in the early twentieth century. He recognizes

Tender Buttons as the product of a scientific experiment, but his concern is that it will not be recognized as such by all readers. The article betrays an anxiety that the experiment of the scientist can be confused with the experiment of the writer. Here, Skinner invokes Stein's association with Pablo Picasso and Henri Matisse, suggesting that her engagement with these artists prompted her to confuse her earlier scientific experiments with art: 'With such an experience behind one, it is not difficult to accept as art what one has hitherto dismissed as the interesting and rather surprising result of an experiment' (55). In Skinner's version of events, Stein made a definite methodological break when she left the psychological laboratory and started a literary career. However, developments within the artistic world led her – mistakenly in Skinner's opinion – to see artistic value in the products of her scientific experimentation. An alternative account would suggest that Stein did not make such a stark move away from scientific experimentation. This would be to suggest that the practices of science and literature were not mutually exclusive – that writing offered Stein ample opportunity for scientific experimentation. Steven Meyer gives a detailed account of this: 'Instead of being modelled on scientific experimentation, her [Stein's] writing turns out to be a form of experimental science itself. It is not just that her ideas about writing were influenced by science; she reconfigured science *as* writing and performed scientific experiments *in* writing' (Meyer 2001: xxi, emphasis in original). For Meyer, Stein's move to literature was not a complete methodological break. Rather, writing is seen as a new form in which Stein could continue to perform 'experimental science'.

Samuel Beckett and the psychological experiment

Stein's literary experiments came to the attention of Samuel Beckett, and what Beckett recognized in Stein's writing was the way in which it brought language down to earth, making it material and permeable. In a much-discussed 1937 letter to Axel Kaun, Beckett contrasted James Joyce's 'apotheosis of the word' with Stein's 'Logographs' in which 'the texture of the language has at least become porous' (Beckett 1983: 172). What I think Beckett apprehends in Stein are, in Armstrong's phrase, 'moments of linguistic breakdown or systematic overload' – moments in which the capacity of language to make sense is stretched. Stein's writing, for Beckett, is notable for its capacity to change understandings of what language is and does. It does not extend the boundaries of artistic practice so much as it interrogates our conception of a specific topic: language. In this way

Beckett's understanding of Stein's writing is close to my understanding of a literary experiment.

Stein, Beckett speculates, produced her experiments on language 'quite by chance' and retained a naive view of language: 'The unfortunate lady (is she still alive?) is doubtlessly still in love with her vehicle' (172).[3] For his own part, Beckett suggests that he wants to bring the word into disrepute 'with full knowledge and intent' (172–3). In the same letter, he suggests that language appears to him 'like a veil which one has to tear apart in order to get to those things (or the Nothingness) lying behind it' (171). There are a number of directions in which this idea could be taken, and I would argue that these directions correspond to significant developments in the history of Beckett criticism. In the Kaun letter, Beckett states that language is material and questions what lies behind this 'terrible materiality' (172). But what does Beckett think lies behind language? In one phase of Beckett criticism, it might have been thought an immaterial space of the mind. This phase is what Ulrika Maude calls 'the first wave of Beckett scholarship', which 'read Beckett as a transcendental writer who subscribed to a Cartesian dualism' (2009: 1).[4] Alternatively, one might accentuate Beckett's speculation that there is nothing behind language and could therefore adopt the more poststructuralist view exemplified in studies such as Steven Connor's *Repetition, Theory and Text* (1988) and Leslie Hill's *Beckett's Fiction: In Different Words* (1990). This would be to argue that Beckett (aporetically) apprehends the absence of a transcendent meaning and is concerned with the interminable play of language and signs – the instability of verbal meaning. In this study, though, I want to follow a more recent trend in Beckett scholarship. This trend, represented by critics such as Anthony Uhlmann (2006), Ulrika Maude (2009), Laura Salisbury (2012) and Dirk Van Hulle (2014), thinks beyond readings of Beckett that portray him as a kind of nominalist. In these studies, Beckett's work does not pursue a metaphysical essence behind the veil of language, and neither does it wholly accept that there is nothing beyond language and discourse. Instead, Beckett's interest in language forms one part of a wider investigation of human experience. In this line of thought, Beckett is concerned with the failure of linguistic meaning, but also with other kinds of meaning that might exist alongside, or emerge out of, this failure. Beckett's concern with speech and writing, here, can coexist with interests in other kinds of human activity.[5]

This interest in human activity, I contend, is where we might find a close relationship between Beckett's work and the practices of experimental psychology. Armstrong is right to point out that experimental psychology has always been interested in the 'limits of language' (how language is, or is not, understood, produced or learnt), but much psychological research has obviously also been carried out on a variety of non-verbal aspects of human experience. In this study, for instance, I will assay the ways in which psychologists have gone about studying processes such as learning, visual and auditory perception, selective attention and mental imagery. Though I will point out some differences, it is my contention that there are striking similarities between experimental psychology's investigation of these processes and the practices of Beckett. But if this is the case, one might ask, from where did this commonality derive? Certainly, Beckett's personal engagement with early psychology was not as substantial as Stein's. The evidence for Beckett's interest in experimental psychology is limited to some notes taken from R. S. Woodworth's *Contemporary Schools of Psychology* (1931) and Jean-Paul Sartre's *L'Imagination* (1936) (Feldman 2006: 102–13; Van Hulle and Nixon 2013: 210–11). Woodworth offers a broad summary of early psychological theories and methods, while Sartre's study briefly outlines early psychological approaches to the image. Thus, especially during his later life, Beckett's knowledge of experimental psychology was presumably both minimal and outdated. Nevertheless, engagements with experimental psychology have been recognized throughout the oeuvre. Matthew Feldman has argued that 'the entire opening exchange in *Murphy* is an artistic rendering of Beckett's 1930s notes on Gestalt psychology' (2006: 103). And Laura Salisbury has suggested that, in later works such as *Watt* (largely written during the Second World War but first published in 1953) and *Molloy* (1951), Beckett challenges gestaltists by 'drawing attention to the sheer fatiguing work involved in sifting figure from ground' (2010: 357). Similarly, as we will see momentarily, Ulrika Maude has argued that Beckett's late drama consistently draws on the behaviourist psychology pioneered by John Broadus Watson (Maude 2013: 85–7). To say that Beckett's work engages with experimental psychology, then, would not be novel or controversial.

However, my interest lies in the extent to which the psychological experiment comes to inform Beckett's own experimental methods, and ultimately what these methods can be seen to achieve. One school of thought on the subject would suggest that, for Beckett, psychology merely acted as 'fodder for the writing process' (Feldman 2006: 102). This is the view put forward by Rubin Rabinovitz who highlights a tension between Beckett's introspective methods and those used by psychologists: 'Modern psychologists seldom use introspection when gathering data for analysis. Given that individuals have direct access only to their own minds, introspection does not provide the intersubjectively verifiable data necessary for scientific generalizations. Hence psychologists prefer to observe others' (1992: 184). In Rabinovitz's view, the modern psychologist observes others and analyses their behaviour in order to make 'scientific generalizations'. For Beckett though, Rabinovitz continues, this method was unsuitable. This is because Beckett's literature is concerned with 'the most profound levels of mental reality', and in these levels there 'are issues that can no longer be dealt with logically': 'The mind deals with flurries of fleeting images confused, distorted, and disorganized. Consequently, there comes a time when Beckett turns away from rational methods and employs a more subjective approach' (185). Rabinovitz suggests that, in Beckett's oeuvre, there is a preference for the observation of inner self over the observation of others. Psychological concepts, from this perspective, might have served as inspiration, but they could not give Beckett the insight into the 'profound levels of mental reality' that his art required. Rabinovitz concludes: ''Though Beckett sometimes touches on a wide range of psychological concepts, he is also ready to abandon them when they become superfluous' (186).[6]

I agree with some aspects of Rabinovitz's argument. I will not be arguing, for example, that Beckett's work is concerned with producing 'physical models to describe mental reality' (184). Nevertheless, there are a few points with which this study will take issue. First, Rabinovitz assumes that Beckett is exclusively concerned with 'the most profound levels of mental reality'. I am not sure this is the case. I agree that some of Beckett's 'characters are engaged in solitary quests that represent journeys of self-discovery', and that some 'of the disputes between shadowy figures can be interpreted as inner arguments within a single mind' (185). But I don't think this means Beckett's work completely eschews an interest in how subjects interact with the external world. Indeed, I will argue that this process becomes a central theme in Beckett's work. More simply, if Beckett is purely interested in introspection and uninterested in the external world, why produce work for others? To some extent, Beckett's putting his work 'out there' must imply a need to find out how particular stimuli affect the external world. To take one example (which I discuss in Chapter 2), Beckett's stipulation that the speech in *Not I* should be 'addressed less to the understanding than to the nerves of the audience' (Harmon 1998: 283) suggests an engagement with the audience's physiological and psychological response to the given stimulus. Thus, I do not think Beckett's process is so far removed from that of Rabinovitz's 'modern psychologist'. Second, partly because of the time at which he was writing, Rabinovitz gives a problematically limited account of 'the modern psychologist'. He seems to define the psychologist by the attitude taken towards introspection, suggesting that, by definition, the modern psychologist is largely uninterested in introspection. This may be true for a behaviourist such as John Broadus Watson, but it certainly does not hold for psychology as a whole. Methods of introspection were practised by early psychologists such as William James, Wilhelm Wundt and Edward Titchener, all of whom Beckett read about in Woodworth. Though, as we will see, the advent of behaviourism saw these methods fall out of fashion in the early to mid-twentieth century, they are now recognized to have made an important contribution to modern psychology. In a recent survey of the practices of scientific psychology, for example, Tim Shallice and Richard Cooper call the phenomenological work carried out by early psychologists: 'Islands of progress in a sea of ignorance' (2011: 3). Shallice and Cooper go on to bemoan the fact that the 'ideology of behaviourism' meant that these advances were ignored for a large part of the twentieth century (3). Rabinovitz's notion of 'modern' psychology probably reflects mid-twentieth-century psychology's discounting of introspection. But, for psychology as it stands today, introspection is not such a dirty word. As we will see, particularly with regard to the topic of mental imagery, introspection has been an important, if not central, part of experimental psychology throughout its history. More fundamentally, for both the aesthetic and the psychological experimenter, introspection is a source of ideas. In the genesis of their experiments, each necessarily draws on their own experience for inspiration and then envisions how an experiment would work in the laboratory, or on page, stage or screen. Thus, I do not think Beckett can be distanced from psychology on the grounds that Rabinovitz uses. This study will be a reassessment of the relationship between Beckett's process and the process of the experimental psychologist. I hope that it also contributes to a wider discussion of twentieth-century literature's relation to the scientific experiment.

Beckett, experimental psychology and psychoanalysis

It is important to note that Beckett's reading of experimental psychology ran closely alongside his study and experience of psychoanalysis and psychotherapy. Indeed, in Beckett's reading, psychoanalysis and psychotherapy were nowhere near so far removed from experimental psychology as they are often thought to be.[7] In Woodworth's book, for example, psychoanalysis is defined as a school of psychology along with behaviourism and gestalt. Like behaviourism, Beckett noted, psychoanalysis was a 'reaction against "consciousness" psychology of 19th century' and, he continues, both approaches sought to 'humanise psychology' (Feldman 2004: 314). It is my contention, then, that Beckett did not read psychoanalysis and experimental psychology as distinct disciplines but as different ways of investigating human experience, each having strengths and weaknesses. In this way, he did not have to decide between behaviourism, psychoanalysis and any other school, but could merely pick out the bits that he found interesting from each. Furthermore, as Matthew Feldman points out, 'Beckett's notes on psychology must be viewed in terms of a larger self-education process during the interwar years', which took in philosophy, theology and other branches of science (2006: 78). 'No inflexible barrier', Feldman argues, 'should be erected to separate the "Philosophy-" from "Psychology notes"'; and neither set of notes should be severed from the 'vital period in which they were transcribed' (80). Beckett's study of psychology, then, may well be seen as one part of a broad intellectual survey which enabled him to eventually find his own methods of experimentation. With this being said, I want to argue that psychology offered Beckett a particularly important set of ideas. Psychology introduced Beckett not only to a collection of methods with which to explore conscious experience but also to the idea that human activity extended beyond consciousness. This is evident at the beginning of the Woodworth notes. Psychoanalysis, Beckett writes, practises the 'apotheosis of unconscious', while behaviourism moves towards the 'rejection of consciousness altogether' (Feldman 2004: 314). Beckett knew that psychology was historically interested in consciousness. He would go on to note the methods by which introspectionist psychologists such as Edward Titchener had sought to explore conscious experience empirically. However, it is crucial to note that psychology showed Beckett a series of methods by which one could study human activity without focusing on consciousness.

Of course, different schools of psychology sought to do this in very different ways. Psychoanalysis, Beckett learnt, worked with the view that much of one's psychic material is repressed and so ordinarily unavailable to conscious experience. Thus, in the analytic situation, through methods such as relaxation and 'talking out', one aimed to 'repeat as a current experience that which has been repressed' (Feldman 2004: 319). Behaviourist psychology, by contrast, took its cues from physiology and sought to study human performance without reference to conscious experience. As Beckett noted, this approach was given great impetus by Ivan Pavlov's finding of the conditioned reflex in his famous experiments with dogs. In Pavlov's experiments, dogs were exposed to a certain sound every time they were given food, and eventually the sound alone was enough to make the dogs salivate. Consequently, the sound became an instrument with which to exert control over the dogs (Woodworth [1948] 2013: 56–8). Watson's behaviourism, Beckett noted, applied the 'conditioned reflex concept to all human habit formation' (Feldman 2004: 315). The crucial point here is that the individual (human or animal) responds to many stimuli without having to think about it. Thus, as Watson put it, human activity can be studied, not in terms of consciousness, but 'in terms of stimulus and response, in terms of habit formation, in terms of habit integration and the like' (1913: 166–7).

Of these two approaches, Beckett criticism has evidently tended to acknowledge the influence of the former over the latter. There is an expansive body of commentary that considers Beckett's relationship with psychoanalysis,[8] but considerably fewer critics have addressed the significance of behaviourism and other branches of experimental psychology. There are two main reasons for this. First, historically, literary critics have been more interested in literature's relationship with psychoanalysis than with other branches of psychology. Judith Ryan writes: 'When we think of the relation between psychology and literature most of us think of Freudian psychology or one of its more recent modifications, such as that of [Jacques] Lacan' (1991: 1).[9] Second, in the case of Beckett, there is good biographical evidence to highlight the author's interest in psychoanalysis and psychotherapy. It has long been known that Beckett undertook psychotherapy with Wilfred Bion at the recommendation of his friend Geoffrey Thompson (Feldman 2006: 88). Moreover, Beckett's 'Psychology' notes were compiled during the time of these sessions, and the overall weighting of the notes shows a clear bias towards psychoanalysis. As Feldman observes, it is only the presence of notes taken from Woodworth's book that allows us to call this 'corpus of material the "'Psychology' notes" rather than the "Psychoanalysis Notes"' (102). Despite this imbalance, it would be unwise to discount the importance of other forms of psychology to Beckett's work. To be clear, I do not see this as a matter of either/or. The practices of psychoanalysis and psychotherapy were undoubtedly influential for Beckett, and they continue to help us come to an understanding of Beckett's texts (as well as literature more generally). This, though, should not lead us to ignore the relationship between literary writers such as Beckett and experimental psychology. In the context of Beckett's work, it is my argument that the approaches were frequently drawn together by a common interest. In psychoanalysis, as in experimental psychology, there is a concern with positioning and stimulating the human body in ways that facilitate new understandings of experience and performance. In psychoanalysis, this manifested in stipulations regarding the therapeutic setting. Here the aim was to induce experience which might bring to the level of consciousness that which had been repressed. In experimental psychology, though, the idea is taken further. Experimenters have continually found new and innovative ways of testing and manipulating the human body, with the aim of finding out what the human can do and how this performance is experienced. Through experimentation, the psychologist aims to bring to light hitherto unknown capacities, effects and affective responses. This is the tradition in which I want to place Beckett's work; in the final part of this introduction, I will begin to demonstrate this through a reading of the television play *Ghost Trio* (1976).

Stimulus-response and the influence of psychoanalysis in *Ghost Trio*

Ghost Trio incorporates Beckett's interest in both the interpersonal investigation of subjectivity that proceeds within psychotherapy and the more objective approach of the behaviourist stimulus-response experiment. There is some critical precedence for this reading. Critics such as Catherine Russell (1989) have recognized the play's resonances with psychoanalytic theory (particularly that of Lacan), while more recent critics have noticed the influence of behaviourism throughout Beckett's later drama. Ulrika Maude, for example, recognizes the influence of behaviourism in the way that Beckett subjects 'his characters to stimulus-response experiments' (2013: 85). Maude, here, points to 1963's *Play* in which the three protagonists appear to be 'trained to spew out language at the instigation of the beam of a spotlight, conditioned to speak when the light hits' the giant urns in which they reside (86). I find the link with behaviourism convincing here (and will discuss it further in Chapter 1), but one might also recognize elements from Beckett's study of psychoanalysis. As Beckett noted, the 'free association' or 'talking-out' method was fundamental to psychoanalytic practice (Feldman 2004: 319), and this undoubtedly resonates with the verbal expulsions of *Play*. Similarly, in *Ghost Trio*, Beckett's protagonist seems to be subjected to a kind of stimulus-response experiment, but one can still see the influence of psychoanalysis. In the play, a female voice (V) observes and commentates on the behaviour of a male figure (F). In part 1 of the play, the 'Pre-action', V introduces the 'familiar chamber' and the few things within it: a window, a door, a pallet, the floor (Beckett [1986] 2006: 409). She seems to have complete control over this space. Critics such as Graley Herren (2007) and Colin Gardner (2012) have compared this controlled environment to that of the television studio. I would add to this the setting of a scientific laboratory. In a description of Pavlov's conditioning experiments, Woodworth describes Pavlov's use of 'a special conditioned reflex laboratory' for his experiments (2013: 58).

The conditioned response, it was observed, could be '*inhibited* by any distracting stimulus such as disturbs the dog or makes him investigate' (58, emphasis in original). To counteract this, Pavlov made 'elaborate provisions for excluding extraneous sights, sounds, odors, gusts of air, etc'. (58). The environment in *Ghost Trio* also seems set up to exclude extraneous distractions. More generally, the defining of the environment is important in the context of an experiment because it allows for the study to be repeated and the results verified. There is emphasis on the idea that the action to follow is not limited to one geographical position but can be repeated anywhere if the same elements are put in place. I am not trying to argue, here, that the scene of *Ghost Trio* is definitively a Pavlovian laboratory (there are numerous interpretations one could make), but I would suggest that elements within the 'Pre-action' recall the approaches taken by Pavlov and Watson.

What one might also question with regard to the Pre-action is whether the audience are themselves subjects in a stimulus-response experiment. At the beginning of the play, V seems to address a television audience directly: 'Good evening. Mine is a faint voice. Kindly tune accordingly. (*Pause.*) Good evening. Mine is a faint voice. Kindly tune accordingly. (*Pause.*) It will not be raised, nor lowered, whatever happens' (Beckett [1986] 2006: 408). The behaviour of the television audience is brought into question here. When asked to 'kindly tune accordingly' it is implied that there is the possibility that the addressee could be unkind and not tune accordingly. If the addressee is assumed to be a television viewer, Beckett seems to be drawing attention to the viewer's freedom to adjust the settings on the television set. Colin Gardner suggests something of this when he argues that *Ghost Trio* 'introduces the idea of the televisual *mise en scène* as a pure abstract object, something which may in principle be manipulated by the viewer through controlling volume, colour, hue and brightness' (2012: 126). But the possibility for manipulation works both ways. There is also a sense in which V's request speaks to the television's capacity to control the human subject. When V states that her voice is faint and asks her addressee to 'tune accordingly' there is the implication that her voice can only remain faint if the volume is not increased. If the voice is going to be faint, the addressee must cooperate. However, as Steven Connor suggests the 'optimum' volume demanded is 'slightly uncomfortable' (2014: 79). In the usual way, one uses the volume so as not to strain to hear what is being said on the television. V is asking her addressee to set the volume to a level at which they will have to strain. The voice is asking the addressee to do something quite unintuitive and giving no reason for her demand. She does not explain why her voice is faint, only emphasizes that it should be so. Beckett is experimenting with the television's capacity to manipulate its audience.[10]

The link with the stimulus-response experiment becomes even more salient in the second part of the play. The 'Action' presents V's attempt to fulfil Watson's stated aim of predicting responses to certain stimuli. Through stimulus-response experiments, Watson argued, psychologists could 'learn general and particular methods by which behaviour may be controlled' (1913: 166–7). In this account, learning how to control human behaviour must be carried out through a process of observation. The individual is exposed to certain stimuli with responses being monitored. If this is done enough, the school will eventually ascertain: 'Such data and laws that, given the stimulus psychology can predict the response; or, on the other hand, given the response, it can specify the nature of the effective stimulus' (167). This process of predicting responses to certain stimuli is played out in *Ghost Trio*. V can predict the behaviour of F when he is exposed to a certain sound. V tells us that F 'will now think he hears her' (Beckett [1986] 2006: 410). A sound has been introduced but the audience is not exposed to the sound that F hears. It is clear only that it is a sound which F associates with an anonymous 'her'. V has control over the application of this sound and knows that it is not 'her' in reality. There is an element of conditioning in this. V has identified a sound that F associates with 'her'. The use of this sound alone now prompts F to exhibit the behaviour appropriate to hearing her. This behaviour takes the form of a movement: F 'raises head sharply, turns still crouched to door, fleeting face, tense pose. 5 seconds' (410). Importantly, the prompting of this behaviour is repeatable. V gives the stimulus twice and both times it gets the same response. After the second response, V can predict a series of movements that F will make around the chamber: 'Now to door' (F goes to door), 'Open' (F pushes door open), 'Now to window' (F goes to window), 'Open' (F pushes window open) (410). This is Watson's ideal. V seems to have acquired the knowledge of F's behaviour to be able to predict his responses to a certain situation. So much is this the case that it might appear as though V has total control over F. However, this level of prediction and control does not persist. After going to the pallet, as V predicted, F goes to a mirror and looks at his face in it. V gives a '[surprised] Ah!' She has not predicted this (410–11).

Now, within the experimental environment, the fact that V has not been able to predict F's behaviour completely is not a major problem. V, it seems, is still ascertaining empirical data about the habits of F through continued observation. Thus, the change in behaviour may be seen to aid the establishment of more thorough models of prediction and control. Things become more complicated, though, when one considers the mirror to which F is drawn. First it should be noted that V did not introduce the mirror when she was outlining the environment in the Pre-action. Unlike Pavlov, who made sure that any 'distracting stimulus' was removed from his laboratory, V has allowed an alien object to interfere with her controlled environment. We do not know how the mirror has got into the chamber, and its mysterious presence gives the space an uncontrollable specificity. But F's interest in the mirror also hints at his own self-reflection.[11] There is the sense that we are moving from the objective approach of behaviourism towards the more interpersonal investigations of psychoanalysis.

This coincides with an increased focus on F. At the beginning of the play, we are invited to speak of F largely in terms of behaviour. F is presented mainly through a long shot and the emphasis is on what he does: '*F is seated upon a stool, bowed forward, face hidden, clutching with both hands a small cassette*' (Beckett [1986] 2006: 409, emphasis in original). However, in the second part of the play we see a close-up of F's face in the mirror, and at the end of the play the face becomes the focal point: '*With growing music move in slowly to close up of head bowed right down over cassette now held in arms and invisible. Hold till end of Largo. Silence. F Raises head. Face seen clearly for second time. 10 seconds*' (413–14, emphasis in original). In the published text Beckett gives no direction to illuminate F's expression. However, in the German production he breaks into a smile, of sorts. I will address the question of facial expression in Beckett's drama more thoroughly in Chapter 3 but here I merely want to suggest that the increasing focus on the face in *Ghost Trio* indicates a move away from the stimulus-response experiment towards the psychoanalytic case history. We move away from V's concern with F's behaviour and are instead given a more intimate perspective on F. Key here is the question of who the 'her' that F thinks he hears might be – a lost love perhaps – and how he feels as he waits for her. But the link with psychoanalysis is stronger than this. As Friedrich Kittler observes, the case histories of psychoanalysis were distinguished from literary productions by the fact that they interrogated the 'depths of the soul' without portraying 'the identities of the persons described to readers' ([1985] 1990: 287). They sought to reveal psychic realities while concealing biographical detail. *Ghost Trio* works in this tradition. F is an anonymous figure and we know nothing of his background, but we do observe him as he awaits a lost other and, by the end of the play, his face is presented in intimate detail.[12] In Beckett's literary experiment, elements of the behaviourist stimulus-response experiment are interwoven with elements of the psychoanalytic case study.

The scope of the study

Ghost Trio is positioned at the heart of this study's period of focus, and it encapsulates many of the concerns that will run through the following chapters. To some extent, it is an experiment on how the human subject learns to respond to the environment in which it is positioned. Chapter 1 will consider this point further by positioning Beckett's plays of the 1950s and 1960s in relation to the psychological learning debates of the early twentieth century. Here I will argue that in works such as *Happy Days* and *Play*, an experimental Beckett emerges to complement an avant-gardist one. The plays, I suggest, can be seen as experiments on learning, but these experiments have an avant-gardist concern, namely the attempt to fashion an avant-garde subjectivity in opposition to expansive humanist and reductive behaviourist models.

Ghost Trio might also be viewed as an experiment on the way in which we perceive and attend to sensory information. We have seen the extent to which the play is concerned with the capacities of both F and the audience to see and hear. Chapters 2, 3 and 4 of the study will consider this element of Beckett's work further through the reading of three theatrical works of the 1970s: *Not I* (1972), *That Time* (1976) and *Footfalls* (1976). In Chapter 2, I will consider the case of *Not I*, focusing on speech perception and comprehension. Chapter 3 discusses face reading and selective attention in the context of *That Time*. Finally, Chapter 4 looks carefully at the concept of inattention in twentieth-century culture and argues that *Footfalls* contributes to the study of this concept. All three of these works, I will argue, show perception and attention as effortful, straining and partial processes. In this way, Beckett helps us understand the fallible labour involved in apprehending and comprehending the world. But, as was the case with *Ghost Trio*, it will also be my argument that these plays engage with a tradition concerned with the representation of an individual's life.[13] Thus the chapters will all consider how two aspects of modernity interact within Beckett's plays: the modernity of information processing (how we perceive, attend to and perform in the world), and the modernity of self-authorship (how we construct ourselves as unified – and marketable – individuals).

If the first four chapters of this study consider the ways in which we form impressions of the world in real time, the final two focus on how these impressions stay with us when the original sensory stimuli have been extinguished. These chapters focus on the topic of mental imagery. In *Ghost Trio*, as we have seen, F thinks he hears a mysterious 'her'. However, because this 'her' never materializes, there is a question of whether F is perceiving a sound which he thinks is 'her', or whether he is imagining or recalling the sound. It is this problematizing of the distinction between the percept and the mental image that animates the final chapters of this study. Chapter 5 assesses the ways in which the mental image has been defined in Beckett criticism, placing Beckett's image between the aesthetic ideas of the Romantics, and more scientific attitudes towards mental imagery. This is punctuated by a reading of the 1982 television play *Nacht und Träume*. The approach defined in Chapter 5 is then developed in Chapter 6. The chapter argues that the late trilogy of prose texts – *Nohow On* – *Company* (1979), *Ill Seen Ill Said* (1981) and *Worstward Ho* (1982) – constitute attempts to find a perspective from which to investigate the mental image, as well as a vocabulary with which to discuss it.

A final point to make in this introduction is one of period and medium. Though this study will take in the entirety of Beckett's oeuvre, I will concentrate mainly on a series of texts that begins with 1959's *Happy Days* and runs through to Beckett's very late works in the 1980s. I have chosen this late period of Beckett's life because by this time he was producing work for a wide variety of media. In addition to his famous works for page and stage, Beckett, during the period in question, worked with film (1965's *Film*), radio (e.g. 1959's *Embers*) and television. Thus, as well as using words as a vehicle with which to 'get to those things (or the Nothingness) lying behind' them, Beckett was working with the aesthetics of sound and vision. If these developments did not exactly allow Beckett to move beyond the 'terrible materiality' of words, they certainly presented him with alternatives. As we have seen, *Ghost Trio* employs words, but it also uses the medium of television to experiment on topics such as sound, body movement and facial expression. It will be my argument that Beckett's adaptation to a variety of media in this period allowed him to experiment in a sense that goes beyond aesthetic innovation. Beckett's aesthetic experiments, I suggest, have the potential to enrich our understanding of how the human perceives, attends to, and imagines the world.

1

Experimental transitions

'Let us be very sure of one thing', writes B.S. Johnson in a 1964 review for *The Spectator*, 'Samuel Beckett is out there in front' (2013: 422). This comment, which forms part of Johnson's largely positive assessment of *How It Is*, does much to identify Beckett as an author of the avant-garde. Marjorie Perloff reminds us that the term 'avant-garde' 'was originally a military metaphor', referring to 'the forerunners in battle who paved the way for the rest' (2006: 20), and Johnson's comment seems to be working with a variation of this metaphor. We are invited to see Beckett pressing on into new writerly territory, with other authors following in the same general direction. Perloff also suggests that avant-garde writing is 'invariably oppositional' (20), and the oppositional aspect of Beckett's writing is recognized by Johnson. At the end of the review, Johnson states that it is Beckett's 'example (towards truth and away from storytelling) which makes it clear that almost all novelists today are anachronistically working in a clapped-out and moribund tradition' (2013: 422). Johnson is positioning Beckett on one side of a writerly political divide. Beckett is part of a progressive minority of novelists that are working to undermine the conventional methods of the 'almost all'.

In the first part of this chapter, I want to think carefully about the ways in which the Beckett of the late 1950s and 1960s positions his work as part of an avant-garde. Focusing on two of Beckett's major theatrical works of the period, *Happy Days* and *Play*, I will argue for the oppositional tendencies of Beckett's writing. This discussion will lead to the main concern of the chapter. I am interested in how this oppositional, avant-garde Beckett relates to the experimental Beckett that I began to identify in the Introduction. Glancing back to Johnson's review, it is worth noting that Beckett is portrayed as part of a movement not only 'away from storytelling' but also 'towards truth'. If one looks to the beginning of Johnson's review, it becomes clear that Johnson conceives this movement towards truth in psychological terms. *How It Is*, Johnson writes, 'is the nearest any writer has ever come to the accurate literary transcription of a man's thoughts in all their chaotic complexity, with all their repetitions and hesitancies: conscious mind continually diffused by the inconsequential, illogical, irrational interjections of the subconscious' (2013: 420). Beckett's writing, this account makes clear, is not only interested in subverting popular conventions and changing literary culture; it is also fundamentally concerned with defining the mind.

Here, a scientifically experimental aspect of Beckett's work emerges alongside the avant-gardist one. This scientifically experimental aspect of Beckett's work is not necessarily antithetical to the avant-gardist tendency. Perloff notes that the 'prototypical avant-garde movement' tends to see itself as working in consonance 'with the new technology, science, and philosophy' to produce 'genuinely new and revolutionary' artworks (2005: 22). But I think there is a distinction to be made between the scientifically experimental Beckett and the avant-garde one. Beckett's avant-gardism is political; it is concerned with the way in which humans relate to each other and the role of art in setting the terms for these relations. His experimentalism, by contrast, is epistemological – primarily concerned with finding something out about the nature of human experience. Later chapters of this study will suggest that from the 1970s onwards the scientifically experimental aspect of Beckett's writing becomes prominent. This chapter, though, seeks to mark Beckett's theatrical work of the 1950s and 1960s as points of transition where the political and epistemological sides of Beckett's writerly practice are equally apparent. In these plays Beckett is writing against convention and working towards a kind of psychological knowledge.

But what is the particular type of psychological knowledge that Beckett's plays of the period are working towards? I will suggest that they can profitably be seen as experiments on a process that occupied a prominent place in psychological debate during the first half of Beckett's life: learning. The question of how, and under what conditions, individuals learn most effectively prompted a great deal of debate within experimental psychology from the late nineteenth century to the middle of the twentieth. Jerome Bruner notes that the so-called 'learning theory wars … came to dominate the psychological research scene from the latter nineteenth century until a decade after World War II' (2004: 14). And, as the 'Psychology' notes make clear, Beckett had a good degree of familiarity with these disputes. The notes Beckett took from R. S. Woodworth's book identify the major parties in 'the learning theory wars', namely the associationist, behaviourist and configurationist schools (the latter represented largely by the gestaltists). Beckett, I will propose, took his knowledge of the learning theory debates and incorporated them into theatrical experiments that investigate the human's capacity to learn.

It might be useful here to draw a rough sketch of the debate around learning that developed in early experimental psychology. The debate revolved around a question of whether learning was achieved through practice and repetition, or insight. Associationist theory emphasized the mind's capacity to learn from experience, arguing that learning takes place through the linkage of sensations, perceptions, ideas and memories. Here learning becomes a matter of making connections between one mental phenomenon and another. One learns, for example, that an object is dangerous through the repeated co-occurrence of a perception of that object and a feeling of pain. This theory of learning was taken on in adapted form by the behaviourists who continued to emphasize the importance of repetition but, as we saw in the last chapter, excised the associationist language of experience (perceptions, ideas, feelings, memories etc.) in favour of a language of stimulus and response. The behaviourist approach to learning was characterized by extensive experimentation (generally using animals as subjects) that investigated what individuals could accomplish if prompted to perform the same task over and over again. As Bruner puts it, 'The burden of the behaviorists' findings, taken collectively, was that repetition of a task, with suitable reinforcement for completing each trial, improved performance' (17). The configurationist view contrasted with the others insofar as it downplayed practice and repetition, instead privileging insight. Beckett noted this in his reading of Woodworth's section on the gestaltist approach: 'Insight essential in learning: this view opposed to that of associationism, with its conception of learning as made up of linkages, native & acquired, between stimuli & responses' (Feldman 2004: 319). This reading evidently stayed with Beckett for many decades. Much scholarship has observed that he would make obvious use of it in the 1957 mime *Act Without Words I*. James Knowlson (1996), Matthew Feldman (2006) and Ulrika Maude (2013) have all noted the resemblances between the action and setting of Beckett's mime and Wolfgang Köhler's experiments with apes, which Beckett read about in Woodworth. In this chapter, I will take these resemblances as a starting point in making the argument that works such as *Act Without Words I*, *Happy Days* and *Play* attempt to acquire knowledge about the way in which human subjects learn to make sense of the puzzling environments in which they are placed.

If, as I suggest, these plays conduct experiments on learning, it is worth noting the relevance of the particular moment at which they were produced. Beckett's 'Psychology' notes were taken at a time when the learning debate was ubiquitous within experimental psychology. By the period of the theatre pieces, however, the learning theory wars had ended amid what was later termed the 'cognitive revolution'. Bruner notes:

> It was the cognitive revolution that brought down learning theory or, perhaps, focused attention elsewhere. After 1960, say, stimulus-response learning theory seemed quaintly stunted, hemmed in by its own self-denial. As for more molar, cognitive learning theories, many of their ideas were restated and absorbed into general cognitive theories … . By the latter 1960s, learning was being translated into the concepts of information processing, with no compulsion to elevate one kind of learning over another in terms of its 'basic' properties. Certainly, the old wars were over. And so, interestingly, were the old rat labs and their ubiquitous mazes. (2004: 19)

Over the course of the 1950s and 1960s, then, experimental psychology was transitioning from the 'stimulus-response' paradigm to that of 'information processing'. Beckett's theatrical experiments should be seen as part of this transition. They are undoubtedly cognizant of the behaviourist method, but Beckett is by no means hemmed in by the 'self-denial' of behaviourist orthodoxy. Beckett may draw on the stimulus-response experiment, but he is also interested in how his subjects store and analyse the sensory information to which they are exposed. Beckett's learning experiments, in other words, synthesize the approaches of the behaviourist and the configurationist in a way that anticipates the cognitivist revolution. In view of this, the final part of this chapter will read Beckett's plays alongside the work of a number of psychologists who adopted behaviourist methods but remained open to concepts such as perception, memory and reflection. Given Beckett's reading, it is notable that R. S. Woodworth's 1927 article '"Gestalt" Psychology and the Concept of Reaction Stages' is often seen as a forerunner of this view. But I will focus particularly on the work of Edward Tolman whose idea of 'cognitive maps' is often seen as crucial to the transition from the behaviourist to the cognitivist era. I will suggest that Beckett and Tolman are exploring similar territory. In my readings of his theatre of the period then, Beckett will emerge as both an avant-garde and a psychological experimentalist – a writer that is working against the mainstream view of art and literature while investigating the human's capacity to learn.

Avant-garde Beckett?

My arguing for an avant-garde Beckett may seem uncontroversial, perhaps even redundant. But over the last few decades a number of critics have brought into question Beckett's continued avant-garde status, or at least stressed that Beckett's avant-gardism needs to be defined in specific terms. In particular, since Beckett's centenary year in 2006, S. E. Gontarski has repeatedly questioned whether the canonization and assimilation into popular culture of Beckett's work suggests the blunting of its 'avant-garde edge' (2006: 1). To be clear, Gontarski is not suggesting that Beckett was never part of a historical avant-garde. He is questioning whether, given that Beckett is now 'alluded to in television sitcoms' and made the 'subject of TV quiz shows', we can claim avant-garde status for the 'Beckett' that has emerged after Beckett (1–2). It is Gontarski's suggestion that the loss of the avant-garde Beckett would be regrettable and should be resisted – elsewhere he argues that theatrical adaptation is an area where this resistance can take place (2017: 178). Gontarski, here, sees the popularization of Beckett's work as part of the 'commodification' and ultimately degradation 'of the avant-garde in general' (2010: 2). If Beckett's status as an avant-garde writer is under threat, for Gontarski, so is the status of the avant-garde itself.

P. J. Murphy disputes Gontarski's argument in 'Saint Samuel (á) Beckett's Big Toe', a 2016 article which introduces the collection *Beckett in Popular Culture*. Murphy suggests that Gontarski is being overly pessimistic regarding Beckett's relationship with popular culture, but the article's main concern seems to be with Gontarski's use of the term 'avant-garde'. He suggests that in Gontarski's argument and elsewhere the term is being used too loosely. How, Murphy asks, can one speak of the loss of the avant-garde Beckett without properly establishing the nature of Beckett's perceived avant-gardism. At this point Murphy draws attention to an earlier argument that he made in *Reconstructing Beckett* (1990), which set out the nature of Beckett's relationship with avant-gardism. There, drawing on Peter Bürger's theory of the avant-garde, Murphy makes the case for viewing Beckett as part of an 'attack on the autonomous status of art' which began to take place in the 1920s and 1930s (1990: xiv).

To elucidate Murphy's argument, it is necessary to give a brief summary of Bürger's theory. Bürger's essay attempts an outline of the history of artistic production, dividing art into three categories: the 'Sacral' (Bürger gives the example of 'the art of the high middle ages'), the 'Courtly' ('example: the art at the court of Louis XIV') and the 'Bourgeois' (typified by the modern novel) (1984: 47–8). The crucial point Bürger makes is that there is a fundamental difference between 'Bourgeois' art and other forms. Put simply, 'Bourgeois' art is distinguished from the former two categories by the way in which it detaches itself from the 'praxis of life' (48). 'Sacral' and 'Courtly' works of art, for Bürger, are put to a specific use and one receives them from within a collective. They operate as part of the social rituals of a religious or aristocratic society. Bourgeois art, by contrast, is received by 'isolated individuals' within a realm that is conceived to be cut off from social reality:

> In bourgeois art, the portrayal of bourgeois self-understanding occurs in a sphere that lies outside the praxis of life. The citizen who, in everyday life, has been reduced to a partial function (means-ends activity) can be discovered in art as 'human being'. Here, one can unfold the abundance of one's talents, though with the proviso that this sphere remain strictly separate from the praxis of life. Seen in this fashion, the separation of art from the praxis of life becomes the decisive characteristic of the autonomy of bourgeois art. (48–9)

In the case of bourgeois art, then, the receiver is encouraged to imagine a better world, a better self, but these imaginings are confined to the autonomous world of art. What cannot be achieved in reality within a capitalist society can be achieved imaginatively through artistic productions: 'All those needs that cannot be satisfied in everyday life, because the principle of competition pervades all spheres, can find a home in art, because art is removed from the praxis of life. Values such as humanity, joy, truth, solidarity are extruded from life as it were, and preserved in art' (50). According to Bürger, the avant-garde is the body that becomes conscious of this development and attacks it. And it is Beckett's role in this attack that, for Murphy, positions Beckett within the avant-garde tradition.

In Murphy's view, Beckett responds to the avant-garde movement by writing a realism 'of a new sort': one that 'reconstitutes the human being within the fictional world of the text' and verifies 'the ontology of this other' (xvi). This realism is structured around a 'power struggle between the conflicting claims of "author" and "other"' (xvi). In effect, then, Beckett's writing, more specifically his prose, is seen to bring life into art by asking us to take seriously the existence not just of the author but also of the others which the author constructs. In this way, Beckett's writing is seen to make a move beyond metafiction. Like metafiction it foregrounds its own artificiality by dwelling on the existence of an author constructing its fictional entities. But it moves beyond this by asking us to treat these fictional entities as live beings that struggle for power with their author. The latter move, Murphy suggests, is 'the strangest and most bizarre aspect of Beckett's remarkable art', but also the basis for Beckett's contribution to the avant-garde. By asking us to treat transparently fictional entities as real, Beckett is continually erasing and retracing the distinction between art and the praxis of life. This, Murphy concludes, is what affords Beckett's works, 'at points revolutionary perspectives on our world'. By taking the existences of author and others seriously, Murphy suggests, Beckett's writing allows new insights on 'real-world' questions of 'power, authority, the expropriations of language, the silencing of others, and the struggle to find a voice' (xvi–xvii).

Now, Murphy makes some very important points. A particular strength of his argument lies in the contention that Beckett's writing affirms a 'traditional view that fiction can … deal with real people', but only after offering 'a devastating critique of the conventions by which the writer of fiction has conditioned us to a willing suspension of disbelief' (112). This is important because it allows us to see the way in which political and epistemological concerns can work together in Beckett's writing. In Murphy's construction, Beckett is offering a 'devastating' critique of convention as well as insights into 'real-world' questions. What should be noted about Murphy's argument, though, is its almost exclusive focus on Beckett's prose. It does not offer a consideration of the ways in which Beckett's drama might deal with reality while engaging in critiques of convention. If, as Murphy argues, Beckett's prose affirms the view that fiction can deal with 'real people' what might be said of the theatre which very literally deals with real, flesh-and-blood people, in the guise of actors and audiences? I want to suggest that in the 1950s and 1960s Beckett uses the fleshliness of the theatre both to intensify an attack on the conventions of bourgeois art and to further his experimental investigations on the nature of human experience.

In making this argument, it is important to note the particular way in which Beckett's writing for theatre developed after the success of *Waiting for Godot* and *Endgame*. As Gontarski convincingly argues in *The Intent of Undoing* (1985), the manuscripts of Beckett's theatrical writing of this period reveal a movement from a parodic style that adopts and subverts the realist conventions of bourgeois literature, towards a more overtly formalistic approach which privileges pattern and structure. For instance, Gontarski notes that, in later versions of *Play*, Beckett 'de-emphasized the clichéd, parodic plot' that had been prominent in early drafts, focusing instead on the musicality of the piece (1985: 92). Gontarski seems to be identifying a conflict between Beckett's avant-garde impulse which drives him to parody bourgeois art, and his penchant for a more disinterested type of formal experimentation – the latter ultimately winning out.

However, when one considers the published versions of *Happy Days* and *Play* (as well as Beckett's approach to staging the plays) it becomes clear that this conflict was not easily resolved. Certainly, the manuscripts testify to a process of vaguening in which Beckett seems to strip his texts of moments that address the specificities of mid-twentieth-century life.[1] But in spite of these modifications, a parodic thread runs through *Happy Days*, even in later versions. This is evident in the description of the play's backdrop in the published version: 'Very pompier trompe-l'oeil backcloth to represent unbroken plain and sky to meet in far distance' (Beckett [1986] 2006: 138). Here Beckett is clearly working to parody a familiar kind of realism. Indeed, in a 1961 letter to Alan Schneider Beckett describes the play's scenery in these terms: 'What should characterize whole scene, sky and earth, is a pathetic unsuccessful realism, the kind of tawdriness you get in 3rd rate musical or pantomime, that quality of pompier, laughably earnest bad imitation' (Craig et al. 2014: 428). It might be suggested that, in working to produce this 'unsuccessful realism', Beckett is engaging in a kind of postmodernist pastiche – blankly adopting the recognizable style of the '3rd rate musical or pantomime'.[2] But there seems to be a particular avant-garde purpose behind Beckett's use of the backcloth. In presenting this landscape, he is setting his play up in opposition to a more successful kind of realism, and by successful here I mean a realism that transports the audience to a fictional sphere in which they can live vicariously. If bourgeois art can be defined by its attempt to affect a wilful suspension of disbelief, Beckett works towards an art that opposes the bourgeois by self-consciously failing to produce this effect.

The oppositionality that is to be found in the stage directions continues in the script of *Happy Days*. So much becomes evident when one considers the passages that are devoted to Shower or Cooker, a couple that are uttered into existence by the protagonist Winnie (who is uncertain of which name they go by). In the letter to Schneider, Beckett is clear about his intentions regarding Shower/Cooker, stating that they 'represent the onlooker (audience) wanting to know the meaning of things' (Craig et al. 2014: 429). Beckett, then, is constructing an audience to supplement the one seated in the theatre. Why? Reading the descriptions of Shower/Cooker alongside Bürger's theory of the avant-garde might move us towards an explanation. It is important to remember, here, the emphasis that Bürger's arguments place on questions of audience. His discussion of the differences between sacral, courtly and bourgeois art, for example, is less concerned with contrasts of content than reception. Bourgeois art is set apart from earlier forms primarily because it is received by isolated individuals who draw from it an imaginative self-understanding that lies outside the praxis of life. Avant-garde art, in turn, is defined by its attempt to trouble this bourgeois mode of reception. The Shower/Cooker passages of *Happy Days* are instances in which Beckett plays a part in this avant-garde programme.

To illustrate this, it is worth returning to the Schneider letter. Importantly, here, Beckett does not state that Shower/Cooker represent an audience per se. Rather they are an audience that wants 'to know the meaning of things'. At this point, Beckett is clearly referring to the questions asked by the male voice of Shower/Cooker upon viewing the submerged figure of Winnie: 'What's she doing? he says – What's the idea? he says – stuck up to her diddies in the bleeding ground – coarse fellow – What does it mean? he says – What's it meant to mean?' (Beckett [1986] 2006: 156). Shower/Cooker voices the desire to extract a meaning or idea from the work of art. As such, he is working in the bourgeois mode of reception outlined by Bürger. Shower/Cooker expects the work of art to hold within it some kind of value and is trying to access it. Eventually, he seems to find this value by casting himself as the hero of the drama and thinking about what he would do if confronted with a half-buried Winnie: 'I'd dig her out with my bare hands' (157). The work of art allows Shower/Cooker to construct an imaginary realm in which he is a hero. Beckett, however, is clearly working to disrupt this mode of artistic reception. This becomes apparent through the words of the female Shower/Cooker voice. When the male voice questions what Winnie is meant to mean, the female voice responds:

> And you, she says, what's the idea of you, she says, what are you meant to mean? Is it because you're still on your two flat feet, with your old ditty full of tinned muck and changes of underwear, dragging me up and down this fornicating wilderness. (156)

The male Shower/Cooker voice is using art to discover himself as a heroic human being. The female voice, however, reduces him back to his functions (walking, mucking etc.). By undermining the male Shower/Cooker voice in such a way Beckett steers a theatrical audience away from Bürger's bourgeois mode of reception. Rather than producing a space in which they can imaginatively 'unfold the abundance' of their talents, the play asks them to remember what functional beings they are in everyday life. In the Shower/Cooker passages of *Happy Days*, then, Beckett invites the audience to perceive themselves reductively. Rather than human beings required to make meaning from art, Beckett casts his audience as material entities who exist to carry out repetitive acts, eat 'tinned muck' and soil their underwear.

This materialization of the theatrical audience is continued in *Play*. In the later work, however, this process is not carried out through (loosely) named characters, but a spotlight. Beckett effectively writes this piece of theatrical equipment into his text by giving it the power to provoke the speech of the three urn-bound players: W1, W2 and M ([1986] 2006: 307). Rather than a mere apparatus facilitating a theatrical production, the spotlight of *Play* is conceived as part of the environment inhabited by the players. As Beckett puts it in a direction, the light 'must not be situated outside of the ideal space (stage) occupied by its victims' (318). Here, as Katherine Weiss notes, 'It is tempting to link the spotlight directly to the eyes of the audience' (2001: 187). The spotlight could, in other words, be seen as a textual representation of the theatrical audience, whose eyes stimulate the players into performance. This, though, as Weiss recognizes, oversimplifies things: the spotlight does not present the audience in general, but an audience of a particular type: one that watches the play mechanically without being able to critically reflect on it and make meaning. Here the spotlight can be contrasted with the male Shower/Cooker voice in *Happy Days*. Where Shower/Cooker tried to draw meaning from Winnie's situation, the spotlight appears to be, in the words of M, 'mere eye. No mind. Opening and shutting on me' (317). The light, as Weiss puts it, 'swivels from one image to the other not hearing or seeing them. It is a precise and automated eye that authoritatively switches the voices on and off but does not see or hear the nuances of the performance' (189). Weiss reads this aspect of *Play* in relation to Walter Benjamin's argument that, over the course of modernity, the gaze-altering power of technologies such as the camera has produced absent-minded, uncritical audiences. For Weiss, however, Beckett's audience is not supposed to identify with Benjamin's absent-minded viewer. On the contrary, they are supposed to resist this identification and become more critical viewers, by questioning 'the reproductive and manipulative structures in the production of a play' (192). In the same way that the male Shower/Cooker voice worked to steer the theatrical audience away from Bürger's bourgeois mode of reception, the spotlight is seen to prompt the audience to resist becoming absent-minded, automated viewers. This becomes clear in the final lines of the play where the protagonists seem to address their viewer directly and speculate about the level at which this viewer is attending to their actions. There is the possibility, M suggests, that the viewer is 'looking for something. In my face. Some truth in my eyes' (317). But ultimately M is brought to question, in the final line of the script, whether he is 'as much as … being seen' (317). The audience is left to question whether they, like the spotlight, are unseeing, automated viewers or whether they are pursuing truth or insight from the situation with which they are presented. The audience is left with the critical problem of positioning themselves in between the bourgeois and the mechanical viewer.

Taken together, *Happy Days* and *Play* showcase Beckett's avant-gardist attempt to draw his audience into a kind of resistance. He does this largely by inviting his theatrical audiences to construct themselves in opposition to the audiences that are represented in the fiction of the plays. In *Happy Days* the undermining of the bourgeois onlooker represented by Shower/Cooker reminds the audience that finding meaning in art does not compensate for an everyday life in which one is, in Bürger's words, 'reduced to a partial function (means-ends activity)'. The audience is asked to resist the response of the bourgeois viewer of art and reflect on the way in which aesthetic experience relates to everyday life. In *Play*, the spotlight plays the role of fictive audience. Here, rather than being asked to recognize their existence as functional subjects, the audience is invited to resist it and, in doing so, reflect on their own relationship with the theatrical production. By foregrounding the spotlight as a functional viewer – a 'mere eye' – Beckett prompts the audience to question the level on which they are engaging with events on stage. Are they just 'opening and shutting' on the action, or are they 'looking for something ... some truth' in what they are shown? Ultimately, then, the plays attempt to fashion an avant-garde subjectivity that takes shape through opposing itself to the bourgeois subject that is searching for insight from art and the mechanical subject that responds to it passively.

Experimental Beckett

Beckett's avant-gardism in *Happy Days* and *Play* has been seen to reside in the capacity of the plays to place their audiences in opposition to bourgeois or mechanistic models of aesthetic spectatorship. In this way, the plays have a political concern. The theatre of the 1950s and 1960s, however, also shows a more epistemological concern with the ways in which humans learn. Here Beckett evidently draws on his knowledge of early-twentieth-century psychology, engaging with the major models of learning that he encountered in his reading: the behaviourist and the configurationist. As has been noted, the relationship between proponents of these two models was fractious – the debates have been characterized as 'wars'. Beckett's experiments on the learning process, however, are largely detached from the internal politics that characterized institutional psychology of the period. Beckett is not trying to decide between behaviourist and configurationist models of learning. Rather, the plays seem to synthesize different elements from the schools that he had encountered, without favouring one over the others.

Beckett's largely non-partisan approach to the psychology of learning is unsurprising when one considers the main source of his knowledge of the learning debates. As the title of the book suggests, R. S. Woodworth's *Contemporary Schools of Psychology* is a work which deals with a plurality of psychological approaches to various topics without seeming to give overall privilege to any one approach. Of course, this can be partly put down to the book's status as an introductory textbook, but Woodworth also favoured this non-partisan perspective when writing for more specialist audiences. For example, '"Gestalt" Psychology and the Concept of Reaction Stages', a 1927 contribution to the *American Journal of Psychology*, sees Woodworth set up 'four men of straw', each of which is a caricature of a particular school of psychology: 'The sensationist, the perceptionist, the intentionist, and the motorist' (63). Each of these men of straw 'represents a fruitful line psychological investigation', but because each adheres strongly to a system that privileges a single aspect of psychological activity (sensation, perception, etc.) each gives an account of psychology that is 'obviously false' (64). 'It is absurd', Woodworth continues, 'that psychologists generally should be expected to choose between one-sided and fanatical systems' (64). There is a need for a system that has a place for 'every sort of scientific psychological work'. Such an integrative system is what Woodworth is working towards in his article.

A system capable of synthesizing multiple competing approaches to psychology, in Woodworth's view, must be underpinned by the idea of 'reaction stages' (64). Woodworth, here, is advocating a type of stimulus-response psychology but one that is more expansive than that of the behaviourists. There are, he suggests, multiple processes or stages that come between a human's exposure to a stimulus and the motor response they make to it: 'When an external stimulus impinges on the organism and elicits a motor response, there is undoubtedly a series of intraorganic processes intervening between stimulus and movement, sometimes a relatively short series, as in reflex action, and sometimes a long series, as in the skilful handling of a complex situation indicated by the stimulus' (62). Psychologists, for Woodworth, need to pay attention to all of these stages and not just the ones that fit into their chosen system. In this way, he is straying from the behaviourist model by stating that psychologists need to study reaction stages that 'may be called "mental"' in addition to those characterized by motor activity (62). But he is also opposing the gestaltist doctrine which denies 'the reality of sensation' in its attempt to emphasize perception (67).[3] Contemporary historians of psychology tend to see the importance of Woodworth's article in terms of the way in which it anticipates the cognitive models that would supersede behaviourist doctrine in the second half of the twentieth century. As David Carroll suggests, Woodworth seems to be outlining 'what would later be called information processing stages in which a sensory stimulus is analyzed in various ways' (2017: 178). Beckett's reading of Woodworth, then, would have given him insight into the transition from behaviourist to cognitive psychology, and the plays of the 1950s and 1960s reflect this.[4] Beckett's dramatic experiments on learning bear the influence of Woodworth in the way in which they work to stand outside of any one school and interrogate the various stages that make up an individual's response to a given stimulus.

In no play is this influence more apparent than 1957s *Act Without Words I*. Originally, written for the Parisian cabaret, *Act Without Words I* is a one-act mime which presents a single man in a desert being frustrated by an unseen force as he attempts to either escape or obtain water and shelter. It is also the work of Beckett's that was most overly influenced by his reading of experimental psychology. James Knowlson recognizes that the mime reflects 'Beckett's reading of behavioural psychology when a young man', pointing particularly to the probable influence of gestalt psychologist Wolfgang Köhler's 1921 book *The Mentality of Apes* (1996: 419). Similarly, Matthew Feldman suggests that Köhler's study acted as inspiration for the setting and events of the play – though, having looked at the 'Psychology' notes, Feldman concludes that Beckett did not encounter Köhler directly, but through his reading of Woodworth (2006: 107). Finally, Ulrika Maude suggests that 'much of the imagery' of the play 'is strikingly similar' to Köhler's illustrations of his study (2013: 89). All three critics recognize surface resemblances between Beckett's play and Köhler's experiments.[5]

However, too little critical attention has hitherto been paid to the fact that Beckett encountered *The Mentality of Apes* through Woodworth, a psychologist who was interested in synthesizing different schools of psychology. This detail is important because it is reflected in the structure of *Act Without Words I*. The play consists primarily of the responses of the man in the desert to a whistle. After he is initially flung onto the stage/desert at the beginning of the play, we are immediately shown that the man is disposed to follow the direction of a whistle. There is a 'whistle from right wing' and the man 'reflects, goes out right', only to be 'flung back on stage' (Beckett [1986] 2006: 203). Beckett seems to have had a long-standing interest in the idea that humans could be trained to follow the direction of a whistle. In 'Fingal', an early story from *More Pricks Than Kicks* (1934), the inmates of a mental asylum visited by the protagonist Belacqua seem to have been trained to the whistle: 'Now the loonies poured out into the sun, the better behaved left to their own devices, the others in herds in charge of warders. The whistle blew and the herd stopped; again and it proceeded' (Beckett 2010: 22). The 'herd' of inmates seem to respond to the whistle reflexively in a way that brings to mind Pavlovian conditioning.[6] There is a sense that the whistle of *Act Without Words I* is operating in the same tradition. It might be argued that rather than Köhler's configurationist, we are invited to see the nameless, wordless protagonist of the play as a Pavlovian/Watsonian behaviourist subject. There is, however, an important difference between the 'loonies' of the early story and the later protagonist: where the 'loonies' are limited to making immediate responses, the protagonist shows the capacity to also make the responses that are founded on reflection. For example, when a 'little tree descends from the flies', a whistle comes from above at which the protagonist 'turns, sees tree, reflects, goes to it, sits down in its shadow, looks at his hands' (Beckett [1986] 2006: 203). When exposed to the whistle, the protagonist still makes an immediate, reflex response (he 'turns'), but there is also an act of perception ('sees tree'), and then an act of thought ('reflects'), before another motor response. Staged here is a model of human action that seems in close confluence with the model of reaction stages favoured by Woodworth. Though *Act Without Words I* evidently draws inspiration from Köhler, the mediating presence of Woodworth is observable in the way in which the text synthesizes the reflexive behaviourist subject with a subject that is more reflective.

The play also synthesizes behaviourist and configurationist approaches in the way in which it stages the process by which the mime learns. Critics of the play have often noted that, in contrast to Köhler's apes, Beckett's mime does not attain the objectives of water and shelter. From this it has often been concluded that Beckett's play critiques, or at least complicates, configurationist ideas about learning.[7] This conclusion, though, ignores the degree to which Beckett's protagonist is shown to learn over the course of *Act Without Words I*. Beckett's protagonist may be frustrated in his attempts to acquire water and shelter. But it seems clear that he does, over the course of the play, attain insight into the nature of his condition and modify his actions in accordance with this insight. In his reading of Woodworth, Beckett noted that in the gestaltist view, one learns to achieve a goal, not by a continual process of trial and error, but 'by perceiving the situation as a pattern with a central feature' (Feldman 2004: 319). In Beckett's play, the protagonist does not achieve the goal of attaining water and shelter, but he does seem to move beyond a process of trial and error to ultimately perceive a pattern. For example, at the beginning of the play, he tries out many different ways of attaining the carafe of water that is placed above his reach – piling up cubes, making a lasso from rope and so on. However, no matter what he does, an invisible force seems to keep the carafe out of his reach. If the protagonist was working purely by trial and error in this situation, he would simply carry on attempting to attain the carafe by different means. This is not the story Beckett tells. Instead, the protagonist seems to attain the insight that an invisible force is keeping the carafe away from him and thus gives up on the attempt to attain it. This becomes apparent at the end of the play when the carafe first 'comes to rest a few feet from his body' and then 'dangles and plays about his face' ([1986] 2006: 206). Rather than reaching out for the carafe, the protagonist continues to lie motionless on the floor. He has learnt the hopeless lesson that the situation is rigged against his acquiring the carafe, and so no longer tries. After a period of behaviourist trial and error, a process of insight-based learning has occurred. Beckett shows an interest in the human subject's, often reflexive, motor responses to given sensory stimuli, but he is also concerned with the frequency with which these motor responses are mediated by reflection and insight.

Cognitive maps in rats and audiences

Act Without Words I, then, does much to place Beckett in the psychological tradition of Woodworth – a tradition that is drawn to behaviourist ideas of stimulus-response, but also sympathetic towards more mentalistic approaches. In light of this, it is also worth viewing Beckett's psychological experimentation in relation to the psychologist that is frequently seen to develop and refine the ideas of Woodworth: Edward Tolman. Now, there is no archival evidence to suggest a direct link between Beckett and Tolman, so my argument here is not one of influence. Rather my case will be that the two writers share an interest in exploring the way in which sensory information is stored, and how an archive of this sensory information impacts future behaviour.

Tolman's definitive discussion of these questions comes in his influential 1948 article 'Cognitive Maps in Rats and Men'. The article is largely devoted to summarizing the findings of a series of experiments carried out by Tolman and others on the capacity of rats to learn to navigate mazes. But Tolman makes clear from the beginning that he is concerned with 'the significance of these findings on rats for the clinical behavior of men' (1948: 189). The rat experiments themselves are used as evidence to support the particular theory of learning advocated by Tolman, namely field theory. The field theorists, Tolman explains, are characterized by their belief 'that in the course of learning something like a field map of the environment gets established in the rat's brain' (192). He defines this school of thought in opposition to a more strictly behaviourist school 'which believes that the maze behavior of rats is a matter of mere simple stimulus-response connections' (190). The field theorists, Tolman goes on, 'agree with the other school that the rat in running a maze is exposed to stimuli and is finally led as a result of these stimuli to the responses which actually occur' (192). But the evidence acquired by the field theorists suggests that 'the intervening brain processes' are more complex, patterned and autonomous than the more strictly behaviourist school would suggest (192).

Tolman describes five empirical findings that support field theory: '(1) "latent learning," (2) "vicarious trial and error" or "VTE," (3) "searching for the stimulus," (4) "hypotheses" and (5) "spatial orientation"' (193). There is not enough space here to discuss all five of these findings, so I will focus particularly on the two that seem most relevant to Beckett's theatre: vicarious trial and error, and latent learning. Essentially, these two findings suggest that, when placed in mazes, rats do not simply respond to the environment reflexively, but deliberate about their different options, engaging in what the experimenters call vicarious trial and error. What is more, this deliberation seems to be informed by past experience – the rats are seen to store previous experiences in the maze and access it when making decisions. In terms of vicarious trial and error, Tolman notes that 'hesitating, looking-back-and-forth-type' behaviour is frequently observed in rat experiments (196–7). His discussion though emphasizes that these moments of deliberation can be observed and measured in order to support the theory that 'in the critical stages – whether in the first picking up of the instructions or in the later making sure of which stimulus is which – the animal's activity is not just one of responding passively to discrete stimuli, but rather one of the active selecting and comparing of stimuli' (200).

This selecting and comparing of stimuli is seen to be informed by experience. So much is made clear in Tolman's description of a contemporaneous experiment carried out by K. W. Spence and R. Lippitt at the University of Iowa. In this experiment rats were run down a straight path that eventually led to two goal boxes, one on the left containing food and one on the right containing water. The rats were placed in this 'Y-maze' in two different scenarios: an initial training period when they were 'neither hungry nor thirsty' and a second test in which half of the rats were kept hungry and half thirsty (195–6). In the initial training period, the rats did not show any tendency towards either the left or the right box. However, in the second test those that were hungry showed a strong tendency to go to the box in which the food had been and those that were thirsty went to the water box. Although they seemed to respond randomly to the maze in the initial training period, the rats had all the time been learning about their environment. As Tolman puts it, they had been building up 'a cognitive map to the effect that food was to the left and water to the right' (196). What is more, they showed the capacity to put this cognitive map to use when motivated to do so at a later point in time. Taken together, then, latent learning and vicarious trial and error evidence two points. First, that rats store sensory information and can retrieve it at a later point. Second, that this retrieval process can frequently be read on the bodies of rats in the form of 'hesitating, looking-back-and-forth-type' behaviour.

In his theatre of the 1950s and 1960s, Beckett experiments on both points, though his subjects are audiences rather than rats. *Act Without Words I*, for instance, can be read as a study of the way in which reflective thought is read, or misread onto the human body. Undoubtedly, the play stages instances that resemble Tolman's account of vicarious trial and error. One thinks particularly of the moment towards the beginning of the play when, having just been whistled towards the left wing and promptly flung back on stage, he is again whistled to the left. At this moment, 'He reflects. Goes towards left wing, hesitates, thinks better of it, halts, turns aside, reflects' (Beckett [1986] 2006: 203). Clearly, this is the 'looking-back-and-forth-type' behaviour that Tolman perceives in rats, but Beckett is not merely interested in the phenomenon of hesitating movements. What also seems crucial for Beckett is that these moves be staged live in front of an audience. There is a clear interest in the process of observing the acting out of thought. This is evident in a 1957 letter to Barney Rosset in which Beckett rejects the idea that *Act Without Words I* might be made into a film. The reason for this rejection, Beckett suggests, is that the play requires that the 'last extremity of human meat – or bones – be there, thinking and stumbling and sweating under our noses' (Craig et al. 2014: 64). Like Tolman, Beckett is working to counter the behaviourist eschewal of mental processes by materializing thought, presenting it as an action that goes on right 'under our noses'.

One might argue, here, that the audience members are cast in the role of experimenter – that they are asked to observe the human's movement of vicarious trial and error and use it to build up a model of human subjectivity. This, though, does not seem quite right. The scripted nature of the play's action, I would suggest, complicates things for the audience and makes it more appropriate to think of them as the subjects of the experiments. Behind the man on stage, there is an actor/mime artist following a set of instructions. Unlike Tolman's rats, Beckett's mime is not really hesitating over what to do next; he is simply exhibiting that behaviour. What is under scrutiny in this experiment, then, is not the behaviour of the actor, as that has already been determined. It is the response of the audience. Though the mime may appear to be deliberating over what to do next, a look to their cognitive maps should show the audience that they are attending a play and the mime is following a script. Nevertheless, as many audience members have reported, trying to hold onto this information is difficult. One frequently gets caught up in the perception that the thought that is staged is really happening. As a reviewer of the Las Vegas production puts it: 'Every thought seems to register on his face. You never get the sense that this is only about movement' (Del Valle 2007). In question in Beckett's play, as in the experiments discussed by Tolman, is the capacity of subjects to use stored information when processing a given sensory stimulus. Does the knowledge that this is 'only movement' prevent us from perceiving that thought is going on 'under our noses'?

In later plays, Beckett would continue to examine the way in which reflective thought is exhibited. However, he brings into view a behaviour that Tolman does not: speech. Unlike Tolman's murine subjects, humans, of course, do not need to rely on 'hesitating, looking-back-and-forth-type' behaviour to evidence their capacity for reflective thought. They can translate their thoughts into words. However, in works such as *Happy Days* and *Play* Beckett scrutinizes the degree to which speech evidences reflective thought. *Happy Days* is exemplary in this regard because of the way in which the speech seems to combine reflectivity with reflexivity. Ulrika Maude has pointed out the frequency with which Winnie's speech seems to be delivered 'in the manner of a reflex, mouthed mechanically, devoid of semantic content' (2013: 87). And this is suggested in Beckett's instruction to Alan Schneider that Winnie should speak with the 'same tone throughout, polishing mechanically' (Craig et al. 2014: 428). However, what should not be ignored are the many points of verbal back-and-forthing that seem to indicate Winnie's capacity for reflective thought. A good example of this is the moment where Winnie speculates on whether 'the earth has lost its atmosphere':

> The earth ball. (*Pause.*) I sometimes wonder. (*Pause.*) Perhaps not quite all. (*Pause.*) There always remains something. (*Pause.*) Of everything. (*Pause.*) Some remains. (*Pause.*) If the mind were to go. (*Pause.*) It won't of course. (*Pause.*) Not quite. (*Pause.*) Not mine. (*Smile.*) Not now. (*Smile broader.*) No no. (*Smile off. Long pause.*) (Beckett [1986] 2006: 161)

The frequent pauses and changing facial expressions, combined with the way in which the succession of phrases modify each other ('not quite', 'not mine', 'not now'), give the sense that we are witnessing a moment of reflective thought here. But the mechanical nature of the delivery never quite allows us to trust this sense. It reminds us of what we should already know – that Winnie is a stage entity delivering a script. Beckett is scrutinizing the capacity of his audience to learn that Winnie's speech is not the product of reflective thought.

Another example of this tension between reflectivity and reflexivity manifests a few lines later. At this point, Winnie seems to voice a degree of insight into the way in which she responds to the bell that has been seen to trigger her action:

> The bell, (*Pause.*) It hurts like a knife. (*Pause.*) A gouge. (*Pause.*) One cannot ignore it. (*Pause.*) How often … (*pause*) … I say how often I have said Ignore it, Winnie, ignore the bell, pay no heed, just sleep and wake as you please, open and close the eyes, as you please, or in the way you find most helpful. … But no. (162)

Again, Winnie seems to be reflecting on her situation, and even tells us what she has said to herself. But Beckett is again emphasizing reflexivity. Not only is the speech delivered in a mechanical way, but its content also testifies to Winnie's lack of agency – whatever she tells herself Winnie will still respond to the bell in the same way. Furthermore, the fact that the bell is the stimulus to which Winnie reflexively responds emphasizes the scripted nature of Winnie's speech; the bell connotes the sound that is used to inform the theatrical audience that a play is about to begin. Thus, the audience is again caught between the knowledge that the performance is a scripted action, and the sense that they are watching an acting out of thought.

The idea that Beckett is experimenting on the audience's capacity to draw on stored information is reinforced by his use of repetitions in *Happy Days* and *Play*. Each play is made up of an initial stage in which a set of actions unfold, and then a second stage that bears a striking resemblance to the initial one but has some key differences. *Happy Days* consists of two acts, but both present the same scene: a barren landscape with scorched grass in which Winnie speaks to Willie but gets little-to-no response. The major difference between the two acts is that the first act presents Winnie 'embedded up to above her waist' in a mound, where the second act sees her 'embedded up to neck' (Beckett [1986] 2006: 138; 160). This difference necessarily means that less can happen in the second act – as Winnie, the central source of action, is less mobile. Pervading the second act, then, is a sense of entropy. The characters' situation becomes more hopeless, and there is decreased potential for dramatic action. In developing this structure, Beckett is experimenting on the richness of his audience's cognitive maps – the extent to which they use sensory information stored during the first act to enrich their experience of the second. The extent to which Beckett conceived the play in these terms becomes apparent in a 1960 letter to Schneider. Speaking of the relationship between the two acts, Beckett writes: 'I am counting a lot on memory of 1 for 2, which is stupidly said, I mean a kind of physical post image of 1 all through 2' (Craig et al. 2014: 383).[8] A divide, thus, emerges between Beckett's protagonists and his audience. The protagonist of *Happy Days* does not seem able to store and retrieve sensory information. As Beckett put it in his theatrical notebook, Winnie moves 'from one inextricable present to the next, those past unremembered, those to come inconceivable' (qtd. in Knowlson 1985: 150). The experience of the audience, however (and consequently the success of the play), depends on their capacity to produce a cognitive map through which to relate the present and the past. Underlying the structure of Beckett's play is a question of how his audience use information from one moment to inform their experience of the next.

Steven Connor recognizes that 'the [above] comments Beckett applied to Winnie … might seem to apply just as well to the characters in *Play*' (1988: 180). *Play*, of course, sees Beckett go even further than *Happy Days* in scrutinizing the connection between speech and reflective thought. We are presented with speech that is delivered in toneless voices and that does not seem to derive from the protagonist's intentions; it occurs at the instigation of a spotlight that might be seen as a successor to the whistle of *Act Without Words I* and the bell of *Happy Days*. This manifests in Beckett's stage directions which emphasize that the 'response' of the players to the light 'is immediate' ([1986] 2006: 307). It becomes clear that, in Ulrika Maude's words, 'the players … lack a sense of agency, or intentional subjectivity. What remains is merely obedience to compulsion' (2013: 87). The players, Connor suggests, exist in a hell of 'unrecognised repetition', in which they are denied even 'the satisfaction of seeing themselves doing the same thing over and over again' (180). In view of this, Connor suggests that the audience is 'crucial to *Play*, for it is they, and they only who realize what is happening' (180). This reading takes as its starting point the repetition that is written into Beckett's play, which, for Connor, not only gives the sense that the players 'must go through their stories again and again' but also changes understandings of the light: 'The effect of the repetition is to reveal that the light is no freer than they [the players] are, but is itself forced to repeat the inquisition, having learned nothing' (180). The audience, then, is crucial because they are placed in a position where they can potentially learn something over the course of the play. It should be emphasized, though, that this learning depends on an audience's capacity to store and retrieve sensory information. If they are incapable of relating the first act and the repeat, the message Connor outlines will not emerge. Beckett's play, I suggest, is an experiment on the existence of this capacity for cognitive mapping; it does not assume that it exists *a priori*.

The sense that Beckett was trying to find something out about the capacities of his audience through the staging of *Play* manifests in the concerns he voiced over the repeat. In his correspondence on *Play*, Beckett frequently questioned the degree to which an audience was likely to comprehend the play the first time they saw it, and how this would affect the experience brought about by the repeat. For example, in a 1963 letter to German literary publisher and audience member Siegfried Unseld, he relates a concern about the repeat:

> It may be that the *da capo* is a mistake. It was justified in my mind, technically speaking, by the necessarily imperfect understanding, on a single hearing, of such broken and rushed speech. It is obvious that if the delivery does not have the required speed, repetition is likely to be wearisome. There has to be a bewildering outburst of light and speech fragments. (Craig et al. 2014: 560)

Beckett is clearly working with a model of latent learning here. He is concerned with the degree to which an audience will learn to (imperfectly) comprehend the play when first exposed to it and then use this information to help perfect their understanding during the *da capo*. However, in this letter, he worries that if the play is easily understandable 'on a single hearing' there will be nothing left for the audience to learn during the repeat. Through the repeat, Beckett wishes to take his audience from bewilderment towards a good level of understanding. However, this theatrical method requires a knowledge of the human capacity for learning that can only be acquired through staging the play and seeing how audiences respond. As it turned out, the things Beckett learnt on staging the play caused him to revise the script, which had been published by Faber before Beckett had worked on it in the theatre. Beckett eventually moved from a direct repetition to a repeat that contained variations in the ordering of the speeches. Through staging *Play*, Beckett seems to have realized that the human capacity for speech comprehension and latent learning was stronger than he assumed, and consequently made the task he set his audience more challenging.

In a later letter to Unseld explaining this change, Beckett seems to recognize the degree to which his idea of what a play does is informed by theatrical staging. In it, he vows that he will never 'give another theatre text … to be published until I have worked on it in the theatre' (Craig et al. 2014: 598). The staging of *Play*, then, was a means through which Beckett acquired knowledge of human capacities, which in turn informed later versions of the play. Finally, it should be noted that Beckett became open to the modification of the conditions of his experiment. He (somewhat uncharacteristically) gave licence for different directors to adapt the repeat differently. The stage direction on which he ultimately settled reads as follows: 'The repeat may be an exact replica of first statement, or it may present an element of variation. In other words, the light may operate the second time exactly as it did the first (exact replica) or it may try a different method (variation)' (Beckett [1986] 2006: 320). The play is set up to allow future directors/experimenters to look for new and varied ways to investigate their audience's capacity for latent learning.

Conclusion

This chapter has tried to distinguish an avant-garde Beckett from an experimental one. But it has also identified a degree of confluence between these two figures. Both Becketts produced in the chapter are defined by the way in which they think about interactions between a theatrical audience and the events that unfold on stage. The avant-garde Beckett is concerned with the capacity of an audience to resist the models of viewership that were dominant in the twentieth century. In *Happy Days*, the audience is incited to oppose themselves to the bourgeois model that is represented by the male Shower/Cooker voice. In *Play*, by contrast, the audience is prompted to react against an unreflective, mechanical mode of artistic reception that is embodied by the spotlight. How does this avant-garde Beckett coexist with an experimental Beckett that is highly concerned with the psychological processes by which humans learn? In some sense, these two Becketts are working at cross-purposes. There is a degree of discord between the political concerns of the avant-garde Beckett and the experimental Beckett's epistemological concerns. The former seems to want to instil his audience with a critical consciousness, where the latter is, to some extent, treating them as a means through which to carry out an autonomous pursuit of knowledge. One might argue that there is something a little bourgeois about Beckett's scientifically informed experimentation. There is then a tension at work within the theatre of the 1950s and 1960s that is (as the following chapters will indicate) less noticeable in the theatrical works that would follow *Play*.

Nevertheless, there are some clear overlaps between Beckett's avant-garde and experimental concerns. Both the avant-garde and experimental Becketts that have been constructed in this chapter are interested in showing their audience that they can be (and are) defined as functional, stimulus-response units. Starting from this base, both Becketts try to negotiate the terms on which the human subject can be conceived as more than this. At this point the experimental aspect of Beckett's work becomes very important. Beckett's theatre does not assume that humans possess cognitive capacities for intention, reflection and interpretation, and merely attempt to represent these capacities on stage. Instead, his theatrical practice scrutinizes the degree to which these capacities are enacted by a theatrical audience, asking audiences to prove that they are more than mere nerves, meat and bones. The experimental Beckett, then, is serving an avant-garde purpose by working to construct an expansive human subjectivity that is not bound up in humanistic, bourgeois assumptions.

2

Attention and speech perception in *Not I*

In *Suspensions of Perception* (1999) Jonathan Crary notes that there was 'an explosion of research and debate' on the topic of attention in the late nineteenth century (1999: 23). Attention, Crary suggests, 'is not just one of many topics examined experimentally by late nineteenth-century psychology' (25). Instead, 'a subject whose attentiveness was the site of observation, classification and measurement' was presupposed in most of the discipline's key areas of research (25). For Crary, this emphasis on attention marks a fundamental cultural shift. He argues that, in Western society, 'new imperatives of attentiveness' were emerging which aimed to make the perceiving body 'productive and orderly, whether as a student, worker or consumer' (22–3). It is no coincidence, by Crary's account, that psychological research on attention emerged alongside an economic system that demanded the 'attentiveness of a subject in a wide range of new productive and spectacular tasks' (29). Inattention, 'within a context of new forms of large scale industrialized production[,] began to be treated as a danger and a serious problem' (13). The 'nascent field of scientific psychology' worked within a culture where the human subject was asked to attend to 'an endless sequence of new products, sources of stimulation, and streams of information' (13–14).

As Crary suggests, the concept of attention has retained a prominent place within institutional empirical research since the 1880s. However, there have been significant changes in the study of attention between the end of the nineteenth century and today. First, the rise of behaviourism undoubtedly lessened the degree to which psychologists studied the concept of attention in the early twentieth century.[1] Attention was problematic for behaviourists because, unlike overt responses, attentional processes are not directly observable. One cannot measure a drop in attentiveness to an object in the same way as, say, a drop in body temperature. Thus, the concept of attention did not fit easily into the early-twentieth-century behaviourist paradigm. The concept, however, becomes important again in the period after the Second World War. Crary glosses the suggestion that 'problems related to the efficient human use of new technology during World War II were in part responsible for a new wave of research into attention' (34). Similarly, Shallice and Cooper point to 'a modern approach to the area' of selective attention that begins after the Second World War (2011: 29). For example, the world wars had seen the advent of aviation as a mode of war, and it was desirable that the pilots operating planes kept contact with those on the ground. It was asked: 'How many channels of contact can be maintained with a pilot?' (29). As we will see, this question triggered a wave of research attempting to tackle questions of how we are able to focus on a single task for an extended period of time or attend to multiple tasks simultaneously.

For a variety of theoretical and practical reasons, then, the concept of attention has been prominent in the history of experimental psychology. In the next three chapters, I want to consider the extent to which it influenced twentieth-century aesthetic experimentation, particularly that of Samuel Beckett. Focusing on three of Beckett's plays from the 1970s – *Not I*, *That Time* and *Footfalls* – the chapters will compare the way in which attention is approached in experimental psychology to the way in which it operates in Beckett's work. The current chapter will begin by suggesting that Beckett's approaches to attention and those of experimental psychology (as well as more psychoanalytic approaches) are rooted in the ideas of the German philosopher Arthur Schopenhauer. It will then move on to an extended discussion of *Not I* in which I consider the play both as a theatrical performance that makes certain attentional demands of its actors and audience, and as a narrative which attends to the life story of a protagonist. The chapters that follow will then consider how we attend to faces in *That Time*, and inattention (how we miss things that are right in front of us) in *Footfalls*. At the heart of this series of chapters are two main concerns. First, the way in which both aesthetic and scientific interests in attentional processes fit into the debates surrounding reductive and expansive models of human subjectivity discussed in the last chapter. Second, how Beckett's concern with attention works alongside his other aesthetic, political and philosophical concerns.

Schopenhauer, attention and the limits of consciousness

As well as emphasizing the degree to which the rise of attention studies coincided with the advance of capitalism, Crary suggests that developments in philosophy over the course of the nineteenth century played a significant role in inspiring interest in the concept. A key protagonist in this, Crary suggests, was the German philosopher (and favourite of Beckett) Arthur Schopenhauer. Schopenhauer, Crary writes, was one of the first to emphasize 'the unstable and specifically *temporal* nature of perception' (1999: 55, emphasis in original). What Schopenhauer brought to nineteenth-century thought, then, was an increased awareness of the limitations of the human capacity to attend to the world. In the second edition of *The World as Will and Representation* (1844), he stressed the extent to which the human was only capable of concentrating on one thing at a time, and that the human could only concentrate on one thing for a limited amount of time. 'The intellect', Schopenhauer writes, 'apprehends only successively, and to grasp one thing it must give up another' ([1844] 1966: 137). But even the one thing that is grasped cannot be held for very long:

> Just as the eye, when it gazes for a long time at *one* object is soon not able to see it distinctly any longer because the outlines run into one another, become confused, and finally everything becomes obscure, so also through long continued rumination on *one* thing, our thinking gradually becomes confused and dull, and ends in complete stupor. (137–8; emphasis in original)

These observations register what Crary calls 'the *physiological* conditions of knowledge' (1999: 56, emphasis in original) – the idea that perception, thought and knowledge are subject to the materiality of the human body. In contrast to Kantian theory, which posits a unifying mechanism that gives coherence to successive perceptions and reflections, Schopenhauer's line of thought suggests that any semblance of intellectual coherence is contingent upon the workings of a will that is closely linked to the body, and of unstable character. Instead of a set of *a priori* principles, human experience is unified by, what Beckett calls in his 'Philosophy Notes', 'the <u>absolute unreason of objectless will</u>' (Feldman 2004: 308, emphasis in original).

For Crary, the ideas of Schopenhauer not only worked towards 'the overturning of a Kantian model of synthesis' but also prompted an interrogation of the primacy of consciousness in human subjectivity (1999: 57). By emphasizing distraction, forgetfulness and the stupor, Schopenhauer pointed to the limits of conscious experience, beginning a line of thought which questioned the hitherto inevitable 'congruence between subjectivity and a thinking "I"' (58). In effect, Crary is making the argument that Schopenhauer's work anticipates psychological movements such as psychoanalysis and behaviourism which emphasized non-conscious forms of human activity. But if Schopenhauer's work gave impetus to the study of a non-conscious subjectivity, it was left for later psychologists, clinicians and artists to put this study into practice. For example, Schopenhauer writes: 'The idea that is now vividly engrossing my attention is *bound* after a while to have slipped entirely from my memory' (1966: 137, emphasis in original). This statement raises a series of empirical questions: To what extent does his being engrossed by the idea imply obliviousness to other matters? For exactly how long does the idea engross attention? And when an idea has slipped from memory can it be retrieved in the future? These were the kinds of questions that would animate both experimental and therapeutic psychology, as well as the aesthetic experiments of Samuel Beckett.

Experimental psychology has done much to address the questions raised in the Schopenhauer quotation. Most notably, since the end of the nineteenth century, experimenters have investigated the extent to which a subject's attending to one task or stimulus implies the failure to register anything else. For early evidence of this, we need only look back to the experiment of Stein and Solomons (discussed in the Introduction). And for more recent examples one can look to influential experiments by Donald Broadbent (1958) and Neisser and Becklen (1975) which tested whether subjects could select one perceptual channel and inhibit others. These experiments questioned whether the human apprehends only successively or is able to pay attention to multiple things at once, but they also consider what humans perform without conscious attention: what tasks or stimuli can be carried out, or responded to, without the subject's thinking about them.

Schopenhauer's anticipation of psychoanalytic thinking is perhaps more commonly recognized. Much critical discussion has evaluated the continuities between Schopenhauer's will and the Freudian unconscious.[2] The resemblance between the two thinkers is most obvious in the degree to which each foregrounds what Sebastian Gardner calls the 'superficiality of consciousness' (1999: 376). In a particularly evocative passage, Schopenhauer compares consciousness to a surface of water, suggesting that the most substantial workings of the mind occur beneath this surface but on occasion 'rise from those depths unexpectedly and to our own astonishment' (1966: 135–6). it is not hard to see why the link between Schopenhauer and Freud has been made so frequently but one must be careful not to overstate the connection. While acknowledging the points of contact between his own thought and Schopenhauer's, Freud never suggested that Schopenhauer's work had a major influence on psychoanalysis (Gupta 1975: 721; Hamlyn 1988: 5; Gardner 1999: 379). Indeed, though both emphasized the prevalence of the unconscious in human subjectivity, Freud's work is more systematic, explanatory and, in a sense, scientific. As D. W. Hamlyn points out, Schopenhauer's work has a limited aim: it might be thought of as a 'notable attempt to bring a great number of facets of experience under a unifying conception' (Hamlyn 1988: 10). Schopenhauer, Hamlyn continues, presents 'a way of seeing things' which may or may not ring true, 'but he does not seek to explain particular phenomena' in the manner of a scientist (10–11). Freud, by contrast, produced hypotheses regarding the laws and nature of the unconscious and worked with the assumption that these hypotheses could be evidenced and refined in the analytic situation. One might doubt Freud's methodology but (along with the experimental psychologists) he is addressing questions of systematic detail in a way that Schopenhauer is not. Schopenhauer's philosophy raises questions about the unconscious which Freud's work attempts to answer through practice.

Beckett's literary experimentation might usefully be placed in this tradition of practically investigating Schopenhauer's 'way of seeing things'. As was the case with experimental psychology, and psychoanalysis, Beckett's aesthetic productions seem to explore the way in which the human apprehends only successively and is prone to missing things. But Beckett's investigation is distinct from the others in important ways. Rather than seeking to establish exactly what tasks the human subject can (consciously or unconsciously) perform in the manner of a behavioural psychologist, or attempting to define the structure of the unconscious, Beckett worked to enrich our understanding of the temporal nature of conscious experience. This interest can be traced back to the 'Psychology' notes. As well as engagements with psychoanalysis and behaviourism, Beckett's notes evidence an interest in 'Existential' or 'Introspectionist' psychology which was primarily concerned with the study of conscious experience. In this approach, 'the essence of psychology is the description of the individual experience. Experience equals existence. Individual is an experiencer, not a performer' (Feldman 2004: 314). Matthew Feldman argues that this approach was more 'favourably received' by Beckett than behaviourism (2006: 104), and what I think Beckett saw in the methods of introspective psychology was a way of exploring the unstable and temporally defined experience that Schopenhauer conceptualized. This manifests in Beckett's note on the 'impression method':

> <u>Impression Method</u> for defining operation of sense organs by means of subject reactions to stimuli of various kinds. E.g. the 'negative after-image': if you steadily look at a coloured spot for 20 or 30 seconds, & then turn your eyes upon a plain grey background, you see a spot of colour complementary to that of original spot – purple for green, blue for yellow, etc. (Feldman 2004: 314, emphasis in original)

A subject is required to steadily look at a spot for an extended period, and this process of sustained viewing creates fluctuations and confusions in the subject's vision. This, to some extent, enacts Schopenhauer's account of vision. As in Schopenhauer's account, an extended period of gazing results in things seeming to 'run into one another'.

Like Schopenhauer, Beckett's interest goes beyond questions of perception. Beckett's writing is interested in the analogy between strains of perception and strains of thought. This can be seen in the unpublished prose fragment 'Long Observation of the Ray' (1975–6). As the title of the piece suggests, the text is concerned with the sustained observation of a mysterious ray of light. The ray is notable for 'its saltatoriality or erratic transfer from one point to another' (Beckett qtd. in Connor 1992: 80–1). As the subject continuously stares at the ray, it appears to move or jump around. This recalls Beckett's note about the 'Impression Method' insofar as concern lies with the effects of extended visual fixation. We are brought to question whether the ray is objectively moving from one point to another, or whether this is an illusion produced by prolonged viewing. The eye, one might speculate, is strained because it has nowhere else to look. There are no 'changes of scene' so the eye is unable to refocus, and this causes the ray's 'erratic transfer' (80). However, this straining of the eye is mirrored in the thinking of the narrating subject, who is drawn to ruminate continually on the movements of the ray. As Steven Connor puts it, the 'eye must "strain" as the mind "struggles"' (1992: 93). Beckett's theatrical experimentation would consistently interrogate these struggles and strains of perception and consciousness. If introspective psychology aimed at the 'description' of conscious experience, and psychoanalysis and behaviourism focused on what goes missing from this description, Beckett's writing falls between these approaches. It investigates the conscious experience of missing something – the moments in which one becomes conscious that consciousness is straining to keep up with, or make sense of, the world. Here, Beckett continues to integrate reductive and expansive models of human subjectivity. On the one hand, he is drawing attention to the physiological basis of human experience and the partiality of consciousness. But on the other he is experimenting on the human capacity to consciously reflect on this partiality.

Not I and the problem of attention

Connor links 'Long Observation of the Ray' to the 'ghostly experiments' that Beckett produced for theatre (1992: 86–7). For Connor, 'It is as though Beckett were observing the movements of the spotlight in *Play* at some post-theatrical point long after the three characters which it interrogates have vanished' (86). The prose piece can be seen as part of Beckett's move in the 1970s towards organizing works around the sustained observation of a single stimulus. One thinks of Listener's face in *That Time*, May's pacing in *Footfalls*, and particularly the speaking mouth in *Not I*. In the original version of *Not I*, the mouth was accompanied by the hooded figure of the Auditor. In later versions, though, the figure was removed leaving an elevated mouth alone on stage. Beckett manipulated lighting conditions in an attempt, one might assume, to fix the audience's eyes on this mouth. In the auditorium, as James Knowlson puts it, 'everything is blacked out except for the illuminous mouth' (1996: 592). Famously, Beckett and other directors of the play have even requested that the exit signs be turned off (Oppenheim 1994: 111). If the theatrical production is successful, the only source of light should come from the mouth.

In this stipulation of darkness, Beckett's work engages with an aesthetic tradition that stretches back to at least the nineteenth century. Crary points out that Richard Wagner was the first to use darkness as a way of exercising 'control over the attentiveness of an audience' (1999: 251). Experimental psychology, though, gives a new perspective on this use of lighting. This can be seen in an experiment carried out in 1912 by Henry Foster Adams on an illusion known as the 'autokinetic' effect. The illusion works as follows: when only one source of light is available to the eyes, this source of light will appear to move around even though it is objectively still. Adams attempted to capture and measure this effect in an experimental environment. A stationary light was projected on the centre of a wall in a light-tight box at a distance of 200 centimetres from the observer (Adams 1912: 3). The head of the observer was then secured 'firmly in a mouth-bit head rest' and all the lights were turned off (3). 'After a sufficient interval had elapsed for him to get rid of the bright after-glow and after-images', the subject focused on the light on the wall and pressed a key every time a '"noteworthy" thing happened to it' (3). The (objectively stationary) light, it was found, moved around significantly for all observers (7).[3]

There is no evidence that Beckett had any knowledge of psychological experiments on the autokinetic effect, but *Not I* certainly produces the illusion. Countless audience members have observed that the mouth seems to move around in the darkness.[4] Furthermore, Beckett's means of producing this effect bear a striking resemblance to those of Adams. Like Adams, Beckett was keen that his stimulus should be presented in darkness at a fixed position. James Knowlson describes a key problem for any production of *Not I*. This is 'ensuring that the actress playing Mouth does not move her mouth even a few centimetres out of a very tightly focussed spotlight' (1996: 592). Both Beckett and Adams aim for objective stillness in the stimulus so as to emphasize the illusion of movement. There is, however, a major difference between Beckett's play and Adams's experiment. Adams is keen to measure the illusions – documenting exactly how far the light appears to move and how long one must be in darkness before the illusion takes effect. Beckett, by contrast, is not interested in measuring the effect; he merely controls conditions so that an audience is exposed to it. In *Not I* Beckett produces a visual illusion that tells us something about human performance, namely what happens to vision when one, in Schopenhauer's words, 'gazes for a long time at one object'. The primary concern of Beckett's play, however, is not with the effect of sustained observation on the observer's performance. Instead, Beckett is interested in an experience in which the individual feels the strains of sustained focus and may begin to doubt their eyes – an experience in which we feel the partiality and materiality of our subjective impression of the world.

Another point to make, here, concerns the nature of the work that darkness performs in *Not I*. Up to this point, I have tended to assume that darkness necessarily draws attention to an illuminated stimulus – that the darkness in *Not I* simply fixes attention on the illuminated mouth. This assumption has also been seen in Crary's account of Wagner's use of darkness, and it is observable in accounts of cinematic experience. For example, Steven Shaviro writes: 'The darkness of the movie theatre isolates me from the rest of the audience, and cuts off any possibility of "normal" perception. I cannot wilfully focus my attention on this or that. Instead, my gaze is arrested by the sole area of light' (1993: 47). Surrounding darkness is frequently assumed to fix attention on that which is illuminated. But darkness can also compete for attention. In the case of *Not I*, the intensity of the darkness that Beckett stipulates for the auditorium is so effective that it can pull against the audience's attention to the speaking mouth. Darkness here might be seen to function as what Stephen Kern has called 'positive negative space' ([1982] 2003: 153), a supposed background that threatens to overshadow the nominal foreground. This effect of darkness can work in different ways. One can become occupied by the ways in which darkness engulfs the body. Charles Spencer of the *Daily Telegraph* tells us that, in the performance, 'you can't see the hand in front of your face, just the moving lips as the speaker gabbles' (2014). Attention, here, seems to be divided between the speech itself and the effects of the darkness. Thus, even as Beckett seems to rid the theatrical environment of distractions by producing complete darkness, a problem of selective attention arises because the darkness itself becomes a channel to which one might attend.

The darkness can also be a more chronic distraction. It can be terrifying and produce an impulse to get away from the performance. Indeed, it has been reported that conditions in the auditorium during Not I have induced panic attacks in members of contemporary audiences (Lane 2014). In this way, the darkness in Not I does not necessarily serve to fix or control the audience's attention. It does not, as Crary puts it in reference to Wagner's work, 'impose a uniform mode of perception' (1999: 248). Rather, the darkness serves to splinter the audience. The potential for darkness to distract from the performance will depend on the individual audience member's capacity to adapt to it. For some, the surrounding darkness will heighten the attention paid to the speaking mouth, but for others it will serve as a significant distraction from events on stage. Any appreciation of the play depends on the nature of an individual's capacity (or incapacity) for sustained gazing and adaptation to darkness. Beckett is emphasizing the physiological conditions of aesthetic experience and staging Schopenhauerian problems of attention.

Strains of speech

In *Not I* Beckett does not just investigate the situation in which one tries to focus on an immobile, illuminated light for an extended period of time. Rather we are presented with a mouth that speaks at a rapid pace. The play is concerned not only with problems of attention but, more specifically, with our perception of and attention to speech. In what follows I will look at *Not I* as an experiment, first, on how speakers attend to their own speech and, second, the way in which this speech is encountered by others. Twentieth-century experimental psychology would have much to say on these topics and experimenters were particularly inventive in devising methods with which to study the processes by which we produce, hear, comprehend and even see the spoken word. One such method is the experimental task known as speech shadowing, which has been prominent in psychological research since the 1950s. The experimental psychologist William Marslen-Wilson describes his use of the task in the following way: 'Speech shadowing is an experimental task in which the subject is required to repeat (shadow) speech as he hears it. When the shadower is presented with a sentence, he will start to repeat it before he has heard all of it' (1973: 522). Shadowing, then, is a way of making the subject's perception of speech observable and measurable. If a subject is merely asked to listen to speech silently, it is difficult to monitor the extent to which the speech is being focused on, or how it is being processed. Shadowing is a way of externalizing the process of listening.

Particularly interesting for our purposes is the way in which the shadower is both a perceiver and a producer of speech – they must perceive words and then say them. In his experiment, Marslen-Wilson wanted to measure the proximity at which it was possible to shadow continuous speech, and test whether close-shadowing subjects understood what they were saying. The experiment asked whether 'very close shadowing' made use of 'normal speech perceptual processes' or activated 'some minimal mode of speech processing' (523). Put another way: Were close shadowers simply parroting what they heard, as they heard it? Or, was the speech being processed on semantic and syntactic levels? In the experiment, 'normal prose' was presented binaurally through headphones at a 'normal conversational rate' of 160 words per minute (522). The results showed some variation between individuals. However, seven subjects were found capable of shadowing speech intelligibly at a mean delay of 350 milliseconds with an error rate of less than 7 per cent (522). Marslen-Wilson calculates that these close shadowers were less than a syllable behind the original material.

Next, subjects were given a different passage to shadow, but this time the shadowing task was followed by a memory test. Through the memory test, Marslen-Wilson sought to find out the level at which these close shadowers were processing their speech: 'If the close shadower is not using syntactic and/or semantic structure', Marslen-Wilson states, then 'he should not have available to him information that could only derive from these levels of analysis' (522). As it happened, the memory test showed that syntactic/semantic information is 'available to the shadower irrespective of his shadowing latency' (523). Now, Marslen-Wilson recognizes that shadowers could produce their output – repeat what they hear – based on low-level, phonetic analysis and perform higher-level analysis of what had been spoken later. If this is the case, he reasons, their shadowing errors 'should be constrained by the syllabic character of the material, but not by its semantic or syntactic character' (523). The errors, though, suggested that the shadowers were processing the content on semantic and syntactic levels. He concludes that 'all the subjects analyse the material up to semantic level as they repeat it', and this analysis 'helps to determine the ongoing series of perceptual decisions' underlying their shadowing performance (523).

The first point to make about Marslen-Wilson's experiment is that he is less interested in the experiences of subjects than in what can be inferred from their performances. We are not told whether the subjects felt themselves to be comprehending the words as they shadowed; Marslen-Wilson merely suggests that they showed evidence of comprehension when tested. Here, he can be seen to work in a behavioural tradition that focuses on what processes the human can perform, with or without conscious awareness. We might contrast this approach to the one which seems dominant in the text of *Not I*. In *Not I* the protagonist, we are told, speaks without being able to consciously follow what her words are saying. She is in a field on an April morning when, all of a sudden, things go dark and she starts to lose sentience. After a period in this state, she realizes: 'Words were coming ... a voice she did not recognize ... at first ... so long since it had sounded ... then finally had to admit ... could be none other ... than her own ... certain vowel sounds ... she had never heard elsewhere' (Beckett [1986] 2006: 379). Here, the focus is not on the individual's performance but her experience. Words come to the protagonist and she speaks them, but she is not aware of comprehending the words on semantic or syntactic levels: we are told that she had 'no idea ... what she was saying' (379). Though she can process sounds into words, the protagonist is not aware of the meanings that these words are forming. However, she is aware of the phonetic character of the speech: she can hear 'certain vowels sounds' that distinguish her voice from the voices of others. Thus, as far as the protagonist is aware, she is analysing the speech phonetically but not semantically or syntactically. It is possible that the words the protagonist hears are being processed at higher levels without the individual's awareness. The text, though, focuses on the peculiar, immediate experience of a protagonist who can hear her own speech but has 'no idea' what that speech is saying. Beckett's protagonist is primarily an experiencer, not a performer.

Beyond those of performance and experience, Marslen-Wilson's shadowing experiment questions how we attend to different aspects of our own speech. In experimental psychology this question has been tackled most thoroughly by Willem Levelt (1983, 1989) and more recently Hartsuiker and Kolk (2001). Drawing on the phenomenological observation that humans frequently seek to correct or modify the words they have just spoken, psychological research has frequently emphasized that 'speakers attend to what they are saying and how they say it' (Levelt 1989: 497). Speakers, it is argued, are capable of monitoring every part of their speech from 'the appropriateness of a given word or phrase in the current context' to 'semantic, syntactic, phonological, and prosodic aspects' (Hartsuiker and Kolk 2001: 113–14). However, they do not seem capable of attending to all of these aspects simultaneously. Rather the aspect of speech to which one attends seems to fluctuate depending on the context in which one is speaking. The context of the protagonist's speech in *Not I* raises some interesting questions here. Rather than moving between levels, the protagonist's attention seems to be stuck on phonological and tactile aspects of speech. The protagonist knows the voice is hers because she can feel the words coming out of her: 'She felt ... her lips moving ... imagine! ... her lips moving! ... as of course till then she had not ... and not alone the lips ... the cheeks ... the jaws ... the whole face (Beckett [1986] 2006: 379). The protagonist, then, can feel her own speech, but she cannot understand it. She can hear the sounds and feel where they are coming from, but cannot take in what is being said. Speech is not understood in terms of grammatical meaning, but in terms of sensory content. The protagonist has not decided to focus her attention purely on the feel of speech – she is trying to 'make something of it' – but her focus repeatedly goes back to the 'mouth lip cheeks ... jaws' (379–80). The narrator contrasts the protagonist's speech in this situation with the 'ordinary way' of speaking in which one is 'so intent' on what is being said that speech is 'not felt at all' (379). Beckett's text, here, does not dispute the 'ordinary way' of speech monitoring proposed by the experimental psychologists, in which one's attention switches between sensation and meaning, form and content. But it does present an extraordinary experience, in which a speaker's attention is fixed on the sensations of speech, rather than the grammatical meaning.

The text's concern with how we attend to our own speech carries into the narration of the protagonist's story, and the way in which this narration is staged. With regard to the first concern, the narrator of the text, Mouth, frequently seems to modify the words that she speaks. Levelt notes that this tendency is quite common: when speakers 'make a mistake, or express something in a less felicitous way', he argues, they frequently 'interrupt themselves and make a repair' (1989: 458). This seems to be one of the defining characteristics of Mouth's narration. For example, at first the protagonist is termed a 'tiny little thing', but a few phrases later this is modified to 'tiny little girl': 'In a godfor- ... what? ... girl? ... yes ... tiny little girl' (Beckett [1986] 2006: 376). A contrast emerges between narrator and protagonist. Where the protagonist cannot attend to the content of her words, the narrator does so to the point of near-constant modification. The experience of speaking, however, undoubtedly puts a strain on the attentional capacities of narrator and protagonist alike. As the narrator monitors the semantic content of her speech continuously and struggles to find appropriate words, the protagonist can only attend to her speech on a sensory level, but still strains to 'make something of it' (Beckett [1986] 2006: 380). Beckett's text presents two different ways of attending to speech but, in both, consciousness is struggling to keep up with the words that are being spoken.

In the text of *Not I*, then, Beckett seems heavily concerned with the strenuous processes by which protagonist and narrator attend to their own speech. But what of the actors playing the role of Mouth? How do they attend to their own words and to what extent do their experiences of speaking mirror those of narrator or protagonist? From the evidence surrounding productions of the play, it seems to have been Beckett's opinion that the actors should not attend to the meaning of what they say. For example, speaking of the advice Beckett gave her on playing Mouth in the play's premiere, Jessica Tandy states: 'What it meant was, I found, you must not think what you are saying. It just has to come out' (qtd. in Knowlson 1997: 591). Tandy's emphasis on not thinking about the content of the script seems to have carried through to contemporary performances. Lisa Dwan, who has performed the role numerous times in the last few years, states that as she performs: 'The only way I'm conscious of the script is as a visual aid.. A road map.. All the rest is music, my family, my landscape..me' [sic] (Dwan, e-mail message to author, 28 March 2015). Because she has rote-learnt the script, Dwan needs to apply little mental resource to what she is saying, meaning that she can mentally attend to other matters. Of course, just because the actors are not aware of thinking about what they say does not mean that they are not processing their words syntactically and semantically. Higher-level analysis of speech could be going on without the actor's awareness.[5] Beckett, though, seemed particularly interested in creating a disconnect between the actor's thoughts and their speech. In a 1972 letter to the play's first director, Alan Schneider, Beckett speaks of the distinction between 'mind & voice' in the context of the play, suggesting that the speech should be delivered 'without mental control or understanding' (Harmon 1998: 283). Like the protagonist of the text, we are supposed to get the impression that the speaker onstage has no idea what she is saying. This feeling manifests in Douglas Watt's observation that, in the premiere performance of the play, the voice seemed to have been 'torn from its owner' (1972). Beckett uses the theatrical environment to consider how one might speak without thinking about it and, in doing so, asks his audience to reflect on non-conscious subjectivity.

But if the actor playing Mouth does not think about what the words of the play mean, what of how those words are spoken? This question was raised by Schneider who asked Beckett for advice on a 'proper tone and, and also a proper tempo for the play' (Harmon 1998: 280). Beckett's response emphasized a particular aspect of the speech over others, namely speed: 'I hear it breathless, urgent, feverish rhythmic, panting along without undue concern with intelligibility. Addressed less to the understanding than to the nerves of the audience which should, in a sense *share her bewilderment*' (283, emphasis in original). This stipulation of breathless urgency in the monologue's delivery seems to have been reiterated when Beckett directed the London production in 1973, working with Billie Whitelaw in the role of Mouth. In her biography, Whitelaw writes of herself and Beckett's mutual feeling that the delivery should be very fast. This was in opposition to the producer Anthony Page who wanted the play to be performed at a speed that the audience could easily understand: 'It seems that Tony wanted *Not I* to go slower. I had known from the start that I would have to go at the rate of knots, ideally at the speed of thought' (1995: 127). As was the case in *Play*, then, speed seems to have been a crucial component in Beckett's conception of performances, but what exactly is its function in *Not I*?

Now, the quickening of speech is something that the speaker might do with or without conscious awareness. Drawing on some 1984 experiments by James Deese, Levelt argues that a speaker might accelerate their speech in order to prevent an interlocutor from interrupting them, or to 'express something in a modest, non-assertive way' (1989: 306). Also, in public speaking, it is frequently reported that the pressure of being watched prompts an (often unconscious) acceleration of speech. Of course, in the case of actors, the capacity to moderate one's speech rate is highly prized and actors are frequently asked to vary the tempo of their speech based on character and situation.[6] Attentional resources are frequently stretched here. Speech rate must be monitored, along with other aspects of speech such as volume and prosody, in order for the actor to give a convincing impression of a particular person in a particular situation.[7] In *Not I*, one might think that the actor's attentional process is more straightforward. Unlike more naturalistic works, Beckett's play emphasizes the actor's performance of a theatrical task above the attempt to play a character. As Beckett put it to Schneider, Mouth is 'purely a stage entity, part of a stage image and purveyor of a stage text. The rest is [Henrik] Ibsen' (Harmon 1998: 283). In contrast to actors in naturalistic works such as Ibsen's, the actors playing Mouth do not have to vary speech rate according to character and situation. They only need concentrate on getting the words out with the required urgency.

Such an idea can lead to a view of Beckett's play as a simple trial of human performance, and this perception might be re-enforced by the way in which performances continue to speed up. Jessica Tandy's premiere performance clocked in at around twenty minutes, Whitelaw's was around fifteen, and the contemporary performance by Lisa Dwan is performed in around eight. Reservations about this development are voiced in Jane Shilling's review of Dwan's performance for the *Daily Telegraph*. For Shilling, Dwan's is 'a dazzling technical performance', but the emphasis on speed means that the play lacks the 'eloquence and emotional range' of earlier versions: 'If she [Dwan] were a racehorse or a sprinter', Shilling continues, the performance could be met 'with unqualified admiration'. For Shilling though, 'there is more to art' than pure 'virtuosity', so the play feels 'brilliantly empty' (2013). Whether or not one agrees with Shilling's impression of Dwan's performance, her critique hints at a tension that is crucial to *Not I*'s dramatic power, as well as its investigation of speech. The play does not merely require the actor to concentrate on speaking as fast as possible. Rather, the aspect of speech rate must compete with a pressure for the speech to exude a certain musicality. Whitelaw famously recalls that in *Not I* she felt like an 'athlete crashing through barriers, but also like a musical instrument playing notes' (qtd. in Knowlson 1978: 89). She also speaks of how 'each gradation of the voice' was meticulously choreographed by Beckett and the degree of concentration that is required of the actor when working within this framework (89–90). There is, then, a sense of multitasking embedded in performances of the play. The speech of *Not I* has to sprint and dance simultaneously, and the play finds an aesthetic power in the sense of strain that derives from this. For Shilling, Dwan seems to attend to speed at the expense of prosody, and in doing so strips the play of some of its dramatic power. I would argue, however, that one can find dramatic power in the very tension that Shilling identifies. What we see in *Not I* is an actor straining to deliver both fast speech and music, and this can be very effective. Even if one cannot follow what is being said, the speech communicates an attentional strain that is able (in Beckett's words) to work on the nerves of the audience. In this way, the play might be looked upon both as a study of the human subject's capacity to attend to different aspects of their own speech and as an aesthetic exploration of the strains that derive from these attentional processes.

The performing audience

Beckett's emphasis on speed and musicality raises a question over the extent to which the audience comprehends the words of the play. Evidently, as was the case with *Play*, Beckett felt that the rapid tempo of *Not I* would make understanding its words difficult, but what was to be gained from this difficulty? Is there a sense in which Beckett wished to investigate the audience's capacity to make sense of words that are delivered at a high speech rate? We might tackle this question by comparing Beckett's work with some psychological experiments on the topic. Experimental psychology has certainly devoted a lot of time to the study of rapid speech comprehension. The discipline, however, has had problems in finding a method with which to tackle the question of how well we comprehend rapid speech. In a discussion of an experiment on these matters, Wingfield, Peelle and Grossman observe that 'even trained speakers attempting to speak rapidly introduce subtle and uncontrollable changes in articulatory clarity and in the pattern of linguistically based pauses and intonation contour' (2003: 311). It is methodologically problematic to present increasingly hurried human speech and measure levels of comprehension because one cannot say whether comprehension is being affected by the speed of delivery, or merely the distortions that come with the hurry.[8] Thus, if *Not I* was an experiment on the human's capacity to comprehend rapid speech, it would be a faulty one as Beckett does not remove the distortions and interferences that come with fast speech.

In fact, the distortions are central to Beckett's project. He hears the speech of *Not I* 'panting along', 'feverish' and 'rhythmic'. Beckett, then, was not merely after pure speed; he also desired the interferences that inevitably come with the strains of speaking rapidly. He wanted a speech that was fast, but also hurried. This method has two main effects. First, the high speech rate means that it is very difficult to consciously follow the words. Experiments such as Wingfield, Peelle and Grossman's have shown that humans are capable of processing speech that is presented much faster than in any version of *Not I*. However, the faster the speech arrives, the less able the individual is to consciously keep up with it – the speed of thought struggles to keep up with the speed of processing. We might be able to answer questions on the content of the speech later but that does not necessarily mean that we feel ourselves to be comprehending the speech in real time. Of course, different individuals are more or less capable of consciously keeping up with a high speech rate and there is an extent to which one gets accustomed to faster speech. Nevertheless, the speed of the speech undoubtedly makes conscious understanding more strenuous and one feels as though large parts of the story are being missed. In the words of Ella Walker in her review of the play for *The Cambridge News*: 'By the time I'd adjusted and was capable of deciphering words and the tale, it was over' (2014). Second, the interferences that come with the fast speech (the actor's 'panting along', for example) create a feeling of hurry, panic and fear. As the same reviewer puts it, 'It was so brutal and so fast that I felt sick. It was like being chased down with no escape' (Walker 2014). Instead of attempting to measure the speed at which speech can be processed, Beckett's play allows one to experience the strains that come with attempting to comprehend rapid speech.

When considering *Not I* as a production that investigates the nature of speech perception and comprehension, it is also important to remember that the speech is not purely an auditory stimulus. Beckett presents an elevated mouth with illuminated lips speaking rapidly, while surrounded by darkness. The early reviews recognize the visual power of this presentation. In his review of the 1973 staging at the Royal Court, the visual stimulus jumped out at Michael Billington: '"Not I" (Beckett's latest work) is [...] compelling because it leaves behind an ineradicable image: an endlessly mobile mouth, rimmed by white clown-like makeup pouring out words of agony' (1973). What Billington perhaps undersells here is the degree to which the visuals of an 'endlessly mobile mouth' can influence one's perception of the words that are 'pouring' out of it. The degree to which the visuals of the mouth influence the reception of speech was a question being investigated in the experimental psychology of the period. Research in this area can be seen to take off in the latter half of the twentieth century. As early as 1954, Sumby and Pollack were testing the extent to which seeing 'the speaker's lips and facial movements' helped one to understand their words in a noisy environment' (1954: 212). In his survey of the subject, Quentin Summerfield argues that these experiments showed that visual hearing can 'transform failure to understand into near-perfect comprehension' (1987: 6). However, the impact of visual stimuli on speech perception was not fully appreciated in psychological circles until later. Writing in 1976, McGurk and MacDonald suggest that 'speech perception is normally regarded as a purely auditory process' (1976: 746). They then describe some experimental results that challenge this assumption. Subjects were shown 'a film of a young woman's talking head, in which repeated utterances of the syllable [ba] had been dubbed on to lip movements for [ga]' (746). On seeing this video, most people 'reported hearing [da]' (746). Information 'from the two modalities' – auditory and visual – was 'transformed into something new with an element not presented in either modality' (747). This is what McGurk and MacDonald call a 'fused response' and has come to be known as 'the McGurk effect' (747). The experiment, then, suggests that visual information from the speaking mouth combines (unconsciously and automatically) with the auditory information to specify the speech sounds that are heard.

Ordinarily, the fact that vision and hearing are working together during speech perception should not be a problem. It is not very often that a mouth's movement contradicts the sound it makes, so most of the time eye and ear are helping each other out. In situations where it is difficult to comprehend speech, we can use the capacity to read lips as a supplement to auditory speech perception. It may be expected that Beckett's play would be one such situation. The words pour out so quickly, it might be suggested, that the audience needs to make use of both the aural and the visual modalities. However, this does not always play out in the accounts of the audience. When I first watched *Not I* at the theatre, a member of the audience reflected on the urge to shut his eyes in order better comprehend what was being said. The visuals were perceived as a barrier to comprehension, not an aid. Why might this be?[9] One obvious difference between the speech presented in Beckett's play and the speech presented in many of the scientific experiments is in what is taken away. As mentioned above, Sumby and Pollack state that seeing 'the speaker's lips and facial movements' can help us comprehend speech. In *Not I* we only get access to the former. In no version of *Not I* do we get access to the speaker's face. In this respect Beckett's play asks a question as to whether, in perceiving speech visually, one makes use of the entire face, or just the lips. Experimental psychology has, to some extent, investigated this question. Experiments following on from McGurk and MacDonald's have shown that 'seeing only the mouth area [of the speaker] is sufficient for speech reading and for eliciting the McGurk illusion' (Eskelund, MacDonald and Anderson 2015: 49). An example of this research that is particularly striking for its resemblance with *Not I* is Summerfield's 1979 experiment in which a speaker was presented in darkness and the lips were painted with decreasing amounts of 'luminous make-up' (1979: 317). In this scenario, speech recognition was better when a mouth was presented in darkness than when the viewer was given no visual information (318). However, the removal of other facial features did impair speech perception substantially (318–19). Thus, the research has tended to indicate that facial expressions, as well as lip movements, can aid the recognition of words. The visuals of Beckett's play may well make word recognition measurably more difficult than in face-to-face contact.

Additionally, the specific mouth movements that occur in *Not I* pose their own difficulties for the audience member that is attempting to make out what Mouth is saying. For example, the speed of delivery means that the speaker's drawing of breath comes to the fore. Lisa Dwan, for example, produces very distinct gasps in her version. Here, the double function of the mouth as an organ of speech and breath is emphasized. The words that the mouth shapes are frequently interrupted by the shapes of gasps. Beckett's play, then, foregrounds the way in which the mouth takes in air and gives an output of words. However, the need for input continually interferes with the output. We might compare this phenomenon to the way in which the noisy buzz of electricity sometimes interferes with the music that is played through speakers. One is no longer able to focus purely on the content but becomes conscious of the means by which it is produced. Recent psychological research has indicated that the presence of salient objects in the subject's line of vision tends to weaken the capacity for visual speech perception (Tiippana, Andersen and Sams 2004). In *Not I* the mouth itself is such an object. When the audience member at Dwan's production spoke of his desire to shut his eyes during the performance, it is my contention that his urge was rooted in the distracting power of – in Billington's words – an 'endlessly mobile mouth, rimmed by white clown-like makeup'. The visual element of the mouth may have helped him comprehend the words, but it was experienced as a flickering, gasping, distracting object.

In *Not I*, then, Beckett makes processes such as selective attention and speech perception noisy and, in doing so, draws attention to the physiological conditions of dramatic experience. At the theatre, we are frequently able to attend selectively to events on stage without conscious effort. In *Not I*, though, by presenting only the single figure of a mouth and intensifying the surrounding darkness, Beckett makes our attempts to focus on the action of his play strenuous. Similarly, naturalistic theatrical productions are ordinarily delivered in such a way that we can perceive and comprehend the words of the speakers without thinking about it. This allows us to focus on more traditionally dramatic aspects of the production (e.g. the intricacies of personal narratives). Beckett's play, by contrast, to quote Laura Salisbury, produces interferences that disarticulate 'the idea of language as a clear reflection of a pristine world of ideas where meaning noiselessly resides' (2010: 368). The pace of the speech makes one strain to follow the words, and the mouth becomes a distracting object. Through making us strain, then, Beckett raises our performances of selective attention and speech perception to the level of experience and explores the aesthetic power of these processes. Beckett is still producing avant-garde art in the sense that he is clearly writing against a mainstream, realist tradition. However, Beckett's removal of the Auditor marks a turn away from the avant-gardist concerns with audience that occupied *Happy Days* and *Play*. By presenting nothing but a mouth speaking in darkness, Beckett is conducting a focused, experimental investigation on the nature of human subjectivity. The play scrutinizes the human capacity to consciously comprehend speech.

Strains of interpretation

In *Not I*, then, the strains of focusing on the mouth or comprehending rapid speech draw attention away from things like plot and character. There is, however, no doubt that the work contains these elements; it is concerned with the telling of a personal story. The way in which the play is delivered might lead us to think that the text is a disordered, chaotic, randomly generated stream from which no order and sequence can be gleamed. But when one spends time with the printed text it is not nearly so disordered and chaotic as it may appear on stage or screen. Particularly in the opening section, there is the sense that a life story is being fashioned. In the remainder of this chapter, I want to focus on the process by which we attend to, and interpret, this personal information. In doing this I will move away from experimental psychology and towards more clinical and psychotherapeutic approaches. In everyday practice, the clinician must efficiently register a large amount of information about a patient and structure that information according to a particular set of principles. It will be my argument that Beckett is concerned with the attentional process by which this is carried out and how it translates into a dramatic context.

Perhaps more than anything else the story of *Not I*'s protagonist is characterized by hurry and unevenness. This begins at birth. At the beginning of the text, we are told that the protagonist is cast out into a world that is jealous of its time: 'Out … into this world … this world … tiny little thing … before its time' (Beckett [1986] 2006: 376). In the description that 'it' comes out 'before its time' there is the implication that the time at which the protagonist was born was not legitimately hers. Not only this, but the elliptical style gives the impression that there is no time to spare in the telling. There is also the sense that the protagonist was produced at the expense of as little time as possible: 'Parents unknown … unheard of … he having vanished … thin air … no sooner buttoned up his breeches … she similarly … eight months later … almost to the tick' (376). The parents are marked by their punctuality. They are present until they have performed their reproductive duties, then vanish. The world that is narrated is characterized by time pressure and so is the narration. This is highlighted as the story of the protagonist's life continues. The story starts at the very beginning of the protagonist's life and gives some account of the early years, but then sixty or seventy years are passed over on the grounds that they were 'a typical affair', which produced 'nothing of any note' (376). The life story goes from birth to old age in twelve lines. The story does not lack order – it goes in a familiarly linear sequence from birth to old age – it just goes through this order in a very hurried fashion.

Working with this hurried atmosphere is a sense of unevenness. This can be seen in the attitude held towards parenting. The protagonist's parents are not present for long enough to show any love or affection but, even for those infants whose parents stay around longer, parental affection is seen as an uneven matter: 'So no love ... spared that ... no love such as normally vented on the ... speechless infant ... in the home ... no ... nor indeed ... for that matter ... any of any kind ... no love of any kind ... at any subsequent stage' (376). The notion, here, that the protagonist has been spared having love 'vented' on her gives the sense that love is a kind of waste that emerges out of the reproductive process and is then unevenly – almost violently – discharged on the infant. This unevenness is reflected in the narration. The first seventy (or sixty) years of the protagonist's life go through in a hurry but then a particular morning is described in detail. The protagonist's experience on this morning is the subject of the remainder of the text. The life story fixates on one event that has been deemed noteworthy. The text, then, presents a double drama of attention. On the one hand, we are presented directly with the protagonist's pattern of attention. For example, we get an account of the material on which the protagonist is focusing: 'She fixing with her eye ... a distant bell ... as she hastened towards it ... fixing it with her eye ... lest it elude her' (378). On the other, there is the question of why this moment is the object of attention, as opposed to the rest of the protagonist's life. A phenomenological concern with how one attends to a plethora of stimuli runs alongside a question of how one attends to a body of personal information and makes something of it.

The latter approach is not uncommon in Beckett's writing. In Beckett's work, the personal story frequently loses its status as an aesthetic object that is produced to absorb or intrigue and becomes a mass of material to be moved through quickly and selectively. An example of this can be found in *Rough for Theatre II* (1956). In the play, two men, A and B, examine a case of documents relating to the life of a motionless third man, C, in order (it seems) to establish whether C's life is worth carrying on with, or whether he should be allowed to jump from a building. This operation seems professional. C is defined by A and B as a 'client' who needs their 'services' – though it is also noted that they give out these services for free (Beckett [1986] 2006: 237–46). It is clear from the outset that perusing C's personal information is a laborious process; A, for instance, announces that they are beginning to pay attention: 'We attend' (238). The sense that the two men are 'on the clock' becomes stronger when B fastens onto the 'vital' detail that C has described himself as 'morbidly sensitive to the opinion of others' (242). Exactly why this detail is deemed so important never becomes clear, but it prompts B to read the whole passage in which the detail is embedded. The way in which B carries out this act of reading is very revealing. He begins reading the entire passage but soon loses patience with its wordy style ('What kind of Chinese is that?') and decides to skip the parts that follow the vital phrase until he gets to the 'main verb': '"Morbidly sensitive to the opinion of others at the time...." – drivel drivel drivel – "... I was unfortunately incapable"' (243). As in *Not I*, there is a sense of hurry and unevenness in the way in which personal information is approached. A and B's attention to the life of C is a laborious process that is moved through with haste and involves fishing out 'vital' details from a glut of material.

The production of the personal story in Beckett's work, then, often seems less of an aesthetic exercise and more of a professional one – less about producing something gripping or beautiful than moving through material efficiently and organizing it in a way that fulfils a mysterious set of obligations. This sense of a professional approach to the personal, I think, is part of the reason that Beckett has so frequently been linked with psychiatry, psychotherapy and psychoanalysis. Of course, there is an extent to which this link simply derives from Beckett's preoccupation with unhappiness and mental pathology, but works like, *Rough for Theatre II* and *Not I* evidence a further interest in clinical practice. In the case of *Not I*, Angela Moorjani writes: 'For many, *Not I*'s disembodied mouth spewing words at a silent, shadowy auditor came to evoke an analytic session' (2004: 176). And, more recently, Jonathan Heron and psychiatrist Matthew Broome have drawn a link between *Rough for Theatre II* and the psychiatric encounter. The point of connection, here, lies in the clinician's task of taking in a large body of personal information and organizing it according to certain principles. In 'Recommendations for Physicians on the Psycho-analytic Method of Treatment' (1912), Freud recognizes the strenuousness of this aspect of clinical practice, noting the difficulties of 'keeping in mind all the innumerable, names, dates, detailed reminiscences, associations' of each patient when one is treating 'six, eight, or even more patients daily' (1933: 323). Here, as Jonathan Crary notes, Freud is 'concerned with the physiological and mental limits of a sustained attentiveness' (1999: 367). But in psychoanalytic theory, Crary continues, Freud is also producing 'a technique for dealing with a stream of information that has no evident structure or coherence' (368). Freud, Crary concludes, 'sought to fashion himself (the analyst) into an apparatus capable of engaging a seemingly random sequence of signs (whether language, gestures, intonations, silences) and yet extracting from that disjunct texture some interpretive clarity' (368). This is a concern that extends into contemporary psychiatry. Broome writes:

> One of the problems we have in teaching medical students is that they find taking a full psychiatric history a huge leap from the briefer history-taking that

they learn for medicine and surgery. They feel that the amount of information they are requested to take is almost endless, and further how they order it, divide it up and present it back to a consultant or an examiner as difficult not only due to time constraints in the relaying of information but also in the genuine heterogeneity in clinicians' models of mental illness, which in turn structures the clinical data. (Heron and Broome 2016: 175)

Models of mental illness might offer a structuring principle with which to organize large amounts of personal information, but this leads to the further question of what theory to use. Broome suggests that the action of *Rough for Theatre II* resonates with psychiatric practice in the sense that A and B 'order and marshal' information in a slightly enigmatic way (175). There may be a guiding principle in A and B's practice, but it is never imparted. I want to argue that this analysis extends to the case of *Not I*. The play presents a life story but focuses on a narrow set of events. What, we are left to wonder, is the structuring principle that has led to this set of events being deemed noteworthy?

Even attention and the clinical encounter

During his engagement with psychotherapy and psychoanalysis in the 1930s, Beckett himself seems to have become a little frustrated with the clinician's tendency to focus on a single detail. In a 1935 letter to Thomas MacGreevy, for example, he describes psychotherapist Alfred Adler as 'another one trackmind' (qtd. in Feldman 2006: 101). One can sense Beckett becoming fatigued at a proliferation of explanatory theories. But Beckett's engagement with psychotherapy and psychoanalysis was not purely one of resistance to theory. As Matthew Feldman observes, in Beckett's notes on psychoanalysis 'the overriding impulse is one of attempted self-diagnosis' (100). Beckett, then, may have experienced a frustration with the one-track nature of the theoretical approach, but he also understood the impulse to look to psychoanalytic theory for explanations. This tension manifests in a note Beckett took from Karin Stephen's *The Wish to Fall Ill* (1933): 'If he [the patient] is dominated by unconscious starvation, so that he needs in all relationships to get as much as possible, he will try & get the most out of his hour, irritably demanding explanations' (Feldman 2004: 313). Here the desire to 'get the most' from time in therapy is seen as symptomatic of 'unconscious starvation', an observation that can be looked at in two ways. In one sense, the patient is demanding that the theoretical searchlight works upon him in order to give the best possible view of his problems. But, in another, this observation is a product of the therapist's one-track mind, in which all behaviour is seen in the light of a theoretical insight: if the patient demands explanations, the therapist thinks, it must be because of 'unconscious starvation'. From his engagement with psychotherapy, then, Beckett had some understanding of the desire for efficient insights, but also of the unbalanced attentiveness of the clinician.

Many clinicians have themselves warned against uneven attentiveness, or the one-track mind. In psychoanalysis a tradition can be traced back to Freud's privileging of suspended or diffuse attention – as opposed to critical or deliberate attention – in therapeutic practice. In 'Recommendations for Physicians', Freud argues that the therapist should not make effort 'to concentrate attention on anything in particular' (1933: 324). Rather, the same 'evenly distributed attention' should be maintained regarding 'all that one hears' (324). For Freud, overly concentrated attention works against the acquisition of psychoanalytic knowledge. When 'attention is deliberately concentrated', he suggests, one aspect of the material 'will be fixed in the mind with particular clearness and some other consequently disregarded' (324). This is unlikely to be productive because 'one's expectations or one's inclinations will be followed', and if this is the case, 'there is the danger of never finding anything but what is already known' (324).

Freud's approach to attention became influential in twentieth-century British psychoanalysis, and particularly the work of D. W. Winnicott and Wilfred Bion. Winnicott's approach to this topic can be seen in 'Child Department Consultations' (1942), a report 'on the cases that came through the Child Department of the Institute of Psycho-Analysis in London over a period of one year' (Winnicott 1958: 70). Winnicott, here, describes the initial procedure in which he decides on the best course of treatment for a new case: assembling a history of the patient and assessing whether sustained analysis will be appropriate and practical. To some extent, this is a process in which information must be efficiently processed. The paper covers each case very briefly (fourteen cases in around ten pages), and there is a persistent concern with how long it took to 'get a good history' of each case (71). But within this scenario, where efficiency is undoubtedly important, Winnicott emphasizes a form of attentiveness that goes beyond the efficient extracting of information. For example, he describes one satisfactory case, that of three-year-old Queenie, in which it was always clear that time constraints would cut the analysis short. Nevertheless, 'not wanting to send the child away with nothing but a useless consultation', he went ahead treating Queenie (75). This brings results: 'Quite important work was done, for the material brought by the child enabled me to show sequence and order in it, and I obtained specific results from interpretations' (75). This success, for Winnicott, could only have been achieved 'by an analyst, experienced in long, unhurried analysis in which material can be allowed to force itself on the analyst's attention while he gradually learns to understand it' (76). For Winnicott, the analyst's attention should not be easily acted upon. The presentation of the material alone does not mean that the analyst can attend to it and instil it with 'sequence and order'. Rather material must 'force itself' on attention. This is where the experience of the analyst comes in. The 'experienced' analyst can recognize that material does not work on attention instantaneously or easily and so, despite time pressures, is in no hurry to 'understand' it. There is recognition that the analyst's role is to make something of the material, but the skilled analyst is distinguished by a lack of hurry in going through the process.

In his *Brazilian Lectures* (1973–4),[10] Bion also advocates a patient attentiveness in which one does not look for a 'vital' detail but waits for material to work on the analyst's attention:

> Instead of trying to bring a brilliant, intelligent, knowledgeable light to bear on obscure problems, I suggest we bring to bear a diminution of the 'light' – a penetrating beam of darkness; a reciprocal of the searchlight [...]. The darkness would be so absolute that it would achieve a luminous absolute vacuum. So that, if any object existed, however faint, it would show up very clearly. Thus a very faint light would become visible in maximum conditions of darkness. (Bion 1990: 20–1)[11]

The crucial difference between the 'beam of darkness' invoked by Bion and the 'searchlight' is one of activity and passivity. In the latter, one knows what one is looking for and attention is shifted around until it is found. In the former, by contrast, one attends to the general area and it is the object that makes itself visible. Bion is advocating the latter: a mode in which the analyst does not illuminate the patient's problems but merely attends to a dark space in which the problems can illuminate themselves. The analyst's skill, then, is in shutting out his own insights so that they do not interfere with the insights coming from the patient. The metaphor invokes two related points of difficulty within psychotherapy. The first is the extent to which theoretical knowledge should guide the therapist and outline the objects that are to be looked for. The second is the temporal pressure for something to be found over the course of therapy. The searchlight mode is informed by theory and temporally more efficient. Theory endows the operator of the searchlight with a template of what is to be looked for and objects can be found that resemble this template. Thus, something is likely to be found even if it is not exactly what one is looking for. When using the beam of darkness, on the other hand, one must play a waiting game and there is no guarantee that any object will show up. The approach is not necessarily productive, and the therapist becomes less 'brilliant'. Rather than producing insights, the therapist's role is to create conditions in which insights can (but may not) emerge.

Bion's ideas on clinical practice were, to some extent, drawn from aesthetics and literature. He repeatedly referenced John Keats's idea of negative capability – the capacity, exhibited by writers such as Shakespeare, to tolerate uncertainties and doubts without reaching for fact and reason (Rollins 1958: 193–4). Bion notes: 'If psycho-analysts are to be able to interpret what the analysand says, they must have a great capacity for tolerating their analysand's statements without rushing to the conclusion that they know the interpretations. This is what I think Keats meant when he said that Shakespeare must have been able to tolerate "negative capability"' (1990: 45). Bion seems to suggest that in everyday life we find it difficult to tolerate the statements of others without attempting to interpret whether those statements are factually true, or why that particular person is making that particular statement. The skill of the analyst or a literary writer such as Shakespeare, however, lies in being able to tolerate 'mysteries', 'half-truths' and 'evasions' (46). In effect, Bion is suggesting that a literary mode of attending to personal information can inform clinical practice.

This view relates interestingly with Beckett's aesthetic. As we have seen, Beckett's writing is frequently concerned with the imperfect conditions in which limits of time and attentional capacity pressure us into making hurried interpretations. In *Rough for Theatre II* we are presented with a professional environment in which A and B attempt to structure information efficiently and fish out 'vital' details. In *Not I*, this is taken further. The personal story of *Not I* is presented to the audience in such a way that one feels the physiological and temporal pressures that force uneven attentiveness. The process of following the words of Mouth is so strenuous that it becomes tempting to adopt a one-track mind – to structure one's conception of what is going on around an accessible detail. Here, we might look to an approach that has been taken to language comprehension within experimental psychology. There is a body of psychological thought which emphasizes the extent to which one's understanding of a statement is structured, not only by the statement itself but also by the knowledge that the listener/reader already possesses (Anderson 1978; Ferreira, Bailey and Ferraro 2002). Thus, in situations where the information that we receive is degraded, the listener is likely to draw on theoretical knowledge and long-term memory (what the psychologists call a 'schema'), in order to produce an understanding that is 'good enough' to serve a particular purpose (Ferreira, Bailey and Ferraro 2002: 13–14).[12] Following Freud, and drawing on literary ideas, Bion seems to advocate a mode of attention that eschews this schematic approach to interpretation. Beckett, though, produces an environment in which we are under pressure to take shortcuts. Where Bion is interested in bringing an aesthetic mode of attention into a professional environment, Beckett seems to do the opposite: in *Not I* an aesthetic environment is perforated by the psychophysiological pressures that make us rush to interpretation.

The difficulties of attending to *Not I*'s personal story, however, go beyond physiological and temporal pressures. We are also faced with the absence (or incomplete presence) of the person. This contrast with the approaches of Winnicott and Bion in which the patient's presence and state of emotion, is paramount. In Winnicott's paper, for example, we are told of how the patient interacted with the therapist through play. He is looking to the immediate presence of the child (her activity and emotional state) when making interpretations. Broome suggests that this is also crucial in psychiatric examination: 'In psychiatry it is good practice to review written records alongside the clinical encounter with an individual' (Heron and Broome 2016: 177). It is desirable that verbal histories are encountered in conjunction with a face-to-face examination in which the psychiatrist can register 'things like the person remaining in one place over a period time, levels of motor activity, as well as particular abnormal physical movements' (174). The psychiatrist's sense of a personal story, then, is structured by a theoretical approach, but also by interpersonal contact. In *Rough for Theatre II*, Broome notes, C is almost completely absent and so the interpersonal way of understanding a life story is marginalized: 'We see one mode of understanding as being prioritized at the total exclusion of another and a seeming bureaucratization of practice' (177). In *Not I*, Beckett complicates this idea slightly. We are constantly teased with the notion that the protagonist is telling her own story. Mouth, we are told, is recovering 'from a vehement refusal to relinquish third person' (Beckett [1986] 2006: 375). There is the suggestion that we are not being told about the protagonist's life by an anonymous narrator, but rather the protagonist is telling us about her own life. If this was the case, the audience might feel as though they are encountering the person as well as the report. Beckett, though, never quite allows this: we are confronted with nothing but a mouth and that mouth never says I. Thus, we are not confronted with a case history, but neither are we allowed to appreciate a personal encounter. Part of the play's aesthetic power lies in its refusal to fit neatly into either of these categories. Beckett's play interrogates the audience's capacity to tolerate uncertainties and doubts. Do the psychophysiological conditions of Beckett's theatre pressure us into a schematic interpretation of what is going on? Or, do we exhibit the 'negative capability' of Keats and Bion, and allow the enigmas of the play to stand unresolved? Again, here, Beckett is juxtaposing a reductive and an expansive view of human subjectivity. In a sense the play recruits its audience into a tradition that is interested in acquiring a set of generalized rules to enable the understanding, predicting and modification of human behaviour. But at the same time, it engages with a counter-tradition that emphasizes the uniqueness of a given individual's experience and the difficulties of understanding it.

Conclusion

There are three main concerns that I want to draw from this discussion of *Not I*. First, I have suggested that Beckett's play fleshes out Schopenhauerian conceptions of human experience. Beckett's work can be placed in a tradition that explores, through practical investigation, Schopenhauer's ideas about the limitations of consciousness and attention. Second, I have argued that in *Not I* Beckett manipulates theatrical conditions in order to raise questions about the human capacity for conscious speech perception. The play explores the different ways in which speakers attend to their own speech, emphasizing the strains that come with the attempt to monitor multiple aspects of speech. And, with regard to how we perceive the speech of others, Beckett makes it strenuous for the audience to comprehend speech by (1) insisting on a high speech rate, (2) removing most of the speaker's facial features, and (3) emphasizing the mouth's potential to distract from visual speech perception. Third, the play experiments on our capacity to interpret a body of personal information: *Not I* pits a mode of attention in which one attempts to shut out theoretical insight and tolerate enigmas, against a more professional, time-pressured mode in which we use the knowledge that we already possess in order to make efficient interpretations about what is going on. *Not I*, then, can be considered an aesthetic experiment in a sense that goes beyond its formal innovations or opposition to the 'mainstream'; it works towards a thorough understanding of how the human attends to, comprehends and interprets the spoken word.

3

Face reading and attentional management in *That Time*

During his reading around the psychological learning debates (discussed in Chapter 1), Beckett's interest was captured by a specific dispute between the associationist and gestaltist schools. The matter in question was whether the individual learns to recognize distinct objects or does so intuitively. Beckett took down these details: 'Associationists rejected innate ideas & all native knowledge of objects. Only by experience can we interpret raw material of sense data (e.g. elicit an organised scene from a manifold of coloured spots). Gestaltists admit that we know the properties of objects by experience but deny that we ever had to learn their shapes' (Feldman 2004: 318). The debate, then, centres on the process by which 'raw' sensory material is interpreted. The associationists saw this process as an acquired skill and the gestaltists saw it as a matter of the brain's primary response to stimulation. Beckett's transcription goes on to sketch out the gestaltist view in terms of face recognition: 'A baby does not open its eyes on [William] James's "big blooming buzzing confusion", but singles out a face or other compact visual unit' (318). The face is taken by the gestaltists to be a pattern which the baby is predisposed to single out – a 'compact visual unit' to which humans are intuitively drawn. Beckett also notes the gestalt school's experiments with the face. He copies down the gestalt observation that the subject's interpretation of the same facial movement changes depending on how much of the face is made visible: 'Apparent change in a feature does not mean objective change in that feature. The eyes, when only the upper part of the face is exposed, have a different expression then [*sic*] when the whole face is exposed' (Feldman 2004: 317). Beckett's interest is piqued by an experiment in which the observer's reading of a particular part of the face can be seen to change depending on the way in which the whole face is presented. Here, it should be remembered that Beckett is merely taking notes from Woodworth's summary. He is not necessarily endorsing gestalt notions of perception. Indeed, as

Jean-Michel Rabaté (1984) and Matthew Feldman (2006) have suggested, these notes were incorporated into Beckett's next novel *Murphy* (1938), in which the gestalt approach comes under severe scrutiny. Nevertheless, the transcription certainly shows Beckett's awareness of psychological debates around face perception in the early part of the twentieth century. This chapter will argue that, later in his career, Beckett would develop these ideas in his own theatrical experiments with the face.

Attending to the face

Beckett's facial experiments occur at a time when the human face was the subject of a large amount of scientific investigation. The scientific study of facial expression goes back at least as far as Charles Darwin's *The Expression of Emotions in Man and Animals* (1872).[1] But in their summary of the subject, Dacher Keltner and Paul Ekman suggest that 'two developments in the late 1960s and 1970s galvanized the study of facial expression' (2000: 236–7). First, experimental psychology produced 'objective measures of facial expression', in the form of the Facial Action Coding System (FACS) developed by Ekman and Wallace Friesen in the late 1970s (237). Second, experimenters began to suggest 'universality in interpreting facial expressions' (237). Until the late 1960s, Keltner and Ekman argue, interpretation of facial expression was thought to be 'a noisy, unreliable system with little reliable communicative value' (240). Since then, however, Ekman and others have built the case that humans are intuitively very skilled and efficient readers of facial expression. Debates around the universality of facial expressions are ongoing, and I am not looking for a resolution to the overall debate here. Instead, I will look specifically at the effort and concentration required in the processes of making and reading facial expressions. There is a body of experimental evidence suggesting that facial expressions can be produced and interpreted without a great deal of concentrated effort. However, through a reading of *That Time*, I want to investigate how this effortless mode might interact with a more effortful way of reading faces, as well as how the two modes combine in an aesthetic or dramatic context.

From the nineteenth century onwards, experimental psychology has continually investigated face perception in babies and young children, as well as adults. Contemporary psychology has, by and large, upheld the gestalt notion that, 'immediately after their birth, infants attend preferentially to faces and face-like configurations' (Frank, Amso and Johnson 2014: 13). This preference for the face in childhood is seen to translate into an adult's ability to navigate facial expressions without a great deal of concentrated attention. In their survey of experimental findings on the subject, Vuilleumier and Righart argue that much psychological research has suggested that 'facial displays of emotions are produced involuntarily and perceived effortlessly' (2011: 449). They point to a number of experiments in which subliminally presented faces have been seen to affect behaviour. For example, Winkielman, Berridge and Wibarger (2005) tested 'the impact of subliminal presentations of happy and sad faces on the actions of pouring and consuming a [unfamiliar] beverage' (2005: 122). The study found that subjects who had rated themselves 'thirsty' before the experiment 'poured more and drank more of a beverage after exposure to happy faces' than after exposure to neutral faces (128). The other notable finding was that participants did not report any change 'in their subjective state, even when their mood was assessed immediately after the subliminal primes' (128). This suggests that face reading can be carried out and acted upon, even when the individual has no awareness of being affected. So, it would follow that the individual can process a face emotionally without making any effort to attend to it. Experimenters have also suggested that some facial expressions may be 'detected better, or faster' than others (Vuilleumier and Righart 2011: 453). This has particularly been the case when the face presented can be interpreted as angry or hostile. A common experimental task presents subjects with a series of stimuli: first an expressive face, then – on another part of the screen – a dot. Measured here is the time it takes for the subject to disengage from the face and move onto the dot; the common finding being that it takes longer for subjects to 'disengage attention from threat-related faces, as compared with positive or neutral faces' (454). This has been taken to suggest that 'the processing of facial expression … may be unintentional and arise before the face has received full attention' (455). In other words, one has scanned a face for signs of emotion, before making a concentrated effort to do so. Vuilleumier and Righart conclude that these experiments exemplify a body of behavioural research which indicates 'that facial expressions can be processed in a range of situations that imply automatic abilities, in the sense that these involve a lack of intention, focused attention, or even awareness' (456).

This focus on the effortlessness of face reading in experimental psychology might lead one to overlook a more deliberate mode of interpreting the face. When inspecting a painted face in a portrait gallery, for example, the face can become an enigma and one might spend hours puzzling over it. This is particularly the case when looking at the unresponsive face – the face that stares blankly into the distance and eludes its context. Jonathan Crary finds an example of this kind of expression in Edouard Manet's *In the Conservatory* (1879). In this painting, Crary sees Manet's portrayal of the woman's face in terms of the questions it provokes: 'We are allowed by Manet, who painted this face with uncharacteristic definition, to ask such specific questions. Is she engaged in thought, or vacuous absorption, or that form of arrested (or diverted) attentiveness that borders on a trance?' (Crary 1999: 99–100). The artist's technique is perceived to prompt a sustained reading of the face. Rather than involuntarily scanning the face, the observer is asking questions: What could this woman possibly be experiencing that would give her this face? In the field of experimental psychology there is a concern with proving the existence of a mode of face reading that is not necessarily available to introspective experience or conscious recall. Thus, much less emphasis is placed on this slower, more effortful mode of face reading. The existence of a conscious, effortful mode may be seen as self-evident and therefore not something that needs to be proved through experiment. However, when discussing the face in wider culture it is important to ask the question of how the two modes might interact. A theory supporting this deriving from the psychology of perception would be Daniel Kahneman's two-system thesis. Kahneman characterizes the decision-making process as an 'uneasy interaction' between two systems: the 'automatic' system 1 and the 'effortful' system 2 (2011: 415). For Kahneman, system 2 'articulates judgements and makes choices, but it often endorses or rationalizes ideas that were generated by system 1' (415). Applied to face reading, this idea would suggest that certain interpretations could be generated rapidly and effortlessly by system 1. But this would still leave room for system 2 to make slower more effortful judgements about the face. System 1 might scan the whole face and pick up an overall affect, where system 2 can study each feature sequentially and contextualize the face to a greater degree. However, for Kahneman, it is likely that the effortful judgements deriving from system 2 will be heavily influenced by the initial impression taken from system 1.

Beckett's reading of the gestalt-associationist debate would have given him some grounding on these questions of the temporality of face reading. The debate seems to mark a distinction between two modes of encountering the face. On the one hand there is a skilled, effortful 'associationist' process in which one interprets the face in a deliberate, almost systematic way. But on the other there is the gestalt encounter in which the face simply appears and provokes a response. In the text of *That Time*, Beckett seems to play these two encounters off against each other. This can be seen in the recollection of 'that time in the portrait gallery' (Beckett [1986] 2006: 388). The protagonist goes to the gallery 'to rest and dry off' before getting 'on to hell out of there' (388). The gallery is almost empty: 'Not a living soul in the place only yourself and the odd attendant drowsing around in his felt shufflers' (389). It is seemingly an ideal place for a rest. But, as the protagonist dozes among the paintings, he undergoes a peculiar experience:

> You hoisted your head and there before you when they opened a vast oil black with age and dirt someone famous in his time some famous man or woman or even child such as a young prince or princess of the blood black with age behind the glass where gradually as you peered trying to make it out gradually of all things a face appeared had you swivel on the slab to see who it was there at your elbow. (388)

The passage describes two modes of face reading. The first is the steady deliberate attentiveness exhibited by Crary's reading of Manet's painting. The protagonist appreciates the painting's materiality (the size, the materials used and its condition) and gradually starts to investigate the features of the individual represented (status, age, gender). However, this process is interrupted by the appearance of a face. So begins the second mode of face reading. The text's presentation of this second face leaves a lot of room for interpretation. It could be the protagonist's own face reflected in the glass of the painting, or it could be a ghostly apparition. It could be that a face represented within the painting gradually becomes apparent to the protagonist – having been initially overlooked. Or, it could be that someone has snuck up from behind and the protagonist sees this person's face reflected in the glass. What is clear, though, is that the protagonist interprets the face as a presence at his elbow. This mode of face reading is dramatically different from the first. In the first mode, the protagonist's relationship with the figure remains visual. He peers at it and the figure's face is only implicit as he consciously tries to 'make it out'. In the second mode, by contrast, a face simply appears. There is no effort to make it out. Also, the protagonist has more than a visual relationship with the face. It triggers action, making him 'swivel'. The text of Beckett's play, then, engages with the idea that face reading is a process that can be either effortful or involuntary. One might go through the attentive process of making the face out, or it could simply appear and trigger a response. However, there seems to be the suggestion that the latter process can interrupt the former. The affective perception of the whole face seems to interfere with the slower, more deliberate process of making a face out.

Staging faces

On a textual level, then, Beckett's play certainly speaks to the attitudes towards face reading that were developing in twentieth-century experimental psychology. It is particularly interested in how a steady, aesthetic mode of face reading can be interrupted by a more automatic encounter with the face. In *That Time*, though, Beckett moves beyond textual representation and attempts to stage a live face alone in the dark. Beckett undoubtedly took a great deal of trouble over this staging and, as is the case with the text, he seems to have been concerned with the interaction between deliberate and automatic face reading. We have seen that the painted face features heavily in Beckett's text, and painting also seems to have been a major influence on the staging of his plays. Billie Whitelaw famously compared Beckett's plays of this period to 'moving, musical' Edvard Munch paintings (qtd. in Knowlson 1978: 89), and the link between Beckett's theatrical scenes and particular paintings (or styles of painting) is commonly drawn. Conor Carville, for example, suggests that the use of lightness and darkness that characterizes much of Beckett's theatrical practice derives from seventeenth-century Dutch painting (2015: 76). What I want to emphasize here, though, is the degree to which Beckett recognized that his appreciation of painting was conditioned by temporality and attentional capacity.

Beckett was a well-known lover of the visual arts. James Knowlson states that Beckett began visiting the National Gallery in Dublin regularly as a student and the 'deep love of painting' acquired there 'remained with him for the rest of his life' (1996: 57–8). This appreciation of painting flourished on his trip to Germany in the 1930s. Mark Nixon notes that a reader glancing at the diaries Beckett kept there 'could be forgiven for thinking that they were written by an art critic' (2011: 132). The 'German' diaries are particularly interesting for the insights they give into Beckett's process of attending to paintings. For example, Nixon discusses Beckett's appreciation of Antonello da Messina's depiction of *St. Sebastian* (1475–6): 'The painting inspired Beckett to such a degree that while looking at it he "felt a poem beginning" but was disturbed by "a noisy guide with a party screaming about Raphael"' (146). The poem, here, is recognized as the product of a steady, effortful attentiveness. However, like the protagonist in *That Time*, Beckett's patient, aesthetic attentiveness is disturbed by a reflex response to the guide's 'screaming'. Beckett clearly recognizes that his appreciation of painting is grounded by attentional limits. Another painting Beckett inspected in Germany was Mathias Grünewald's *Sts. Erasmus and Mauritius* (1520–4). Beckett suggests that the painting 'immediately says very little' but it is 'gradually full of psychologies & derisions. Remoteness, contempt, suspicion of Erasmus, social & devout prepossessions in conflict' (148). Here, Beckett identifies the extent to which his interpretations of the painted scene are temporally grounded. Beckett is not aware of getting anything from the painting instantaneously – though it is of course possible that he is sensing more than he knows. As time passes, however, the painting gets filled with 'psychologies & derisions'.

This concern with the temporality of face reading and the possibility of distraction can be observed in the live face that is staged in *That Time*. In one sense, it is a painterly construction that is designed to provoke a patient, aesthetic attentiveness. Like the protagonist in the portrait gallery, the audience are invited to go through the slow, effortful process of trying to 'make out' the face and appreciate its particular qualities. But at the same time, it is a noisy stimulus that is likely to trigger automatic reactions. For evidence of the extent to which Beckett thought about the psychophysiological impact of the face we might turn to the genesis of the play. Beckett's primary concern during this process seems to have been a question of whether the listening face alone was enough of a visual element. He states in a manuscript note: 'To the objection visual component too small, out of all proportion with aural, answer: make it smaller on the principle that less is more' (qtd. in Knowlson 1996: 602). The extent of Beckett's deliberation over this aspect of the play becomes apparent in his letters to director Alan Schneider. He stated that there was 'not much' to be done to the play in September 1974, but was deliberating on the problems of imbalance between aural and visual components up until August 1975: 'The delay in parting with it [*That Time*'s manuscript] is due to misgivings over disproportion between image (listening face) and speech and much time lost in trying to devise ways of amplifying former. I have now come to accept its remoteness and stillness' (Harmon 1998: 328). Beckett's deliberation over whether or not the face needed to be amplified, and how this might be done, implies a question of the extent to which face reading occupies attention. Beckett's conclusion in the manuscripts that 'less is more', suggests he came to think that the less the face does, the more it will occupy the audience. But he was obviously not always entirely sure about this. He spent some time thinking about how a face might be made to arouse attention. S. E. Gontarski gives one example of this. In the opening holograph, Beckett mooted two potential movements for Listener:

> The first, which no doubt would have caused an unbearable burden for the actor was: 'No blinking. Eyes staring wide open as long as possible. Then closed as or longer.' In revision, Beckett noted an alternative 'eyes open only in silence'. And

it is the alternative that Beckett retained in the second holograph version and essentially maintained throughout composition. (1985: 155)

Note that Beckett did not set a maximum duration for the stare. Instead, the eyes were to 'stay wide open' for 'as long as possible'. Beckett had used this kind of instruction before. In the 1971 Berlin production of *Happy Days*, he had asked the actress playing Winnie, Eva-Katharina Schultz, to stare the audience out 'unblinkingly for as long as possible' (Knowlson 1996: 584). She was, Knowlson states, 'almost blinded' and needed eye drops (584). This method evidently puts certain somatic strains on the actor and one can see how these strains might produce a noisy affective stimulus. However, the alternative that Beckett settled on in the case of *That Time* brings up a different set of concerns. Rather than amplifying the visual stimulus and arousing the audience with a bodily spectacle, Beckett produced a play that tests the capacity of the face to command attention. In the final version, the audience is presented with a face that does almost nothing. The eyes are closed and Listener is inactive for nearly all of the play. His activity amounts to a few ten-second blocks of silence in which the breath becomes 'audible' and the eyes open for three seconds (Beckett [1986] 2006: 388–95). Then, a final flourish in which there is a five-second 'smile, toothless for preference' (395). The face is live but it is not particularly lively. What demands does this live but almost inactive face make on audience and actor?

In terms of the requirements put on the actor, the facial movements of *That Time* give the actor temporal, as opposed to interpretive tasks. Beckett is not asking the actor playing Listener to be consciously expressive with his face. In fact, he is distracting the actor from expressiveness. First, there is the deceptively arduous task of keeping the eyes closed for long periods. Ruby Cohn observed the 'strain within repose' in Patrick Magee's face when he performed the role at the Royal Court (1980: 268). But there is also the task of opening the eyes at precisely the right moment and for precisely the right duration. There is no necessity for the actor to react to the meaning of the text. Instead the demands of the role are largely temporal and somatic – doing the right thing at the right moment. Cohn's recollection of Magee's statements around the time of the Royal Court performance is telling in this respect. She remembers Magee mocking 'earnest academics who dig through Beckett's texts for buried gold' and maintaining that Beckett's directions were 'so simple and specific that any idiot could follow them' (267–8). As Magee saw it, his role was not to engage with the text and make emotional interpretation through his face, but to simply follow specific instructions. In a sense, then, Beckett is discouraging a naturalistic mode of face reading in which the actor deliberately produces facial expressions for the audience to interpret. Instead, he is asking the actor's face to work in an almost mechanical way.

However, regardless of intention or attention, the actor simply cannot present a blank face. As Bernard Waldenfals states in relation to Emmanuelle Levinas (of whom we will hear more momentarily), 'We cannot close our face as we close our eyes' (Waldenfals 2002: 64). Each performance will bring with it a particular set of unscripted facial movements: the lips might quiver; the eyebrows might raise or lower and there may be tensions and relaxations of the jaw. From his experience directing *Not I*, Beckett would have been very aware that the human face finds it difficult to stay still. *That Time* experiments with this difficulty by leaving room for unscripted expressions. The actor's face is bound to present some involuntary movement and, by presenting the face as the sole visual stimulus, Beckett emphasizes these flickers. The live stimulus of the actor's face always threatens to disturb the scripted face. Beckett's play can be seen as an experiment that draws attention to the face's status as both a site of aesthetic interpretation and an affective psychophysiological stimulus.

Face culture

If Beckett's play can be thought of as an experiment on face reading, it might be useful to place this experiment in a broader historical context. In the modern period the face has increasingly become a point of contention. This is noted by Crary in his discussion of Manet's painting. Crary suggests that Manet's portrayal of the woman's face in the conservatory can be placed within the context of cultural developments in the later part of the nineteenth century. The period, for Crary, saw 'a new regime of faciality' take shape after a long historical period in which 'the meanings of the human face were explained in terms of rhetoric and language' (1999: 99). The central question in Crary's discussion seems to be one of whether the face can be managed. Crary suggests that within nineteenth-century culture there was an assumption that the inability to manage one's face was a sign of insanity or inhumanity. This assumption, though, came into conflict with developing evolutionary and physiological conceptions of facial expression, which emphasized the general uncontrollability of facial features.

The face has continued to occupy this precarious position through the twentieth century and beyond. This is evident in the work carried out by Ekman and others into 'micro-expressions' – 'very brief facial expressions' that 'occur when a person either deliberately or unconsciously conceals a feeling' (2015a).

There is the idea that, as socialized beings, humans will inevitably try to mask certain spontaneous expressions of emotion (the teacher, for example, might try to hide anger from students). But these spontaneous expressions will still manifest as flickers on the face. The face, Ekman's psychology suggests, will betray even the most socialized of individuals – it can never quite be controlled. Western culture is still seduced and disquieted by the idea that facial expressions can mark us out as both physiological organisms and socialized individual subjects. Ekman's research is interested in showing that faces cannot be completely mastered, but the dissemination of his work plays on a need for mastery. For between US$40 and US$200, one can purchase Ekman's training tools, which promise to teach you how to 'read micro-expressions', 'spot concealed emotions' and 'manage the expression of your own emotions' (2015b). There is ongoing tension between the recognition that facial expressions are frequently produced involuntarily and uncontrollably, and the individual's desire to attain some level of control over them.

This interest in face management can be found throughout twentieth-century culture. Within twentieth-century psychotherapy and psychoanalysis, there was a continuous interest in the face, and particularly the potential dangers and benefits of face-to-face interaction. As Crary suggests, nineteenth-century psychiatry commonly treated facial expressions as markers of mental pathology. The most prominent example of this can be found in the images of patients produced in case studies of hysteria. These images often highlight the facial expression as a key symptom of the condition. Sander Gilman notes that the case studies of the period make some effort to obscure the identity of their subjects through the 'use of initials or masked names' (1993: 349). However, the face itself is still usually presented – often emphatically – because it is deemed to give crucial insight into the condition: 'There is the assumption that the face (its structure or its expression) is so important that it does not need to be masked' (349). In *The Invention of Hysteria* (1982) Georges Didi-Huberman notes that photography was used for its potential to capture aspects of the face that the naked eye might miss. Speaking particularly of the neurologist Jean-Martin Charcot, he argues that it is 'on the basis of photography's capacity for (diagnostic, pedagogical) certification and (prognostic scientific) "foresight" that Charcot's *iconographic impulse*, as it has been called, must be understood' ([1982] 2003: 33, emphasis in original). Representations of the face, then, were an integral part of nineteenth-century psychiatry's diagnostic procedure. In twentieth-century psychotherapy and psychoanalysis, however, the face is not only looked to for diagnostic purposes. There is also a growing sense that facial interaction between patient and therapist/analyst might function as a more or less useful part of treatment.

Discourse on this topic might be seen to begin with Freud who evidently recognized the potential significance of face-to-face interaction to psychoanalysis but wanted to manage interaction in a particular way. In 1913, Freud recommended that face-to-face contact between analyst and patient be avoided. He stipulated a therapeutic environment in which the patient reclines 'on the sofa while one sits behind him out of his sight' (1933: 354). This situation is preferable, he reasons, because when listening to the patient the analyst resigns their self to the control of 'unconscious thought' (354). Freud thinks that this unconscious thought will be expressed on the therapist's face, and that these unconscious expressions might affect the patient. This state of affairs is undesirable: 'I do not wish my expression to give the patient indications which he may interpret or which may influence him in his communications' (354). Freud undoubtedly recognizes that much can be gleamed from the face (and stipulates an environment in which analyst might look to the face of the analysand), but he is not interested in making use of two-way facial interactions within the therapeutic environment.[2]

However, as the century goes on – and non-Freudian methods of psychotherapy become more prominent – there is a growing interest in the way in which facial interaction might affect therapeutic relations. Psychoanalytic therapists such as H. F. Searles began to incorporate face-to-face interaction and suggest that the 'analyst's facial expressions are a highly, and often centrally, significant dimension of both psychoanalysis and psychoanalytic therapy' (Searles 1984–5: 47). Describing the case of a forty-year-old female patient, Searles recognizes that the patient's 'attunement' to his face proved to be a 'far more significant emotional avenue for the unfolding of the transference, than did the realm of words' (64). The facial expression, here, is seen not only as a window to pathology but as the primary medium through which patient and therapist communicate. Thus, whether in Freudian practice or face-to-face psychotherapy, the face was of high importance in twentieth-century therapy. Freud took the analyst's face out of the equation (perhaps because of an awareness that his face would make expressions that he could not control). Later therapists, on the other hand, have tried to incorporate the spontaneity of facial interaction into their approach. As in the work of Ekman, there is the recognition that facial expressions will be produced and interpreted involuntarily but also a desire to filter out, identify, modify or make use of this unmanageability.

This concern with the face in psychology spilled into twentieth-century philosophy. In *A Thousand Plateaus* (1980), Gilles Deleuze and Félix Guattari[3] note that 'the face has been a major concern of American psychology, in particular the relation between the mother and the child through eye-to-eye contact' ([1980] 2004: 188). However, their discussion opens out into a wider consideration of 'faciality'.[4] The face, they argue, comes into being when the head 'ceases to be part of the body' and becomes a 'screen with holes' – a 'white wall' punctuated by black holes (188–9). Here, Deleuze and Guattari argue, an 'abstract machine' produces 'faciality' (189). This operation begins with the head being 'decoded' and 'overcoded' by the face and, eventually, 'the entire body' also 'comes to be facialized as part of an inevitable process': 'When the mouth and nose, but first the eyes, become a holey surface, all the other volumes and cavities of the body follow. An operation worthy of Doctor Moreau: horrible and magnificent. Hand, breast, stomach, penis and vagina, thigh, leg and foot, all come to be facialized' (188–9). Deleuze and Guattari are keen to distinguish this process from one in which parts of the body are simply seen to resemble the face. They are interested, instead, in 'a much more unconscious and machinic operation that draws the entire body across the holy surface' (189). In this process, instead of experiencing the body as a proprioceptive, volume-cavity system, one begins to scan it in terms of the way in which holes are presented on a wall. Is this hole too big? Is that hole the wrong shape? Should the other hole even be there? Deleuze and Guattari, then, do not take the face as a given. It is not, they argue, related to 'evolution or genetic stages' and nor is it 'universal' (190–6). '*Certain* social formations' 'need face' and 'there is a whole history behind it' (200, emphasis in original). In 'primitive societies', Deleuze and Guattari argue, 'there is very little that operates through the face' (195), but in modernity the face has become an entrenched, habitual, often violent way of perceiving otherness and endowing it with degrees of sameness.

Deleuze and Guattari's account has been influential but perhaps the twentieth-century philosopher best known for his emphasis on the face is Emmanuel Levinas.[5] As was the case with Deleuze and Guattari, the face to which Levinas refers is not merely the collection of features situated at the front of the head. Rather it seems to refer to a way of encountering the other's presence more generally. For Levinas, 'The face is a living presence; it is expression' (66). The face, then, is not cut off at the neck. As Bernard Waldenfals notes, Levinas is not suggesting that there is some aspect of the other that is 'condensed in the face' (Waldenfals 2002: 65). Instead, 'the whole body expresses, our hands and shoulders do it as well as our face taken in its narrow sense' (65). Thus, both Deleuze and Guattari and Levinas describe the facial encounter as a general mode of experiencing the other. However, there is certainly a distinction to be made between the ways in which this encounter is described in the respective works. For Deleuze and Guattari, the facial encounter occurs through the medium of a 'machinic' system. In the view of Levinas, by contrast, the encounter is much more direct. For Levinas, one can decide to play a particular role when in contact with others, but this role-playing does not preclude a more direct facial encounter. An existent can lie 'without being able to dissimulate his frankness as interlocutor': 'The eye breaks through the mask – the language of the eyes impossible to dissemble. The eye does not shine; it speaks. The alternative of truth and lying, of sincerity and dissimulation, is the prerogative of him who abides in the relation of absolute frankness, in the absolute frankness which cannot hide itself' ([1961] 2013: 66). For Levinas, then, the eyes have a language, but this language is not coded in the way that it is for Deleuze and Guattari. The features of the face are not holes to be processed by an abstract machine. Instead, they have their own language which communicates with frankness and cannot be overcoded. Thus, even as one puts on a mask and 'disposes a theme', the eyes are able to break through and express in a manner that is unquestionable (66). Again, the face is seen as a site of unmanageability – it does not dutifully express what the individual consciously wants it to express. But, for Levinas, this unmanageability is not pathological and nor is it merely seen to interrupt a verbal encounter. Rather, it is the site at which meaning might emerge. Meaning, as Levinas describes it, is not 'produced as an ideal essence; it is said and taught by presence' (66). Thus, in the facial encounter with the other, one is changed: the other's presence 'dominates him who welcomes it, comes from the heights unforeseen and consequently teaches its very novelty' (66). If the encounter with the other's facial presence is welcomed, Levinas suggests, the self is de-stabilized and becomes receptive to meaning.

Twentieth-century psychology, psychotherapy and philosophy, then, offer a wide range of approaches to the face. There are differences between disciplines. Ekman's FACS would likely be anathema to a philosopher such as Levinas, for whom giving meaning to one's presence is 'irreducible to evidence' (66). But there are also differences within disciplines. Freud filtered facial interaction out of the analytic session where Searles made it the focal point of his psychoanalytic method. There are also disagreements on whether the face is a cultural construct or a matter to which humans are innately drawn. Wherever one looks, though, there is a growing emphasis on the idea that the movements of the face (and our interpretations of these movements) frequently occur outside of the individual's conscious control. For some, such as Levinas and Searles, this offered the hope of ethical, or therapeutic, insight. For others, the face was the product of cultural homogenization and one needed to escape it. Some, such as Ekman, attempted the rational study of the face, and others – like Freud – tried to put facial interaction to one side. All, however, posit a face that is beyond the conscious control of the human individual and question what might be done with it.

Managed spontaneity

How, then, does this concern with the manageability of the face manifest in Beckett's theatrical experimentation? I want to argue that Beckett's writing can be seen to engage with one aspect of twentieth-century facial culture in particular. It registers and resists an attitude that seeks to use the face's perceived unmanageability in order to produce a choreographed sense of spontaneity. This technique of manufacturing spontaneity can be traced back to the theatrical practices of the nineteenth century, particularly the act of flinching. Tiffany Watt-Smith notes that, in this period, flinching 'hardened into a "stage-effect", a piece of "business" in which jerking, twitching and staggering backwards, shielding the face, shrieking and gasping were carefully choreographed in order, paradoxically, to suggest a body involuntarily betraying itself' (2014: 63). The twentieth century would see the rise to ubiquity of another movement in which the body seems to betray itself: the smile. Colin Jones argues that the twentieth century saw a great increase in cultural esteem for the toothy smile, in contrast to the nineteenth century's idealization of 'thoughtfulness, character and demureness' (2014: 180). This, Jones suggests, was triggered by new photographic and dental technologies. Dentistry became accessible *en masse* and the photographic snapshot allowed one to capture the spontaneous, pearly toothed smile in a way that was not possible with paint. With this cultural preference, the smile became a skill to be mastered. It became a way of making friends, getting jobs and selling products – not only a spontaneous expression of happiness but a culturally ubiquitous expectation.

Appreciation for the smile, here, extends beyond the aesthetic practices of theatre or painting. In a wider culture, and particularly in commercial situations, the smile acquired value. The mere act of smiling (say curving the mouth upwards and showing the teeth), though, was not enough: what people were deemed likely to pay for was the evocation of spontaneity. This development is recognized by Arlie Russell Hochschild in her study of the practices of air hostesses working for Delta Airlines. These workers carry out what Hochschild calls 'emotional labour' (1983: 8–9). Smiling is part of their work, but the required smiles are not merely professional; they must seem spontaneous. This attitude, Hochschild notes, is evidenced in a jingle used by Pacific Southwest Airlines: '[On PSA] our smiles are not just painted on' (4). In order to produce this sense of spontaneity, Hochschild continues, hostesses adopt an 'artificially created elation' (4). Their labour does not lie in making themselves look happy but in working themselves into a happiness from which a smile can easily slip. Drawing on Constantin Stanislavski's theatrical theory, she calls this emotional labour 'deep acting' (38). In order to evoke an emotion convincingly, Stanislavski argues, an actor must feel that emotion, perhaps by recalling or imagining an experience that has provoked/would provoke it ([1936] 1965: 57). For Hochschild, the air hostess (and many other participants in modern life) must work in a very similar way (37–43). The individual's facial work lies in looking as though they are not working to produce facial expression.

When the work becomes perceptible, though, we begin to move into the realm of what Sianne Ngai terms 'the zany'. Drawing on Hochschild's study, Ngai argues that in the later part of the twentieth century there was a move in the 'capitalist organization of production' from 'scientific management' to 'performance management' (2012: 201) – from a mode of production in which one merely had to carry out particular tasks, to one in which one had to exude a particular personality or emotion. An aesthetic of zaniness, for Ngai, registers this by emphasizing the ways in which 'affect, subjectivity, and sociability' are being put to work (203). This aesthetic is largely comedic. Ngai suggests that if the earlier capitalist system 'made people laugh at characters incapable of adjusting to new roles and social situations quickly', the later system draws comedic potential from characters that 'seem almost too good at doing so' (174). To exemplify this, she points to a selection of figures that might seem far removed from Beckett's aesthetic, particularly Lucille Ball's character (Lucy) in the mid-twentieth-century situation comedy *I Love Lucy*, and Jim Carrey's character in the 1996 comedy *The Cable Guy*. Unlike these characters, it is difficult to argue that Beckett's protagonists are 'too good' at adjusting to new roles and social situations. Rather, Beckett's writing tends to focus on figures that fail (or refuse) to adapt. The paradigmatic Beckettian figure is not one that continually moves between social roles. Rather Beckett's characters prefer, paraphrasing *Molloy*, to stay where they happen to be (Beckett 2009d: 85). Nevertheless, Ngai's conception of the zany aesthetic evidently encompasses Beckett's writing (or certain aspects of it). Beckett, Ngai states in passing, works in the zany tradition by exploring 'themes of laborious or compulsive doing' (13–14). How, then, can Beckett's – seemingly rather rigid – figures fit into a comedic aesthetic that focuses on subjects that are, in Ngai's words, 'absolutely elastic' (2012: 174)?

Ngai seems to perceive Beckettian zaniness in moments where characters perform ostensibly pointless tasks indefatigably, and with great relish – one thinks particularly of the sucking-stones episode in *Molloy*. But these moments seem to differ from the instances of zaniness that Ngai recognizes elsewhere insofar as characters such as Molloy are not, in any straightforward sense, adapting to new roles or social situations. Rather they are described to be fulfilling their own needs and desires. Molloy, for example, professes a 'bodily need' to 'suck the stones in the way I have described, not haphazard, but with method' (Beckett 2009d: 68). There is not the sense of social or professional obligation that characterizes Ngai's other examples of zaniness.

However, in his use of the smile, Beckett explores questions of social performance in a way that resonates strongly with Ngai's idea of the zany. Now, Beckett's writing frequently considers the smile, and different types of smile can be found across the oeuvre. In some instances, the smile is described as a private phenomenon that affects the mind but may not be perceptible on the face. For example, in a review of Jack B. Yeats's novel *The Amaranthers* (1936), Beckett writes of how, when confronted with Yeats's irony, 'the face remains grave, but the mind has smiled' (1983: 89). Another instant in which the smile is portrayed as kind of mental affect can be found in *The Capital of Ruins* (1946), a short prose piece written for radio in the aftermath of the Second World War which reflects on Beckett's time as a hospital volunteer in war-shattered Saint-Lô. Here Beckett points to a number of moments in which the 'therapeutic relation' between patients and staff faded and there was

> the occasional glimpse obtained by us in them, and who knows them in us (for they are an imaginative people) of that smile at the human conditions as little to be extinguished by bombs as to be broadened by the elixirs of Burroughes and Welcome – the smile deriding, among other things, the having and the not having, the giving and the taking, sickness and health. (1995: 277)

Again, the smile seems to function primarily as the mind's response to a social situation, it can only be glimpsed occasionally on the face. Crucial, here, is the point that no conscious emotional labour goes into the production of these smiles. They are reflex, emotional responses to certain situations which occasionally leave external traces.

In other works, however, these seemingly effortless (often purely mental) smiles are superseded by smiles that show a large amount of facial (though not necessarily emotional) labour. An early example of this can be found in the smile of the character Watt. Watt, we are told, 'had watched people smile and thought he understood how it was done' (Beckett [1953] 2009e: 19). The protagonist's smile is not an involuntary show of emotion, but the product of a deliberate process of studying others in order to master the smile. This process of study has worked to an extent: 'Watt's smile, when he smiled, resembled more a smile than a sneer' (19). But, the narrator suggests, 'There was something wanting to Watt's smile, some little thing was lacking' (19). This lack makes the smile enigmatic: those seeing it for the first time 'were sometimes in doubt as to what expression was exactly intended. To many it seemed a simple sucking of teeth' (19). Also, Watt's smiles tend to linger: 'Watt's smile was further peculiar in this, that it seldom came singly but was followed after a short time by another, less pronounced it is true. In this it resembled the fart. And it even sometimes happened that a third, very weak and fleeting, was found necessary before the face could be at rest again' (21).[6] This comparison is interesting as the smile gets caught between the somatic and the social. A fart is bodily and involuntary to an extent. It can, on occasion, break out from nowhere without one's having the chance to think about it. But at the same time the individual usually has a modicum of control over the process – one can usually pick socially opportune moments. In *Watt* the sense of spontaneity is degraded as the smile is extended through time. The third movement, we are told, was 'found necessary', which gives the sense of a cognitive debate over how long to extend the process. There is the implication that, in the normal way, the smile slips out one time before the face rests. But in Watt's 'peculiar' way, the face is seen to think about its smiling – cognition is seen to override affect. Importantly, here, Watt is not deep acting. He has not worked himself into a state of emotion from which a smile can easily slip. He is managing his facial features in order to produce a particular shape rather than doing the emotional labour that would enable a spontaneous smile. Watt's facial effort is perceptible and so he produces a slightly enigmatic smile which exudes a peculiarly Beckettian zaniness. One sees a subject labouring to adjust to a social situation, but it is the wrong type of labour. In a world in which the subject is expected to manage their emotions in order to produce a spectacle of spontaneity, Watt is only able to manage the machinery of his face.

In *That Time* the audience is presented with a descendant of Watt's smile. The play closes with a five-second smile 'toothless for preference' (Beckett [1986] 2006: 395). It is important to recognize a difference in medium here. In contrast to that of Watt, there is an actor's face behind Listener's smile, and we might question the nature of the relationship between actor and smile. Given that Listener's smile is situated at the end of the performance, it may be seen as the moment at which 'the mask comes off' and the actor relaxes, producing a spontaneous show of emotion. However, as was the case in *Watt*, the smile lingers. It is extended for five seconds 'till fade out and curtain', which signifies that the script is still playing out (Beckett [1986] 2006: 395). This extension through time gives the sense that the smile is being forced and because of this I do not see it as a show of happiness, relaxation or relief. As Shane Weller puts it, the smile provokes a 'labour of interpretation' (2006: 131). There may be a hint of spontaneity in the actor's smile. He may spontaneously show relief at the end of the play. But the extension of this smile over time lends doubt as to what it is expressing, and the primary sense evoked is that of a 'zany' effort. As suggested by the above comments of Patrick Magee, Beckett does not ask the actor playing Listener to perform emotional labour (Stanislavskian 'deep acting') during performances, but to follow simple and specific instructions. In *That Time*, though, he seems to script the moment at the end of a performance where the actor is supposed to stop acting and engage in face-to-face contact with his customers, the audience. In the late twentieth century, the individual was under increasing pressure to make moments of labour look spontaneous. In Beckett's play, though, the moment in which the actor is supposed to look spontaneous begins to look like work. Beckett is writing against a Stanislavskian culture of deep acting[7] and a broader culture of managed spontaneity.

Selective attention and the 'cocktail party' problem

In the presentation of a flickering and often inactive face, Beckett has so far been seen to experiment on the process of face reading and engage with contemporary attitudes towards the face. One should not forget, however, that the face is not the only element of the play. The low-level visual stimulus is accompanied by a stream of aural stimuli. Listener may not speak to the audience, but the audience does listen in on his being spoken to. The action of the play sees three recorded voices, 'A' 'B' and 'C', come to Listener 'from both sides and above' (Beckett [1986] 2006: 388). The three voices give out three different memories, which we might assume are from different periods of Listener's life: 'A' of old age, 'B' of middle age and 'C' of youth. They give out a huge amount of detailed information about what Listener has experienced and how he has experienced it. For example, voice 'C' begins:

> When you went in out of the rain always winter then always raining that time in the Portrait Gallery in off the street out of the cold and rain slipped in when no

one was looking through the rooms shivering and dripping till you found a seat at a marble slab. (Beckett [1986] 2006: 388)

This is not just the gist of a memory but a detailed recollection of lived experience. Without pause, we are given a flurry of particulars. As in *Not I*, these words were intended to be delivered quickly. In an early note, Beckett states that the play should last '15 min' and go at '200wds/min' (Gontarski 1985: 156). Thus, as the visual stimulus gives out very little scripted information, the aural stimulus gives out an abundance of it. This wealth of aural information is also presented in a fragmented manner. The memories are not presented one by one in chronological order. Instead, 'they modulate back and forth without any break in general flow' (388). The first part of a memory is given by A. Then, without break, C takes over and starts to give out a different memory. Next, C stops, and B starts to give out a different memory and so on. In addition to this fragmentation, there is a problem of chronology. The play does not start with the memory of youth and move through to old age but starts with old age and moves back to youth, only to go back to old age again in a loop. Furthermore, the order shifts as the play goes on. If the face provokes 'a labour of interpretation' by giving out a dearth of information, the voices provoke equal labour by presenting a torrent of seemingly disordered detail. In what follows, I will be concerned with the way in which these two sensory channels work together. James Knowlson has observed that in Beckett's drama of this period sight is played off against sound (1996: 624). In a sense, *That Time* is a perfect example of this conflict between ear and eye. As mentioned above, when studying da Messina's depiction of *St. Sebastian* in Germany, Beckett complained of being disturbed by a 'noisy guide'. It may be suggested that in *That Time*, voices A, B and C take the role of this noisy guide and interfere with the audience's study of the face. Conversely, one might argue that the 'labour of interpretation' provoked by the face distracts from the content being voiced by A, B and C. However, the visual and aural stimuli may also be seen to supplement each other. Put crudely, the material presented by the three voices might be seen to represent what is going on in Listener's mind. In other words, the voices might help us interpret the face's expression and the face's movements might also help us to interpret the voices. Two sensory channels are, in one sense, competing for attention but, in another, combining to give the audience a sense of what is going on.

The aural stimulus in *That Time* was not intended as one continuous stream. It is broken up into different channels, and these channels also have the potential to come into conflict with each other. This potential for conflict is evident in the manuscripts. As with the presentation of the face, Beckett toyed with various ideas as to how he would present the aural stimulus. Gontarski recognizes that in early drafts there was a focus on processes of 'interruption' and 'conflict' between the three channels (1985: 156). In the initial draft, Beckett considered a set-up in which there were moments where two of the voices would speak together: 'A beginning stops B or C, but for a moment 2 together. A may persist. B or C yield' (156). Beckett's mooted method bears a striking resemblance to a series of experiments that took place in twentieth-century experimental psychology.

In presenting two recorded voices simultaneously, Beckett would have produced his own experiment on a psychological effect known as the 'cocktail party' problem – the question of how, when presented with multiple voices, the human is able to attend to a certain voice and inhibit others. In his review of the field of selective attention Jon Driver outlines this problem as such:

> In many situations (e.g. a noisy room full of people), many sounds enter our ears at once. How are we able to pick out just those sounds that are relevant to us (e.g. the conversation we are taking part in)? Moreover, what is the difference in processing for such attended sounds vs. unattended sounds (e.g. the other conversations taking place in the room)? (2001: 54)

There are two questions to tackle here. First there is a question of separating signal from noise in any situation – for example, how I manage to attend to the music coming from my speakers and ignore the sounds of cars on the street, or the buzzing of my fridge. This is a question that Beckett had come across in his reading of gestalt psychology. In his interwar notes Beckett informed himself of the gestalt idea of 'figure and ground'. At the same time as he read about the baby's tendency to single 'out a face or other compact visual unit' in the visual sphere, he also noted how this process translated when one is presented with aural or tactile stimuli. A 'noise figure', Beckett notes, will be recognized against a 'noise background' and a 'movement on skin' will be recognized against a 'general mass of cutaneous sensation' (Feldman 2004: 318).

However, in the presentation of the aural stimulus in *That Time*, Beckett is negotiating a slightly different question. In presenting two voices simultaneously, Beckett would not have been asking an audience to separate figure from ground. Instead he would have asked them to choose between two aural figures, a process that became important in the study of attention in experimental psychology. Experiments by Broadbent (1958) and Moray (1959) studied this process through 'selective shadowing' tasks. Here 'two different spoken messages were played at the same time' (Driver 2001: 54). One message was played to each ear through headphones and listeners were required to concentrate on one message rather than the other. Driver isolates two fundamental empirical questions that experiments on this subject investigated. First, 'What differences between two messages are needed' for successful selective attention? (54). Second, if one is able to selectively attend to one message, how much does one know about the unattended channel?

With regard to the first question, Beckett's method poses some problems for selective attention. In *That Time*, the three channels presented are very similar in content so it would have been difficult to attend to one over the others. Voices A, B and C have the same voice and, as Gontarski notes, all are apparently 'memories belonging to the visible head' (1985: 150). The three channels share certain phrases – the titular 'that time', for example; they are presented at similar speeds, in a similar tone; and there is nothing in the text to suggest that one is any more significant than the others. There is, however, one difference that might enable selective attention. Psychological experimentation suggested that, for efficient selective attention, 'there needs to be a clear physical difference between the messages, such as their coming from different locations' (Driver 2001: 54). As he explains in a letter to Alan Schneider, Beckett went down this route:

> The chief difficulty of A B & C being the same voice will be to make clear the modulation from one to another, as between attendant keys, without breaking the flow continuous except where silences indicated. I feel that dissimilar contexts and dislocation in space – one coming to him from left, a second from above, third from right – should be enough to do it. (Harmon 1998: 329)

Beckett's method, then, offers just enough of a physical difference to give a sense of 'modulation', but he also wanted to keep the voices in a continuous flow. In this sense he would have made selective attention possible but effortful. With regard to Driver's second question, it was found that, when one is able to select a particular channel for attention, little is picked up from the other channel. The experimenters found that, given a physical difference between the channels, 'people appear to know surprisingly little about the non-shadowed message' (Driver 2001: 54). They had little idea about the topic of the unattended channel and, in many cases, could not detect a change in language or the repetition of a single word (54). In these experiments, the only changes reported were 'unsubtle' changes in physical properties, such as changes in pitch, or the sudden insertion of a loud tone (54). Thus, if Beckett had gone down the route of presenting simultaneous speech, it would have likely resulted in chunks of A, B or C becoming inaccessible. Performance would have probably seen random parts of the text undone.

Gontarski suggests that Beckett's deciding against the presentation of simultaneous voices was part of a wider move towards formalism in the genetic process. For Gontarski, Beckett moved from 'a pattern of simple hostility among the voices' to a 'harmonious relationship' (1985: 156). Beckett's labour in the writing process, Gontarski suggests, was primarily devoted to 'orchestrating the fragments into increasingly complicated patterns' (157). Here, he continues, 'the analogy with music is particularly apposite' (157). In Gontarski's account, Beckett went away from the idea of presenting a dramatic conflict between three voices, towards one of presenting the voices as three elements of a single musical pattern. He goes on to suggest that Listener's closing smile can be explained in terms of an appreciation of form, rather than content:

> What Listener appears to be responding to at the end of the play is not the content of the voices but their pattern. In the play's first section, Listener hears the ACB pattern broken by the final CAB. In the second section, the CBA pattern is broken by the ending BCA. But in the third section Listener can take some pleasure in the restoration of order, or at least a formal harmony, as the BAC pattern is retained throughout the third part. (158)

Now, the notion that Beckett was occupied by formal concerns during the writing of *That Time* is beyond question. However, I think Gontarski may overstate the case a little. With regard to the smile, as Shane Weller points out, Gontarski assumes that it is 'rooted in pleasure' – downplaying its enigmatic nature (2006: 130). Furthermore, in Gontarski's reading, Beckett seems to overestimate a theatrical audience's capacity to apprehend the pattern that he presents. As an audience member, I would have little chance of locating where each voice is coming from, let alone keeping track of the pattern that unfolds. Though Beckett might overestimate his audience in such a way, I wish to advance another theory. Rather than simply moving from a version of the play which focuses on conflict between voices to one which focuses on pattern, I would argue that Beckett is interested in playing these two versions against each other. Beckett, I suggest, is not producing patterns for their own sake. Rather, the play investigates how we move between attending to three distinct elements and apprehending that those elements are a single continuous whole. Here, we might go back to Beckett's study of gestalt psychology. The major point Beckett took from his notes on the gestaltists was their insistence 'that every act or experience should be studied as a whole & in its setting, rather than analysed into its elements' (Feldman 2004: 314). Beckett's presentation of the aural stimulus in *That Time*, though, does not allow us to do one or the other. In a stage note, Beckett stipulated that the aural stimulus should produce a particular 'effect' in which the switch between voices is 'clearly faintly perceptible' ([1985] 2006: 387). He did not want the aural stimulus to be experienced as a continuous whole, but neither did he want the distinction between elements to be completely definite. Instead, he brings two degrees of attention into conflict. On the one hand, we might appreciate *That Time*'s aural stimulus as a single musical piece that moves through a series of formal progressions. But on the other we are presented with three voices that tell different stories and compete for attention. Beckett, I suggest, was interested in exploring the psychological strains that reside between these ways of attending to voices.

Aesthetic labours of attention

In *That Time*, then, reading faces and selectively attending to voices become psychologically strenuous tasks. Beckett brings an audience to question the way in which they are to attend to the sensory material that is presented. But what is the purpose of all this labour? Put another way, how does the psychological labour transition into aesthetic experience, or theatrical entertainment? There seems always to have been a question in Beckett's mind over *That Time*'s aesthetic credentials. Before it was performed, James Knowlson remembers Beckett telling him that the play would be working 'on the very edge of what was possible in the theatre' (1996: 602). In a sense, here, Beckett seems to understand his work as an attempt to extend the boundaries of artistic practice, and the play might be viewed as an experiment in this sense. But, if this is the case, in what ways are the boundaries being extended? I would argue that Beckett is extending the boundaries of aesthetic experience – working on the edge of what is possible in the theatre – by incorporating traditionally non-aesthetic modes of attention into an aesthetic environment. In one traditional aesthetic mode of attention (exemplified earlier by Beckett's inspection of Mathias Grünewald's painting) the subject devotes attention to a particular object and patiently tries to make out what that object is saying to them. This mode, though, is atypical in a modernity in which novel objects (or new channels of stimuli) frequently emerge to compete for the subject's attention. As we have begun to see (and we will consider this more thoroughly in Chapter 4), experimental psychology is heavily concerned with the subject's capacity to deal with these competing stimuli – the ways in which the modern subject manages their attentional load in everyday life.[8] Beckett's experiment, I suggest, is characterized by the introduction of these modes of attention into an aesthetic environment.

Of course, in modernity aesthetic experience is also increasingly characterized by a kind of divided attention. In the contemporary world, where a room is frequently populated by numerous devices capable of transmitting aesthetic products (books, televisions, smartphones, tablets, laptops, radios etc.), there is always the possibility that one aesthetic product might compete for attention with another. The last time I read one of Beckett's works,[9] for instance, I was intermittently aware of the television drama that was playing on my partner's laptop across the room. The question here becomes one of whether this type of experience can still be labelled aesthetic. *That Time* can be seen to anticipate this question. It presents sensory information in a way that requires the subject to manage or divide their attention and questions whether this process can be aesthetic, or even entertaining. For a response to the play that seems to register this question, we might look to John Pilling's review of Alan Schneider's 1977 production in New York. Unconvinced by the play's aesthetic, Pilling notes that the work often feels 'too languid to be dramatic' and 'nearly always seems too long' (1978: 128). From this, one might infer that Beckett's play does not offer enough content to fill out the time it takes to perform. Pilling, though, is raising a slightly different concern. He suggests that the work might be 'more compelling as a radio play or short prose text' (128). The play is seen to give out too much content. Pilling suggests that it may be more 'compelling' if the visual element was removed and the play became a purely aural or textual matter. There is the indication that less would have been more: the aural stimulus alone would have been enough to occupy Pilling, but when the visual and aural stimuli combine, the play becomes a little boring. Here, Pilling is imaginatively separating the play out into discrete elements (what the speech would sound like without the visual stimuli; how the words would read if they were not being spoken). The play is perceived as a selection of stimuli competing against each other, and Pilling does not feel that this competition is dramatically compelling. Instead, he reckons the play would be better if this competition was extinguished through the removal of certain channels. Rather than an aesthetic experience in which one concentrates on a single channel, the play produces a more laborious, everyday environment in which content comes from multiple sources and attention has to be managed and divided. By Pilling's account, then, psychological labour fails to translate into aesthetic pleasure.

However, this reading ignores a key aspect of the play's aesthetic practice: the telling of a personal story. Beckett's play is ultimately the story of a particular individual, and we might question why Beckett has chosen to tell the story in this particular way. For an answer to this, we might look to the text in a little more detail. The text narrates a series of episodes from a protagonist's life, but (as was the case with *Not I*) it consistently raises the question of why these episodes are particularly worthy of our attention. The title of the play gives an indication that there is one crucial time at the heart of the story, and the text hints that certain moments being described hold significance for the protagonist. At the same time, though, Beckett's text (to paraphrase Patrick Magee) frequently resists the view that one can dig through it to find buried gold. For instance, when voice C describes the (above discussed) time in the portrait gallery, the passage ends with the question of whose face it was that appeared (Beckett [1986] 2006: 389). When C begins again it states that the protagonist was 'never the same after that', hinting that a transformative moment ensued after the appearance of the face (390). However, this potential for insight is almost instantly refuted: 'But that was nothing new if it wasn't this it was that common occurrence something you could never be the same after crawling about year after year in your lifelong mess' (390). The play prompts us to focus in on the episode before insisting that it actually recounts a single 'mess' in which no moment can necessarily be distinguished from the 'blooming, buzzing confusion'. The text, then, seems to disqualify itself as a source that is likely to offer any keys to the protagonist's story.

In the light of this, we might look in search of insight to the presence in front of us, namely Listener's face. As mentioned, the play's presentation may be interpreted to suggest that if one monitors the face for expression and listens to what the voices are saying, an overall sense of the protagonist's situation can be gleamed. However, textual detail and embodied presence do not combine neatly. The face does not respond to the words of the text straightforwardly, and the fragmentation of the play disrupts the sense that one is examining a protagonist in any holistic way. The face is live while the voices are recorded, and the voices themselves are dislocated in space. Furthermore, we are frequently reminded of the distinction between Listener and the actor playing him. Listener, for example, seems to be lying down – he is given 'long flaring hair as if seen from above' – but the actor playing him is presented facing the audience in an upright position (Beckett [1986] 2006: 388). Although *That Time* is ostensibly concerned with the life story of a single individual, the performance of the play gives the impression that many different things are going on simultaneously. In an effort to make out the personal story, one has to divide attention between numerous distinct figures. Thus, *That Time* offers insights on the experience of attentional management, and ultimately investigates how one produces (or fails to produce) narrative meaning amid the competing channels of modernity.

Conclusion

That Time, then, is a work that demands an appreciable amount of psychological labour from its audience, and part of its aesthetic experimentation, I have argued, lies in an attempt to extend the boundaries of artistic practice by incorporating problems of selective and divided attention into a theatrical environment. The play questions whether psychological labour can transition into aesthetic pleasure, and I would argue that this question is still open for debate. In many ways, this is a question that has framed the entire modernist corpus. From the exacting literary projects of Eliot, Joyce and Woolf to the systematic music of Terry Riley, Philip Glass and Steve Reich, prominent modernists all seem to work with the assumption that aesthetic pleasure can be derived from psychological labour. But Beckett's work, with its emphasis on human incapacity and attentional strain, seems to interrogate the relationship between aesthetic pleasure and psychological labour in a much more open-ended way. It is often said that Beckett's writing is 'hard work' (and it would be difficult to argue that Beckett intended otherwise), but the works themselves frequently ask us to consider whether this psychological labour is worth it – whether focusing our mind on this novel, text or play for an extended period of time is likely to deliver an aesthetic pay-off. This question is particularly important in a society in which a single stimulus (aesthetic or otherwise) rarely obtains our undivided attention but competes with a variety of other channels of stimuli. Beckett, then, might be seen to work with many experimental psychologists in exploring the ways in which the modern individual manages attentional loads. Much psychological experimentation questions whether the human can perform multiple, unrelated tasks simultaneously, and analyses different modes of attention. Beckett's play, though, might be distinguished from these experiments insofar as it ties a question of attentional management to individual experience; the effortful, psychophysiological tasks it asks us to perform are all linked to a single personal story. Reductive and expansive models of human subjectivity are, thus, brought into tension as the attentional labour the play requires is geared towards an attempt to unravel the mysteries at the heart of a life story.

4

Inattention in *Footfalls*

In the late nineteenth century, Jonathan Crary argues, a normative observer began to be conceptualized 'not only in terms of the isolated objects of attention, but equally in terms of what is not perceived, or only dimly perceived, of the distractions, the fringes and peripheries that are excluded or shut out of a perceptual field' (1999: 40). Crary cites the Freudian model of 'an unconscious actively denying certain contents to attentive awareness', but also suggests that Freud's theory was one of many in the period to show a concern with themes of 'inhibition, exclusion, and periphery' (40). Here he is referring to the development of numerous theories which suggested that sensory content is generally left inaccessible to consciousness, not in order to prevent psychic rupture, but because it is not task-relevant. In particular, he outlines Hermann von Helmholtz's notion that sensory information which is 'unlikely to be useful or necessary is involuntarily unattended to' (40). To become aware of this inhibited information, Helmholtz suggested, one must make a 'special effort' to reorient attention (40). Thus, one is not – as in Freud's theory – repressing material with the potential to cause psychic rupture. Rather, attention becomes a matter of usefulness and necessity. One registers the material that is likely to be meaningful or useful and remains oblivious of that which is not.[1]

There are two aspects of Crary's discussion of inattention that I want to bring into the context of the twentieth century, and Samuel Beckett's *Footfalls*. First, Crary detects an opposition between theories that emphasize repression (such as Freud's) and those that look at involuntary, task-oriented inattention. Debates around this opposition have undoubtedly continued through the twentieth century, and these debates will inevitably enter my discussion. The opposition, though, will be a secondary concern in this chapter. I am primarily interested in the other concern that comes up in Crary's discussion: the 'special effort' that is required to reorient attention in order to become aware of or retrieve inhibited information. Whether working with theories of repression or involuntary inattention, the twentieth century saw a sustained investigation into this activity. In the psychological laboratory, researchers used new technologies in order to manufacture attentional overload and produce observable moments of inattention. In psychotherapy, there was continued investigation into repression and dissociative states. Here questions of attention spill into questions of memory. With the development of trauma theory in the 1970s, 1980s and 1990s, there was debate around the question of whether it was possible to retrieve memories of experiences that had been inhibited or repressed. Therapists also worked with patients in order to explore the qualitative experience of dissociative states. It is my contention that this is an important context in which to read Beckett's work. Beckett, I will argue, was very interested in 'the distractions, the fringes and peripheries that are excluded or shut out' of a perceptual field. However, his method should be distinguished from those of the psychologists or psychotherapists. He is not working to reorient attention to enable the retrieval of repressed or inhibited information. Nor is he working to decide between those theories that assume repression and those that emphasize involuntary, task-oriented inattention. Instead, in works such as *Footfalls*, he manipulates the theatrical environment in an effort to capture a particular affective state: the experience of perceiving things dimly and feeling as though a large amount of material is being shut out. *Footfalls* offers one the chance to attend to the experience of inattention.

Experiencing nothing: The case of Amy

Towards the end of the text of *Footfalls* there is a moment in which Beckett's interest in the experience of inattention is particularly evident. In the final part of the play, the protagonist, May, tells the story of Old Mrs Winter and her daughter, Amy. There are a couple of things that might be deemed peculiar about this story. For the sake of clarity, I will give my interpretation of these peculiarities before going any further. First, there is a close link between May and Amy. Besides the obvious typographical similarities between the two names, Amy is described to pace up and down in a manner that has been characteristic of May. Second, Old Mrs Winter is linked to the voice of May's mother with whom May has spoken earlier. They each, for example, wonder whether their daughter will ever 'have done ... revolving it all' (400–3). Thus, May's story seems to be a refraction of her life. The story may be deemed a fiction within a fiction but elements of the host fiction seep into the fiction that is being hosted. The strangeness of this situation is enhanced by the way in which it is presented to the audience. May does not tell her story from the beginning but describes it as a 'sequel' (402). The audience, it seems, has missed part of the story. This becomes apparent when May states that 'the reader will remember' Old Mrs Winter (402). Old Mrs Winter has not been introduced to the audience of *Footfalls* previously and nor is the theatrical audience, in any straightforward sense, a 'reader'. Thus, it emerges that May's story is not addressed to the theatrical audience. Rather, the audience is overhearing May creating a semi-autobiographical story for a 'reader'. The audience, then, is informed that it has missed something.

Within this slightly unusual set-up, May narrates an exchange between Mrs Winter and Amy in which Mrs Winter asks Amy whether she observed anything strange at the ceremony. Amy denies having seen anything strange and goes on to say that this is to put it mildly, for in fact she 'observed nothing of any kind, strange or otherwise. I saw nothing, heard nothing of any kind. I was not there' (402). Mrs Winter is puzzled by this as she 'distinctly' heard Amy make responses to the sermon, finally asking: 'How could you have responded if you were not there?' (403). How does one reconcile these conflicting testimonies? One way it can be done is with reference to the distinction between performance and experience made in the 'Psychology' notes. For Mrs W, in this reading, Amy is a performer. She has 'distinctly' heard Amy make the appropriate responses at church and Amy's being there resides in this performance. Amy, by contrast, sees herself as an experiencer. She has not been there because she has not experienced being there. But what, then, was the nature of her experience? Of course, we could take Amy at her word and assume she was physically absent from church – that she did not make the performance that Mrs W describes. Perhaps Mrs W's report is the product of hallucination. The text leaves this possibility open. When she is setting the scene, the authorial voice of May states that Mrs W is 'sitting down to supper with her daughter after worship' (403). She does not affirm that both attended worship, merely that both are sitting down to supper after worship. There is, then, some doubt about the reliability of Mrs W's observation of Amy's performance. It should be noted, however, that Amy does not specify where she was, if not at church. She does not say 'I could not have been at X because I was at Y all the time' – she does not offer an alibi.

The text, then, leaves an open question as to whether Amy was physically absent from church. Beckett, as ever, does not present events transparently. But let us assume that Mrs W was not hallucinating, and Amy was responding at the church. How could she have made these responses without being there? One might suggest that Amy is subject to amnesia. It may be that she was completely present and active at church, but has since, for reasons unspecified, forgotten the experience. However, there is a certainty to Amy's statement that she 'observed nothing of any kind' at Evensong that refutes this. Amy does not have a spot in her memory that is completely blank. Rather than not remembering where she was at all, she remembers not being 'there'. The church, for Amy, is a place in which she positively recalls performing an action of not-being. Amy, then, seems to be recalling a negative experience. This idea of negative experience had long been familiar to Beckett. In his reading of the 1930s, Beckett took notes on Democritus's statement that '"Naught is more real than nothing". Non-Being is as real as Being' (Feldman 2004: 296). These notes pop up frequently in Beckett's work. Shane Weller finds their influence in this passage from *Murphy*: 'Murphy began to see nothing, that colourlessness which is such a rare postnatal treat, being the absence (to abuse a nice distinction) not of *percipiere* but of *percipi*' (Beckett [1938] 2009c: 154). As Weller observes, for Murphy, '"the Nothing" becomes an object of experience' (2008: 70). Amy's account of her own experience may be an example of this phenomenon in which the 'somethings give way, or perhaps simply add up, to the Nothing' (Beckett [1938] 2009c: 154). However, there are differences in the way in which these experiences are presented in the respective works. In *Murphy* we are presented with a narrator's report of Murphy's negative experience, but in *Footfalls* something slightly different is going on. Amy's account of her own experience is placed next to Mrs W's account of her performance. In his use of the Latin terms *percipere* and *percipi* in *Murphy* Beckett seems to hint at this opposition. There is a sense that Murphy can perceive without detecting his own perceptions. In *Footfalls* Beckett develops this idea: Amy is observed to perform something while experiencing nothing. She is unable to attend to her own perceptions and responses. A positive experience of nothing is occupying Amy so that she is unable to experience her own performance at church.

There is also a question of what, if anything, the nothing that Amy experiences is made of. In *Murphy* the narrator wonders whether 'the Nothing' is experienced because the 'somethings' have given way to it or added up to it (154). It could be that 'the Nothing' has overridden the somethings, but it could also be that the Nothing is composed of somethings. In *Footfalls* Beckett also seems to develop this idea. Amy claims to have 'observed nothing of any kind' but Mrs W raises another possibility. She asks Amy: 'Will you never have done … revolving it all … in your poor mind' (403)? This might suggest that Amy's nothing is composed of many somethings – 'it all'. Ultimately, we cannot tell whether Amy is experiencing too much or too little. Either way, though, her experience amounts to 'nothing'. The focus of the passage is not on the specific matters that are occupying Amy at church, but in her experience of not being there, or anywhere else. We are left with the question of how this experience of non-being can be reconciled with a performance that suggests a degree of attentiveness to the ceremony. Here we can see Beckett's study of philosophy tying in with his study of experimental method. Amy undergoes an experience of non-being that recalls Democritus, but this experience is weighed against her responsive performance. The individual, then, is portrayed as both performer and experiencer, and one is left with the question of which constitutes the individual's being 'there'.

Missing something: Inattention in the laboratory

In *Footfalls*, then, Beckett seems to become interested in the individual's capacity to remain oblivious to 'strange' events that occur right in front of their eyes. This was a phenomenon that was also being investigated in the twentieth-century psychological laboratory. Mrs W's inquiry as to whether Amy noticed 'anything strange' at church sounds very similar to the types of question that became crucial to the psychological study of inattention in the later part of the twentieth century. A foundational experiment of this nature was carried out by Neisser and Becklen (1975). Neisser and Becklen essentially took the selective listening experiments discussed in Chapter 3 into the realm of vision. Subjects were presented with two optically superimposed video screens, 'on which two different kinds of things were happening' (Neisser and Becklen 1975: 480). The experiment investigated whether 'subjects would easily be able to follow one episode and ignore the other' (482). In most cases, it was found that subjects 'had little difficulty in following a given episode even when another was superimposed on it' (490). In addition to the video showing standard actions being performed, Neisser and Becklen also videotaped 'a number of "odd" episodes to determine whether unusual events in an unattended episode would be noticed' (484). To give some examples of these unusual events: handshakes were introduced into both the basketball and hand-slapping episodes; a ball was introduced into the hand-slapping game; a ball was taken away from the basketball game; the three men in the basketball game exited one by one to be replaced with women, who were then replaced by the original men (484–5). At the end of the trials, subjects were asked if they had seen anything odd in these events (in progressively more leading ways). It was found that these 'odd' events were 'rarely noticed and then only in a fragmentary way' (490). Out of twenty-four subjects, for instance, only one 'spontaneously reported seeing a handshake in the handgame', and 'only three others mentioned it in the postexperimental inquiry' (491). In the episode where the men were replaced by women, some subjects noticed something strange but could not describe it exactly and questioned their own perception (490–1). One subject, for instance, reported: 'I thought I saw a different person, but I thought it was my imagination' (491). Overall, half of the subjects gave no indication that they had observed or responded to the odd events and, according to the experimenters, the 'most common response to the inquiry was incredulity' (491). Subjects not only missed the strange events but were reluctant to believe that the events happened.

This incredulity implies a feeling of there-ness, or at least the absence of not-there-ness. The subjects evidently felt as though they were, on some level, experiencing both episodes. If they had recognized the extent of their own inattention, they would not have been surprised when told of the events that they had missed. Alternatively, their incredulity could be a retrospective phenomenon – a reluctance to believe that they could have missed something that was right in front of them. In any case, the experiment suggests a gap between performance and experience. In half the subjects' performances, there is no indication that the unattended episode was being registered in any way. However, it seems they did not experience their own inattentiveness. This is the direct opposite of Amy's experience in *Footfalls*. Asked about her experience at church, Amy suggests that she was 'not there', and so 'observed nothing of any kind, strange or otherwise', but, for Mrs W at least, her performance suggested attentiveness. There is a mutual interest, on the part of Beckett and the experimenters, in how an observer can be experientially 'there' without anything in the viewing performance suggesting it. Or, how one can be experientially 'not there' even when one's viewing performance suggests an attentive presence.

The method of Neisser and Becklen was later incorporated into a slightly more striking experiment by Simons and Chabris (1999). In this experiment, subjects were shown a video of a group playing basketball and asked to monitor the number of passes (Simons and Chabris 1999: 1066). There were two teams playing basketball: a team wearing black shirts and a team wearing white. Subjects were asked to monitor the passes of either the white team or the black team. This time there was no second event presented, subjects merely had to attend to the one team and ignore the other (1066). However, two 'unexpected' events were placed into the midst of two separate versions of the basketball episode (1066). In one, a tall woman with an umbrella walked through the scene and, in the other, a shorter woman wearing a gorilla costume did the same (1067). It was found that 54 per cent of 192 observers noticed the unexpected event (1068). Thus, attention to a counting task was found to make 46 per cent of observers blind even to very peculiar, unrelated events. Also, different subjects were shown different videos with the counting task being more difficult in some videos than others. It was found that, as the counting task grew more difficult, subjects became less likely to notice the gorilla, or the figure with the umbrella (1069). Finally, similar results were found in new subjects, even when the gorilla stopped in the middle of the walk through the basketball players, looked to the camera, and thumped its chest (1070). Again, it is crucial that strange events in the unattended channel will be missed even when this channel is on the same visual field as the one that is being attended to: 'Strange events can pass through the spatial extent of attentional focus (and the fovea) and still not be "seen"'(1070). These results have become the most famous proof of an effect known as 'inattentional blindness': the idea that without attention many subjects have no awareness at all of a stimulus object (Mack and Rock 1998). There is no evidence to suggest that Beckett had any familiarity with this branch of scientific study, but his work can certainly be seen to interrogate a related concern. In *Footfalls*, Beckett is not investigating the phenomenon of inattentional blindness exactly. Instead, he is interested in what one might call an attention to blindness: a capacity to experience one's inattention and recognize that one is 'not there'.

Staging inattention

The 'inattentional blindness' experiments are in many ways, dramatic. They present observers with recordings of scripted performances, and these performances make use of various dramatic conventions: performers wear costumes and move in and out of shot. However, the experiments all aim at a kind of mimesis – they are trying to simulate real-life experience. The episodes that Neisser and Becklen produced were, for example, supposed to be 'naturalistic', though they note that the 'unrelated and optically superimposed displays' used in the experiment 'do not occur in ordinary vision' (Neisser and Becklen 1975: 482). Simons and Chabris pick up on this, observing that video superimposition gives the displays 'an odd appearance', and (without endorsing it) rehearsing the opinion that this 'unnatural' presentation might cause inattentional blindness (1999: 1064). There is, though, a frequent insistence within the experimental literature that the phenomenon of inattentional blindness is not limited to the artificial conditions of the laboratory. The literature on the subject is characterized by a tendency to draw 'real-world' analogies. Simons and Chabris describe missing friends waving at a crowded theatre because attention is occupied by the pursuit of a seat (1999: 1059). Jeremy Wolfe describes the failure to notice a change in interlocutor when one is concentrating on giving directions (1999: 1). Cathleen M. Moore describes missing someone doing a back-flip in a crowd because of an attempt to pick out a close friend or, more seriously, 'missing a child in the path of your car because you are carefully focussing your attention on other cars' (2001: 178). Obviously, there is nothing unusual in a psychologist's wanting an experiment to be applicable to the 'real world', but the study of inattentional blindness seems particularly concerned with naturalistic simulation.

This tendency towards mimesis manifests most clearly in an experiment carried out by Chabris and colleagues in 2011. The experiment was based on a specific event. In January 1995 Kenny Conley, a Boston police officer, was chasing the suspect of a shooting. Also engaged in this chase was a plain-clothes police officer, Michael Cox. Cox was mistaken by other police officers for the suspect, assaulted from behind and brutally beaten. In his pursuit of the suspect, Conley ran right past this beating and eventually apprehended his original target. He was later convicted for perjury and obstruction of justice because he maintained that he had not seen the assault on Cox, while admitting that he ran right past it. This was not accepted as possible: 'The investigators, prosecutors, and jurors in the case all assumed that because Conley could have seen the beating, Conley must have seen the beating, and therefore must have been lying to protect his comrades' (Chabris et al. 2011: 150). In the experiment, conditions that amounted to a similar event were created. Subjects were asked to pursue 'a male confederate' for 400 metres. In doing this, they maintained 'a distance of 30 feet (9.1 meters) while counting the number of times the runner touched his head' (151). But an unexpected event was also produced: 'At approximately 125 meters into the route, in a driveway 8 meters off the path, three other male confederates staged a fight in which two of them pretended to beat up the third. These confederates shouted, grunted, and coughed during the fight, which was visible to subjects for at least 15 seconds before they passed by it' (151). Unsurprisingly, given the results of the previous experiments, it was found that 'a substantial number of subjects failed to notice a three-person fight as they ran past it' (153). From this, the conclusion is drawn that Conley may have been truthful in his assertion that he did not see the fight.

Again, this experiment involves numerous naturalistic, dramatic performances. The confederates are being asked to play certain roles: the role of a suspected criminal on the run, or that of a man engaged in a fight. As was the case in the experiments discussed above, though, the observer (the chasing participant) of these performances is being artificially manipulated. Their attention is directed towards the confederate being chased and away from the fight, so that a substantial number of subjects do not notice the latter performance. Thus, the dramatic performance of the fight is only experienced in retrospect. The point of the experiment, then, is not the performances per se but the fact that they can be missed. The experiment produces, in the observer, a retrospective feeling of having missed something.

Footfalls is also concerned with producing a feeling of inattention in observers, but the inattention that Beckett attempts to stage is more present than that of Chabris and colleagues. Beckett is working to capture the qualitative experience of inattention – a feeling of not-quite-there-ness. In the text, the sense of not being 'there' has been seen to arise in Amy's consciousness, but Beckett also attempts to raise this sense in his theatrical audience. This attempt manifests in various methods used in the staging of the play. The material that is accessible to the audience in *Footfalls* is presented at a low, flickering level and one is frequently confronted with the feeling of missing something. The play equips its audience with a slow, fuzzy and narrow field of awareness. The visuals are presented in a light that doesn't exceed dimness, the voices of the characters are 'low and slow throughout', and there is the 'faint single chime' of a bell (Beckett [1986] 2006: 399). There is the sense that background events are being foregrounded without any amplification. These effects manifest in the reviews of Lisa Dwan's recent production of the play. Writing for *The Independent*, Paul Taylor (2014) describes how 'the spectral lighting ... keeps tapering into an almost uncanny faintness', and numerous reviewers describe the sounds of the play as echoes (Martin 2014; Billington 2015). The reviewers can attend to the not-quite-there-ness of the play's sensory material. Here we might compare the experiences produced by Beckett's play with the introspective accounts of Neisser and Becklen when taking part in their own viewing experiments. They suggest that, in the dichoptic presentation task, 'the unwanted episode really does disappear (or parts of it do), and we can *attend to its disappearance*' (Neisser and Becklen 1975: 493, emphasis in original). The experimenters are attending to their own inattention. They know exactly what they should see – they produced the episodes – but can feel themselves not seeing it. However, in Beckett's play there is no primary episode layered on top of the flickering episode. The primary scene is presented as though it were secondary. One hears the faintness of the echo without there being a primary sound.

At the same time, though, attention is drawn to certain bits of this faint scene. For example, the only element that is 'clearly audible' (and not faint) is the 'rhythmic tread' of the feet (399). Similarly, in the visual field May's faint, pacing figure is surrounded by darkness. Billie Whitelaw, who first played the role, describes May as 'caged by one little strip' of light (1995: 109). This does, to some extent, make May's figure stand out, but the figure is not a continuous whole. Rather, the lower part of her body is highlighted: the lighting is 'strongest at floor level, less on body, least on head' (Beckett [1986] 2006: 399). This presentation narrows attention and encourages a focus on the feet and such a narrowing gets across the feeling that one is missing something. What insight, we are left to wonder, can be gleaned from the material in the darkness that surrounds May, or from her barely visible face? This feeling of missing something is mirrored in the play's appeal to the intellect. As mentioned above, May presents the story of Amy as a 'sequel', but we are not presented with the original (402). Thus, Mrs Winter is presented as a character that 'the reader will remember' (402). This brings into question whether something has gone amiss in the previous exchange, or what one is supposed to have read. The audience's confidence in their own attentiveness is interrogated. There is the sense that one is twice removed from events. The scene is not quite there, and one is not quite able to attend to it. As Lyn Gardner puts it in her review, 'It feels like being trapped in somebody else's nightmare' (2014). Both Beckett's work and experiments on 'inattentional blindness', then, are concerned with staging experiences in which one fails to attend to an event or attends to it partially. But why was this conception of the human observer deemed so enticing at this historical moment? In what follows, I will attempt to place the interest in context. Why, I will ask, has the experience of inattention been explored so extensively since the second half of the twentieth century?

Holding something back: Inattention and the failure to witness

There are three contexts with which we might frame the late twentieth century's experiments on inattention: the politics of non-seeing that characterized post-war discourse, the rise of trauma theory, and the demands of capitalist modernity. To begin this discussion, let us return to the experiment conducted by Chabris and colleagues. The experiment addresses a particular historical event. A brutal beating has occurred in the vicinity of a police officer, and he purports not to have noticed it. The experiment takes his non-noticing as an issue of attentional capacity – questioning whether his occupation with other events might have caused him to miss the fight. However, complications arise when one applies the study of inattentional blindness to a divisive historical situation. The experimenters essentially marginalize the political context of the Conley case and proceed from the assumption that Kenny Conley could have been anyone and Boston could have been anywhere. They are not interested in why Kenny Conley would not want to see but in the theoretical question of whether he could have not seen.

Debates around the Conley case, however, were not only concerned with the empirical question of human capacity. The plain-clothes police officer that fell victim to the brutal beating – Michael Cox – was African American, and Conley was white. In the context of late-twentieth-century America this fact was hard to ignore. Boston, in particular, was recovering from a period of severe racial turmoil. From 1974 until 1988, the city had been subject to a court-ordered de-segregation plan, in which children from mostly white neighbourhoods were bussed to schools in mostly African American neighbourhoods, and vice versa (Lehr 2009: 56–7). The implementation of de-segregation sparked a wave of violent protest, and the legacy of these protests affected public perceptions of the Conley case substantially. Kenny Conley was from the Southie area of Boston, a mainly white district which had seen particularly unpleasant protests in the 1970s. Even in 1995, according to journalist Dick Lehr, the area retained a largely negative public image (56). The neighbourhood in which Conley grew up, then, was deemed severely xenophobic and, for Lehr, this affected the way in which Conley's act of not-seeing was judged. Furthermore, in Boston and other parts of America, there had been numerous violent incidents involving white police officers and black victims. Most infamously, in 1991, a video emerged showing an African American, Rodney King, being attacked by a gang of white police officers. Racialized police brutality was (and clearly still is) a national problem, but Boston's police department was particularly heavily afflicted. Lehr, for example, cites the 1992 trial of the 'Brighton 13', a group of Boston police officers who had been seen savagely beating a suspect named John L. Smith. These officers all refused to testify against each other, one going so far as to claim that 'in all his years he had yet to see another officer commit so much as an infraction of the department's regulations' (75). This was true to form. In Lehr's words, when it came to reporting the wrongdoings of other officers, Boston police were known to adhere to one code: 'See no evil, hear no evil, and speak no evil' (75). In the wake of cases such as this, the Boston police force was increasingly perceived as racist, violent and dishonest. Thus, when a black police officer was found brutally beaten on a street occupied solely by police officers, and those officers claimed he had 'slipped on a patch of ice', there was more at issue than the question of human capacity (3–4). In failing to witness, Kenny Conley was seen not only as a police officer protecting violent police officers but also as a white man protecting violent white men.

This context makes little infringement on the experimenters' discussion of the Conley case. Race, in fact, goes completely unmentioned in the paper (though the authors do acknowledge Lehr's book which emphasizes the political context). What are the implications of this omission? The first thing to stress is that the experiment did not exert any influence on Conley's case. By the time of the experiment, Conley had been cleared on other grounds. Another important point is that the authors are not claiming that their study has provided any definitive answers as to what Kenny Conley saw. They note that 'no scientific study can prove or disprove a particular cause of a specific historical event' (Chabris et al. 2011: 153). Their aim, then, is not to limit the possibilities. They conclude that Conley could have missed the fight because of inattentional blindness, not that he definitely did. The text, then, leaves open the possibility that Conley saw the beating and wilfully denied it. The psychologists merely assert the physical possibility of the inattentional blindness explanation based on the performances of a collection of subjects. This physical possibility, though, is not weighed up against an assessment of Conley's identity, motives and testimony. The possibility of wilful denial is not refuted but marginalized. In this way, the experiment concurrently moves towards politics and away from it. A failure to witness is de-politicized insofar as we are prompted to put aside the political context and ask whether Conley's missing the assault was a physical possibility. Kenny Conley, a white police officer from Boston chasing a murder suspect, becomes a man 'running outdoors at night chasing a moving target at some distance' (151). Identity, here, is a kind of background noise that is filtered out in order to establish the mechanics of the situation.

At the same time, there is a kind of politics at work here. The experimenters have chosen to de-contextualize, but also draw attention to, an event that is politically and ethically atrocious.[2] The experiment is clearly informed by the distressing details of the event, but it does not address it directly. One is forced to look beyond the text in order to find it, and this leaves the question of whether the atrocity is being invoked and memorialized, or whether it has been omitted because it does not fit in with the theoretical interests of the researchers. A question such as this is comparable to those that are asked of Samuel Beckett's writing. Beckett's work, particularly that which came after the Second World

War, has frequently been looked upon as de-contextualizing and apolitical. Mark Nixon observes that 'up until the 1990s, Beckett in the eyes of most critics and commentators was a homeless, stateless writer who shunned geopolitical problems and specificity, creating fictional worlds in order to examine the universal nature of human existence' (2009: 31). This perception emerged from the tendency in Beckett's writing to dislocate, or vaguen the places and events that are invoked in his work. As Seán Kennedy puts it, 'The major works that secured Beckett's reputation give the distinct impression that they are set "both anywhere and nowhere"' (2009: 1). The perception that these major works were apolitical saw Beckett attacked in some circles. Most famously, in reviewing Beckett's work for television in 1977, the dramatist Dennis Potter asked: 'Is this the art which is the response to the despair and pity of our age, or is it made of the same kind of futility which helped such desecrations of the spirit, such filth of ideologies come into being?' (qtd. in Knowlson 1996: 636). There is the sense, here, that Beckett's methods fail to respond to particular historical atrocities and, furthermore, might facilitate these atrocities. In effect there is the accusation that Beckett is turning a blind eye, wilfully denying the atrocities of his age. Now, this notion of Beckett's writing is peculiar because, as an individual, Beckett did a great deal to bear witness to, and fight against, the 'filth of ideologies' to which Potter surely alludes. Most obviously, he served in the resistance cell 'Gloria SMH' during the Second World War and risked his life in the fight against fascism, later explaining that 'you simply couldn't stand by with your arms folded' (qtd. in Knowlson 1996: 303–4). In life, then, Beckett did not turn a blind eye to the atrocities that surrounded him, but what of his writing?

As Nixon's statement implies, the last three decades have seen attempts to re-situate Beckett's work in relation to the historical contexts from which it emerged. There has been a critical move to read Beckett's work as a series of responses to particular historical events, many of which the author experienced at close hand. But – if taken as responses – Beckett's responses are rarely direct. They are veiled, oblique and inscrutable in tone. In a discussion of the allusions to the Second World War that are found in *Watt*, James McNaughton outlines the key questions that are raised by this technique: 'First, had Beckett wanted us to consider contemporary history, would he not have written about his, or others' experience in the war directly? Second, is it reasonable to assume that all readers know Beckett's biographical involvement in history, or are willing to take textual hints to the archive to figure out their importance?' (2009: 55). The key critical task that emerges from these questions is one of explaining why, if Beckett's work is a response to the particular historical events that he encountered, it responds to these events in such an oblique way. This is where the critical work that's been done on Beckett's writing can be used to elucidate the experiment of Chabris and colleagues. Beckett's writing seems to invoke particular atrocities that happened in his lifetime. McNaughton, for example, takes the discussion of high barbed wire fences in *Watt* as an allusion to the holding camps that Beckett would have been detained in had the Gestapo caught him when Gloria SMH was betrayed. Beckett, McNaughton points out, does not reference the camps directly but 'trusts that they will re-appear as the elephant in the room, as a guilty and mirthless laugh that obviously relies on the reader's awareness of contemporary history' (53). Beckett, McNaughton suggests, does not represent the atrocity but leaves its effect to be felt by those with the means to feel it.

Thus, as in the inattentional blindness experiment, details of a specific historical atrocity are invoked, but the text occludes key elements. McNaughton sees the methods of *Watt* as an interrogation of the reader's attention. In the novel, he suggests, 'The formal gymnastics distract us from darker interpretations' (52). 'Beckett's experimental style', McNaughton continues, presents the reader, 'in the form of literary and aesthetic conundrums, similar interpretive challenges to those propaganda presents' (66). We are distracted from the atrocity, so we do not believe it is there. In this line of thought, Beckett's concern is not with representing 'what happened'[3] but addressing 'the more important questions of why it happens' (55). Beckett is seen to rehearse the distracting processes of propaganda in an aesthetic context so as to bring into focus the ways in which such processes 'affect us well beyond the literary text' (67). On a similar note, Laura Salisbury draws on the intelligence work Beckett performed during the Second World War and observes that works such as *Watt* arise out of a historical moment in which language is being manipulated in novel ways. At this time, Salisbury suggests, it came to be recognized that language is 'plastic enough to be broken down into bits, the information it carries to be condensed and displaced or submitted to encryption' (2014: 157). In the same way that propaganda seeks to draw attention away from certain unpalatable facts, the coding practices of the twentieth century sought to hide crucial information behind banal appearances. In this environment, Salisbury argues, 'One is forced to submit to very close, very attentive forms of speaking, writing, reading and listening' in order to discern the latent content behind the façade (157). For Salisbury, *Watt* is not a code to be cracked; one cannot access hidden meanings in the text by reading it in a particular way. Rather Beckett is interested in 'materialising doubt' (166) – producing a mindset of multiple channels in which one is aware that something important always has the potential to pass by unregistered. The experiment of Chabris and colleagues can be seen to work in a similar way. They are less interested in what happened than in why these things happen. The point is not merely that we can be distracted from atrocities, but also that we are not sufficiently aware of how easily it happens. They speak, for example, 'of the common but mistaken belief that people pay attention to, and notice, more of their visual world than they actually do' (Chabris et al. 2011: 150). These explorations of inattention may not document atrocities fully, but they respond to atrocities by allowing us to understand how easily they can be missed.

Inattention and trauma

The notion of inattention I have put forward so far leans heavily on an idea of attentional capacity. One is seen to miss an event because of being occupied by something else. In the case of Beckett's reader, 'formal gymnastics' have been seen to distract from 'darker interpretations', and in the case of Kenny Conley the demands of a police chase have been seen to distract from a violent beating. However, it is important to note that the late twentieth century saw the rise of another theory which seeks to explain the failure to witness: trauma. Though the concept of trauma was part of nineteenth-century psychological and medical discourse, it reached popular consciousness more fully in the period after the Second World War. Post-Traumatic Stress Disorder (PTSD), for example, was recognized as an illness by the American Psychiatric Association in 1980. There are two aspects of trauma theory that are relevant to my discussion of inattention. First, there is the question of the subject's capacity to experience, process or recall traumatic, 'stresser', events. It is commonly observed that the individual's inability to bear witness to an event is a sign of trauma. As trauma theorist Cathy Caruth has put it, 'The most direct seeing of a violent event may occur as an inability to know it' (1996: 91–2). Second there is the question of how the traumatic event affects the subject's attentional capacities in the medium to long term. In what follows, I will outline how these questions of trauma are working in the background of both the experiment of Chabris et al. and Beckett's play. But I will also suggest that, in *Footfalls*, Beckett becomes particularly interested in the second of these questions. The play, I will argue, is ultimately not an investigation of the potentially traumatic, missed event but can be seen to capture the qualitative nature of the post-traumatic experience.

With regard to the first aspect, traumatic repression may be put forward as an alternative lens with which to look at the Kenny Conley case. Given the violence of the event that occurred in Conley's vicinity, one might advance the idea that, rather than completely missing the event through inattentional blindness, Conley – to paraphrase Caruth – saw the event directly but was unable to know it. I will not attempt to choose between theories in this space. What I do want to show, though, is the extent to which the events of the Conley case were permeated by questions of traumatic repression. The case unfolded at a time when these questions were hotly debated. The early 1990s saw bitter disputes around the question of whether therapeutic techniques could be used to access repressed memories. Some asserted that techniques such as hypnosis could be used to 'retrieve memories in their pure, objective form', while others countered that 'traumatic events are likely to be the most malleable memories' and are 'particularly open to therapeutic suggestion' (Luckhurst 2008: 73). These debates spilled into the courtroom as psychologists on both sides of the debate were called up as expert witnesses. The relevance of this controversy to the Conley case might be seen in two main ways. First, one might speculate that therapeutic techniques such as hypnosis could be used to unlock Conley's memory of the event. But there would still be the serious question of whether these memories were truly retrieved or merely moulded by the technique.

Second, and more concretely, the cultural salience of these questions at the time is highlighted when one looks to the reason for Conley's eventual reprieve. Conley was cleared because the testimony of the witness who placed him in a position to see the beating was brought under question. Richard Walker, a fellow police officer, gave a variety of different accounts of what he saw that night and when questioned about the inconsistencies 'proposed his own truth-seeking exercise: hypnosis' (Lehr 2009: 264). Writing in 2009, Lehr calls this a 'zany, almost circus-sounding idea' (264), and it is possible that Walker was simply being evasive, but Walker's invocation of hypnosis shows the influence of contemporaneous debates around trauma, the failure to witness, and memory retrieval. The core difficulty, here, lies in a tension between the aporetic nature of trauma theory, on the one hand, and a cultural need for certainty on the other. Roger Luckhurst notes (paraphrasing Bruno Latour) that the debates of the 1990s 'emphasized the extent to which trauma was not "a matter of fact"' but an 'enigmatic thing that prompts perplexity, debate and contested opinion' (2008: 33). This, Luckhurst continues, led to the assertion that 'the authority of psychology, particularly in relation to the natural sciences, is not always secure' (34). The theory of inattentional blindness might be seen as a response to this perceived loss of authority. It offers a framework to explain the failure to witness without producing the aporias that come with trauma theory. The idea that Conley never saw the event is more culturally digestible than the interpretation that he saw the event but does not know that he saw it. This is evident when one compares Lehr's view that hypnosis was a 'zany, almost circus-sounding idea' with the credence he gives the theory of inattentional blindness. Again, it should be emphasized that Chabris et al. are not claiming that inattentional blindness is a definite explanation for Conley's non-noticing, and their research was not used as legal evidence. What the theory does seem to reach for, though, is a more clear-cut way in which psychology might intervene in debates around the failure to witness.

The association between trauma and the failure to witness goes back to the nineteenth century and the advance of industrialization. Wolfgang Schivelbusch has suggested that the railway accident was 'the site of the first attempt to explain industrial traumata' (Schivelbusch 1986: 14). Luckhurst picks up on this, citing an 1862 article in *The Lancet* which suggests that 'the violent jarring of the body in an accident might induce permanent but invisible damage' (Luckhurst 2008: 21). There is the idea that a 'jarring' event such as a railway accident might not leave obvious traces on the individual but is likely to affect them in detrimental ways. In nineteenth-century psychology, this notion developed to incorporate the idea that details of the jarring event might not be accessible to the individual's consciousness. In the 1880s, psychologists such as Pierre Janet began to suggest that particularly shocking events might be held out of conscious recall (Luckhurst 2008: 42). This line of thought did not escape the notice of Samuel Beckett. Beckett may have had some awareness of Janet's ideas,[4] but he seems to have attained the mainstay of his knowledge of repression-based inattention through his reading of later psychoanalytic works. This is most evident in his notes on Ernest Jones's *Papers on Psychoanalysis* (1913):

> Repression & Memory: 'There exist in the mind certain inhibiting forces which tend to exclude (& keep excluded) from consciousness all mental processes the presence of which would evoke there, either directly or through association, a feeling of Unlust. Forces of repression (censors) act at 2 points of junction between unconscious & preconscious & (less important) between preconscious & conscious.' (Feldman 2004: 330)

Beckett, then, was familiar with the idea that 'inhibiting forces' in the mind exclude material that is likely to evoke 'a feeling of Unlust'. However, this idea of 'hedonic repression' is balanced against an idea that one represses material that is not task-relevant: 'Likelihood of primarily hedonic mechanism of repression being appropriated for further purpose of excluding material that is merely irrelevant, without necessarily being disturbing. "Hedonic repression" & "utilitarian repression" – latter derived from former' (330). In Jones's account, task-based inattention (or 'utilitarian repression') is seen to be derived from the 'Hedonic' realm. The process of missing what one would rather not see is privileged over that of missing what is merely irrelevant. Beckett, though, would go on to investigate the boundary between not seeing and not wanting to see – between wilfully denying that one has seen something, repressing it, and simply being occupied by another matter.

This investigation manifests at the end of the radio play, *All That Fall* (1957), when we hear that a little child has fallen 'under the wheels' of Mr Rooney's train (Beckett [1986] 2006: 199). Even though Mrs Rooney has repeatedly inquired about the journey, Mr Rooney has not mentioned this accident in earlier discussions. Instead, when giving an account of his train journey, he suggests that his mind has been occupied by financial matters:

> Alone in the compartment my mind began to work as so often after office hours, on the way home in the train, to the lilt of the bogeys. Your season-ticket, I said, costs you six a day, that is to say barely enough to keep you alive and twitching with the help of food, drink, tobacco, and periodicals until you finally reach home and fall into bed. (193)

Mr Rooney's mind, it seems, has been working on calculating the economies of his working life and so we are left to question whether this task might have occupied him to the extent that he simply failed to notice the train accident. Alternatively, one might speculate that Mr Rooney's silence on the topic of the child's death can be put down to 'hedonic repression'. Finally, it may be suggested that Mr Rooney wilfully refuses to bear witness to the accident – that he noticed it but does not want to talk about it. The text ultimately privileges neither interpretation and the audience is left to question the distinction between wilful denial and 'hedonic' or 'utilitarian' non-seeing. Beckett's writing is interrogating the boundary between can't see and won't see.

In *Footfalls*, this question is again raised. Adam Piette has recognized the parallels between the character of May and a 'traumatized hysteric' of one of Janet's case studies, Irene (1993: 47). In this reading, the mother's death becomes the traumatic event at the centre of *Footfalls*, and May has been unable to witness, or know, this event. Hints of 'hedonic' or traumatic repression can also be seen when May first introduces the pacing Amy. Some nights, when walking up and down the church we are told that Amy 'would halt as one frozen by some shudder of the mind' (Beckett [1986] 2006: 402). Her halting, here, might hint that there is a moment in her past that periodically resurfaces to jolt her mind and trigger a kind of systemic shutdown, but this moment is never identified. Mrs W's suggestion that Amy is continually 'revolving it all' in her poor mind is interesting in this regard. It creates the image of Amy's mind as a kind of wheel in which the same matter constantly rotates. The shudder, though, suggests that the matter does not always rotate smoothly; there is the occasional jolt. The physicality of this image might recall the child who has fallen 'under the wheels' of Mr Rooney's train in *All That Fall*. But in *Footfalls* there is no original event. Instead, we are merely presented with suggestive imagery. Amy's mind is conceptualized as a jolting wheel, but we don't know what, if anything, is causing the jolts. Laura Salisbury has argued that rumination is 'part of the formal signature' in works such as *Watt* as 'the novel becomes entangled in evocations of permutation that force a hiatus in its forward movement' (2011: 75). One can also see the kind of ruminative hiatuses that Salisbury finds in *Watt* in the characters of Amy and ultimately May. For May and Amy, the idea of forward movement is taken away. They are condemned to circularity, revolving it all over and over (embodied in their pacing up and down). But this process is punctuated by jolts; some unspecified mental matter is forcing a hiatus in their circular movements.

However, Beckett again juxtaposes the hints of traumatic inattention with a more utilitarian idea. This can be seen in the portrayal of May's attempt to care for her mother. Here May asks whether her mother requires her to perform a range of acts of care: 'Straighten your pillows? (Pause.) Change your drawsheet? (Pause.) Pass you the bedpan? (Pause.) The warming pan? (Pause.) Dress your sores? (Pause.) Sponge you down? (Pause.) Moisten your poor lips? (Pause.) Pray with you? (Pause.) For you (Pause.)' (Beckett [1986] 2006: 400)? In a sense, May's performance seems compassionate and attentive. However, there is something in her performance that raises a question about her experience: Is she quite there? The acts of care are absorbed into a list of proposals which she can reel off. May does not wait for a response to one proposal before going to the next but recites them mechanically. There is the sense that neither May nor her mother needs to be wholly 'there' in order for May to produce her performance. When questioned about the nature of this exchange, Beckett suggested that May is 'occupied with her story' (Asmus 1977: 87). Beckett is suggesting that May's conversation seems inattentive because, as the exchange goes on, her attention is shifting towards the attempt to re-narrate her life. May's ruminating is seen to distract from immediate experience and give the impression that she is not wholly there. The mother's voice seems to recognize May's state of distraction when she asks the question: 'Will you never have done ... revolving it all?' (Beckett [1986] 2006: 400). Though her performance is dutiful, May is deemed too busy 'revolving it all' to be attentive.

Ultimately, in *Footfalls*, the notion of utilitarian inattention cannot be separated from trauma. If May is 'occupied with her story' it may be argued that this preoccupation is post-traumatic. Her rumination, it is hinted, is triggered by a traumatic event. As is often the case with Beckett's characters, the traumatic event in May's life – assuming there is one – seems to be birth itself. This is gestured towards in the exchange between May and her mother which opens the play. May's mother says to her daughter: 'I had you late. (Pause.) In life. (Pause.) Forgive me again. (Pause. No louder.) Forgive me again' (Beckett [1986] 2006: 400). Beckett had read about the topic of birth trauma in Otto Rank's *The Trauma of Birth* (1924), noting that 'all anxiety goes back to anxiety at birth' (Feldman 2004: 351). And there is the sense in the passage that May's maladies can be attributed to a traumatic birth. What should be noted, though, is that the details of the traumatic moment itself were removed as Beckett went through drafts of the play. S. E. Gontarski notes that Beckett's manuscripts show him going back and forth on how much detail to reveal about May's birth. In an early draft, Beckett included a passage revealing that the doctor delivering May had 'made a mess of it' but this detail was later omitted (1985: 165). Beckett hints at the traumatic event, but the play is ultimately concerned with May's attentional patterns – with whether she is quite there.

Beckett's portrayal of May's not-quite-there-ness certainly seems to echo many accounts of the post-traumatic subject. Evidence of this might be found in the aftermath of the assault on Michael Cox. Post-traumatic stress was a well-established phenomenon in mainstream medicine by the time of the incident, and Cox was, in fact, diagnosed with chronic PTSD (Lehr 2009). Lehr summarizes an account of the effect of the event on Cox, given by his wife in a police hearing:

> Now Mike seemed only partly there. 'If we're having a conversation he'll walk out of the room in the middle of the conversation. I'm talking about one thing and he'll leave that subject and go to something else, or he'll pick up the phone and he'll, you know, start dialling, calling someone on the phone and, like, Hey, we're talking.' (2009: 284)

One can see in this account the kind of jolting attentional pattern that Beckett portrays in *Footfalls*. We do not know that the traumatic event is necessarily revolving around Cox's mind any more than we know what is revolving in the minds of May or Amy. Rather, Cox's wife observes him moving between there-ness and not-there-ness. The traumatic event is in the background; foregrounded is a low level, inattentive atmosphere. Cox's wife draws a clear distinction between the man she knew before the trauma and after the trauma. Her account offers a clear cause and effect. Beckett's text is slightly different in that we are never offered a 'before' moment. The lives of Amy and May cannot be divided so neatly into a pre-traumatic and a post-traumatic period. But in *Footfalls* Beckett is interested in the day-to-day not-quite-there-ness that characterizes the account of the post-traumatic Cox. Again, Beckett is reluctant to represent events directly and in their entirety; this is not a before-and-after trauma narrative. Instead he focuses on the qualities of an experience in which the subject is not wholly attentive to their own life. However, in the conception of the mind as a jolting wheel, there is more than a hint of the post-traumatic in Beckett's presentation of this experience. Where, in the psychological experiment of Chabris and colleagues, trauma theory is excised in favour of a more clear-cut utilitarian theory, Beckett's work weaves together utilitarian and trauma-based theories of inattention.

Inattention and the modern self

Beckett himself linked *Footfalls* to his encounters with psychotherapeutic theory, specifically that of Carl Jung. James Knowlson recalls that the character of May was 'specifically linked by Beckett with the young female patient of Jung, of whom Beckett heard him speak in 1935' (1996: 616). Walter Asmus reports that, during a rehearsal of the play, Beckett suggested the 'connection' between May's character and 'the Jung story' of a girl who 'existed but didn't actually live' (Asmus 1977: 87–8). From this, Knowlson suggests that May is 'Beckett's own poignant recreation of the girl who had never really been born' (1996: 616). Beckett had made more overt links to this lecture in earlier works. In *All That Fall* Mrs Rooney describes attending a lecture of 'one of these new mind doctors', recalling that this unnamed doctor gave the opinion that a patient of his 'had never really been born' (Beckett [1986] 2006: 195–6). Critics have disagreed on the significance of Beckett's repeated invocation of Jung's lecture. David Melnyk (2005) notes the degree to which Beckett adapted and re-contextualized Jung's words and warns against taking Beckett's allusions as evidence of a close relationship between Beckett's work and Jung's theories.

Julie Campbell, on the other hand, makes an argument for a congruence of aim. Beckett's theatre, Campbell argues, shows a Jungian concern with the representation of 'unconscious personalities' and complexes (2005: 165). Now, I hesitate to accept the link Campbell draws between Jung's specific theory and Beckett's dramatic technique. Melnyk is right to point out the way in which Beckett twisted Jung's phrase to suit his own purposes, and I sympathize with the argument that, for Beckett, Jung's idea was more evocative than foundational. However, when one reads Jung's phrase in the context of his discussion, there is a definite relevance to *Footfalls*. Jung's invocation of the girl who (he thinks) has 'never been born entirely' comes in response to a question from an audience member. The audience member has a five-year-old daughter, and he effectively asks Jung to interpret her dreams (1968: 105–6). The girl has had two peculiar dreams: one in which 'a wheel is rolling down a road and it burns me', and one in which the girl is being pinched by a beetle (105). Jung suggests that these are examples of the 'strange archetypal dreams children occasionally have' (106). These archetypal dreams, Jung suggests, can be explained 'by the fact that when consciousness begins to dawn', the child is still close to 'the original psychological world from which he has just emerged: a condition of deep unconsciousness' (106). This closeness is seen to give children 'an awareness of the contents of the collective unconscious' (106).[5] If this awareness of the mythological content of the collective unconscious remains for too long, Jung continues, 'the individual is threatened by an incapacity for adaptation; he is haunted by a constant yearning to return to the original vision' (106). This incapacity produces 'ethereal children' who live their life in 'archetypal dreams' and cannot adapt (107). The patient that had never been born entirely, for Jung, was one such child.

The extent to which Beckett was interested in Jung's overall theory of the collective unconscious is debatable. But he certainly seems to have picked up on the content of Jung's discussion. Two aspects of Jung's discussion surface in *Footfalls*. First, the motif of the rolling wheel emerges in both of the texts in which Beckett alludes to Jung. As noted, in *All That Fall* a little child has fallen 'under the wheels' of Mr Rooney's train and, in *Footfalls*, Amy and May are seen to be 'revolving it all'. Beckett seems to incorporate into his work the archetypal dream content that Jung interprets ('a wheel is rolling down a road and it burns me'). More importantly, though, I think Beckett is interested in the incapacity for adaptation that Jung discusses. Beyond the archetypal contents themselves, Beckett is interested in how these contents produce a kind of not-quite-there-ness – a failure to adapt and attend to the world. As Campbell notes, 'not quite there' was a term Beckett used to describe the character of May (2005: 164), and, in what follows, I want to further interrogate and historicize this idea of not-quite-there-ness. I will suggest that the concept is linked with the need to adapt to a capitalist modernity in which the individual's attentiveness is not just founded on their capacity to perform particular tasks, but also produce a story of self. In this period, there is the emergence of an economy of personality in which the individual is required to construct a self out of their past and make decisions on their future, while giving the impression that they are present and engaged. It is telling that Mr Rooney's failure to witness in *All That Fall* occurs as he is deliberating on the profitability of his job. Questions of the past and future are seen to distract from present experience. Beckett, I will argue, along with therapists such as D. W. Winnicott, can be seen to respond to the challenge of witnessing the present in the context of a modernity in which one is continually pulled from tense to tense.

The question of how present experience is affected by the pressure to negotiate or construct a past or future plays a crucial role in twentieth-century psychotherapy. The psychoanalytic theory of Melanie Klein, for example, emphasizes the ways in which subjects negotiate their past, particularly the 'losing of caring or cared for people' (Segal 2004: 46–7). When a subject feels as though a caring/cared for object has been lost, Kleinian theory argues, the goodness of that object may come under attack (46).[6] Put another way, in order to minimize the pain caused by loss, the subject might come to think that the lost object was never that good in the first place. This denigration of the lost object, for Kleinians, is potentially damaging, and (for good psychic health) one needs to go through a process in which the denigrated object undergoes reparation. This reparation, however, requires a large amount of psychic labour; one is forced to re-narrate one's past. Rina Kim (2010) has argued that this labour is crucial to much of Beckett's later work including *Footfalls*. In *Footfalls*, Kim suggests, Beckett can be seen to represent this act of reparation. If May is occupied by her story in the first part of the text, Kim argues, it is a story in which the mother figure is represented as the attentive Mrs Winter (157). May, it seems, is so consumed by the labours of re-narrating the mother figure that she seems removed from a present in which she performs an act of care. This representation, Kim goes on, served a particular purpose for Beckett. Along with the character of May, Beckett is attempting to reconstruct his feelings towards the mother figure. There is, though, always the sense that the reconstruction of a past can draw one's attention from present experience.

Kim's reading is persuasive in many ways but, again, there is danger of being overly specific when discussing Beckett's approach to not-quite-there-ness. Beckett's investigation of inattention, I suggest, does not hinge on Kleinian ideas of the mother–child relationship, on Jungian notions of a collective unconscious, or on any trauma-based theory. Nor is Beckett purely interested in a utilitarian account of inattention. Rather, Beckett's interest seems to reside in the phenomenology of inattention – how one experiences oneself as inattentive and perceives it in others. To help study this further we might look to one of Winnicott's later case studies. The study is interesting for its analogues with the cases of May and Amy, and as a comparison with Jung's patient. But more than this there is a certain theoretical approach that ties the study to Beckett and to Jung. It is less interested in going back and finding a cause for the patient's not-quite-there-ness, than in investigating the qualitative experience itself. In his 'Psychology' notes Beckett quoted Jung's statement that 'I no longer find the cause of the neurosis in the past, but in the present. What is the necessary task which the patient will not accomplish?' (Feldman 2004: 320). It is this looking to present experience that I think is crucial for Beckett and for Winnicott.

In 'Dreaming, Fantasying and Living', Winnicott gives the case history of a patient who is caught between fantasying and imagination.[7] Imagination, for Winnicott, is a healthy process that enriches life and becomes accessible to the individual either consciously or in dreams. The patient's life, though, has been dominated by the unhealthy process of fantasying. Fantasying, in Winnicott's construction, is an 'isolated phenomenon', which absorbs energy but does not contribute to dreaming or living ([1971] 2005: 36). The key difficulty with fantasying lies in its 'inaccessibility' (36). It takes up the individual's mental resources but cannot be used practically or emotionally. The two processes are very difficult to tell apart qualitatively. Their differences 'can be subtle and difficult to describe' and are not necessarily discernible from verbal reports 'of what goes on in the patient's mind' (36–7): 'The patient may sit in her room and while doing nothing at all except breathe she has (in her fantasy) painted a picture, or she has done an interesting piece of work in her job' (37). In this state she is presently doing something in her fantasy, and her activity in this dissociative state competes against lived activity. By contrast, while still sitting in a room doing nothing observable, she may be 'thinking of tomorrow's job and making plans, or thinking about her holiday and this may be an imaginative exploration of the world' (37) These acts of imagination do not compete against life but hold, supplement and enrich it. In both scenarios the patient is inactive in terms of performance, but there is a difference in experience. Imagination can be held by the individual and put to use where fantasy cannot.

Winnicott goes on to give a (semi-fictionalized) description of the patient's life story. He describes the type of fantasying partaken in by the patient as rooted in the nursery. She had older siblings who had worked out ways of playing together before her arrival, so 'found herself in a world that was already organized before she came into the nursery' (380). Being 'intelligent' she managed to 'fit in' with the way things were organized but could only do so 'on a compliance basis' (38–9). She could play whichever role was 'assigned to her', but this play was 'unsatisfactory' because she did not really have any say in it (39). Others also 'felt something was lacking in the sense that she was not actively contributing' to the play (39). This lack of contribution is put down to a state of dissociation. When she was functioning as a part of 'other people's games' she was 'essentially absent' as the most part of her was *all the time engaged in fantasying* (39, emphasis in original). For Winnicott, this childhood habit became the basis for the patient's life. Her life became constructed in such a way that 'nothing that was really happening was significant to her' and 'the main part of her existence was taking place when she was doing nothing whatever' (39–40). She also disguised this 'doing nothing' with certain 'futile' activities – originally thumb-sucking, but also 'compulsive smoking' and a series of 'boring and obsessive games' (40). The patient has 'health enough' to give promise, but this promise cannot be fulfilled because fantasy has consistently overcome imagination and she has been unable to attend to lived experience (40). For this reason, she is described to be 'missing the boat' (37).

There are certainly some points of comparison between Winnicott's case and Beckett's presentation of May and Amy. In all there is a sense of absence, preoccupation or inattention. We might also detect the 'compliance' of Winnicott's patient in the way that May plays the role of carer to her mother and the way that Amy responds to the sermon at church. May's repetitive pacing might also recall the 'futile' activities that Winnicott's patient uses to disguise her fantasying. The underlying similarity, though, lies in the failure to attend to performance. Winnicott's patient is able to 'fit in' with the way things are organized and is more or less able to function from day-to-day but there is the feeling that something is 'lacking' and that she is 'missing the boat'. She is performing certain tasks but there seems to be the lack of a self being actively engaged in these tasks. Similarly, in *Footfalls* the problem is not what May or Amy do; May seems to perform the duties of caring for her mother and Amy seems to have been responsive in church. Again, though, there is the sense that each is otherwise occupied. Winnicott suggests that his patient is engaged in fantasying and the mothers in *Footfalls* suggest that their daughters are 'revolving it all'. In both cases, a (sometimes unconscious) preoccupation with producing a story of self distracts from immediate experience.

This story of self, though, is rarely optional in capitalist modernity. In *The Experience of Modernity* (1983), Marshall Berman observes the degree to which capitalism 'fosters, indeed forces, self-development for everybody' (1983: 96). In the world of the CV, the interview and the retirement plan there is a continual need to develop a story of past and future, and this inevitably distracts from present experience. One might argue that Beckett's characters are often far removed from the competitive world of employment, but I would contest this. As mentioned above, Mr Rooney is contemplating retirement on the train, and even the text of *Footfalls* draws May in competition with her peers. As May paces we are told that 'when other girls of her age were out at … lacrosse she was already here' (Beckett [1986] 2006: 401). Winnicott and Beckett, then, articulate the pressure that is placed on the individual to be self-present while all the time producing a story of past and future. For practical purposes, the study of inattention that we have seen in experimental psychology tends to be structured around two definite perceptual tasks. Reading these studies alongside the texts of Beckett and Winnicott, though, can broaden our view of inattention. Inattentional blindness is not merely a matter of one terminable task distracting from another. There is another sense in which the interminable story of life distracts from the events that unfold in front of the subject. Beckett and Winnicott's concern with inattention is rooted in the desire to raise awareness about this tendency. This is evident in the case of Winnicott for whom success with his patient comes in the form of her being able to recognize her own inattentiveness. As she discusses her symptoms with him, she interrupts herself to tell him she is slipping into fantasy: 'At this moment she reported that she had already "gone off to her job and to things that had happened at work" and so here again while talking to me she had already left me' (2005: 44). The crucial point is that therapy has enabled the patient to become aware that she is not attending to the conversation wholly. She can recognize and report the experience of inattention. This increased awareness, Winnicott hopes, will give the patient some choice about her way of living. In a modernity in which there is a continual pressure to construct a past and a future, there will always be moments when the individual is not quite in the present. In different ways, though, Beckett, Winnicott and the experimental psychologists can help us attend to and (perhaps) manage a penchant for not-quite-there-ness.

Conclusion

In a recent review of Lisa Dwan's Perth Festival performance of *Not I*, *Footfalls* and *Rockaby*, Van Badham compares her experience of the production to 'watching the re-enactment of a once bold experiment whose conclusions have long been accepted as fact' (2015). One might take this criticism in a couple of ways depending on how the term 'experiment' is understood. In one sense, Beckett's plays are experiments insofar as they are innovative and cutting-edge. In this line of thought, they extend the boundaries of artistic practice and prove that one can produce successful theatre when presenting nothing but a mouth, a face or a pacing figure on stage. If the term 'experiment' is understood in this way, then, it may be fair to argue that the plays were 'once bold' but there is little at stake when they are staged today. We know that these set-ups can work as theatre and so, while we might be impressed with their technique, we cannot be thrilled by their discoveries. They have already extended the boundaries of artistic practice and cannot be expected to extend them any further. It is my argument, however, that we might understand the term 'experiment' in another sense. Rather than focusing on how Beckett's plays extend artistic practice, the last three chapters have treated them as more direct experiments on the nature of modern experience. In this way, I have argued that these plays investigate the processes by which the individual adapts to a modernity in which one is required to attend to, in Crary's words, 'an endless sequence of new products, sources of stimulation, and streams of information' (1999: 13–14). Crucially, the plays do not just test the individual's capacity to perform perceptual tasks, though they certainly do this. Rather, the novel streams of stimuli that Beckett presents are always accompanied by a concern with the production of a story of self. In *Not I* the rapid speech and striking darkness is accompanied by a focus on the production of an I. In *That Time*, one needs to read faces and isolate voices in order to get at a story of Listener's life. And in *Footfalls* we are presented with May whose occupation with her story – her 'revolving it all' – distracts her from present experience. Beckett's plays, then, can be deemed experimental in the sense that they take part in an investigation of the ways in which the modern individual strains to process a given body of material while endlessly developing a sense of self.

5

Beckett and the mental image

In Chapters 2, 3 and 4, the material that Beckett presented in his theatre of the 1970s (the frenetic mouth of *Not I*, the inactive face of *That Time* and the pacing figure in *Footfalls*) was largely discussed in terms of perception and attention. To take the example of *Not I*, the mouth was treated as a projector of sensory stimuli, and the actors and audience were discussed in terms of their capacity to process, attend to, experience and interpret these stimuli. In this respect, I argued that, like many psychological experiments, Beckett's works are spaces in which we can study the responses of human subjects when they are exposed to novel sensory environments. There is, though, a distinction to be made here insofar as Beckett's experimentation works to produce a different, more experiential knowledge to that which is frequently sought in experimental psychology. The psychological experiments I have looked at so far are primarily interested in the human subject's capacity for performance. They are interested, to give some examples, in how quickly speech can be processed; how many voices can be comprehended at once; or how attentional loads affect the subject's ability to notice an event. Beckett's experiments are also interested in the performance of tasks such as speech perception and selective attention, but the concern in the context of Beckett's work is more consistently with the experience of the performing subject – the ways in which the subject becomes conscious of that which they perform. The next two chapters will continue to understand Beckett's works as experiments on subjective experience, but I will focus less on perceptual experience than on what is left behind in the wake of perception: the images that the subject is able to apprehend or recall without direct sensory stimulation. Put simply, I will treat Beckett's works less as experiments on perceptual experience and more as experiments on mental imagery.

What one might question here is the degree to which the percept can be separated from the mental image in the context of Beckett's work. Recent criticism has argued that a large part of the power of Beckett's works resides in their resistance to this categorization of experience. Ulrika Maude, for instance, has suggested that Beckett's works see 'categories such as perception, memory and imagination lose their differentiating characteristics' (2009: 37). This is an important point, and the distinction that will be drawn between perception and mental imagery in this section is most certainly not a sharp one. I will talk about the mental image and the percept as two areas insofar as I hold that there are differences in the extents to which the two phenomena are capable of affecting the sensory world. Here I use William James's observation that the properties of 'real' or perceptual phenomena 'always accrue' consequences on the sensory world, where the properties of mental imagery do not ([1909] 2008: 15). As James puts it, 'Mental triangles are pointed, but their points won't wound' (15). However, my argument will be that Beckett is interested in the moments at which these two areas blur into one another, and it becomes difficult to sift perceptual experience from the experience of mental imagery. The section, then, aims to extend, rather than contradict, Maude's argument. To illustrate this, we might look to the context of Maude's statement. It comes in the midst of a discussion of vision in Beckett's work where Maude suggests that imaginative experience frequently interferes with the perceptions of Beckett's subjects. In a discussion of the short story 'The End' (1946), for example, Maude notes that 'the narrator's observations vacillate between vision and imagination, making the certainty of what is seen precarious and erratic' (2009: 38). Maude, here, is arguing that percept and image blur into one another in Beckett's work, but her focus is on how this blurring affects our understanding of perception. The possibility that images of imagination blur with the narrator's visual perception of the outside world is seen to shed doubt on the reliability of his vision. Beckett's work, in this interpretation, is seen to counter the tendency in the Western philosophical tradition to privilege the objectivity and reliability of sight in comparison to other senses such as hearing and touch. This is a convincing argument, but it does leave an important question unaddressed. In suggesting that Beckett's troubling of distinctions between perception and imagination might affect attitudes towards perception, Maude raises a question of how this strategy might also alter conceptions of the imagination and imagery. If the work of Beckett allows us to see elements of the image in the percept, is the opposite true in the case of the mental image? Does Beckett's work allow us to understand the mental image as an entity that, like the percept, needs to be processed, attended to and interpreted? This is the concern that animates this section.

Beckettian mental imagery

To begin to confront this question we might return to the reception of *Not I* and specifically Michael Billington's observation that the play is 'compelling' because it 'leaves behind an ineradicable image' (1973). In this account, the artistic value of *Not I* lies not just in the perceptual process in which the figure on stage is observed. Rather, the play is adjudged successful because the sensory experience that it presents stays with the observer in imagistic form long after the performance has finished. This contention has also been made in more recent criticism. Drawing on approaches to the image taken by Henri Bergson and Gilles Deleuze, Anthony Uhlmann has advanced the argument that, while all Beckett's works (and presumably the works of other authors) 'make use of images of various kinds', there is a 'true Beckettian image' which possesses a singular aesthetic power (2008: 62). This 'true' image, for Uhlmann, 'is something which appears, or is created, and vanishes, but in vanishing leaves a strong impression, an impression which lingers or even transforms the one it affects' (62). Beckett's images, Uhlmann continues, 'are impressed upon us as we watch and more or less burnt into our retinas, leaving afterimages which linger' (62). The observations of Billington and Uhlmann are useful in helping us distinguish between the object of perception and the mental image in Beckett's work because they help us to identify two separate stages in the reception of a given stimuli. There is a perceptual stage in which we are concerned with what is objectively presented and the observer's capacity to process, attend to and interpret this material in real time. But there is also an imagistic stage in which our concerns are with the quasi-sensory impressions that linger in the observer's consciousness. For Billington and Uhlmann it seems that Beckett's works are distinguished by the emphasis they place on this imagistic stage.

Works such as *Not I*, then, seem to have a peculiar power to leave behind mental images, but what is the nature of these images? Here it might be useful to compare Billington and Uhlmann's accounts of the image left behind by Beckett's work with some other types of mental imagery. Uhlmann implies a link between the lingering Beckettian image and retinal afterimages, suggesting that the image left behind by Beckett's work is a static entity that is stamped down on our minds. This, though, does not account for the 'endless' mobility described by Billington. In Billington's account, the image of the mouth does not seem to be a static representation. Instead, Billington gives the sense that he is involuntarily re-experiencing the visuals of *Not I* as a kind of replay. This might suggest that the imagery he describes is similar to that of the traumatic 'flashback' memory in which individuals frequently report 'a vivid perceptual content' and a sense that this imaginal content is 'happening in the "here and now"' (Speckens et al. 2007: 250). On further inspection, however, it is difficult to argue for a strong link between Beckett's lingering imagery and the imagery of traumatic memory. Neither Uhlmann nor Billington, for example, report the 'feeling of travelling in time' that is common with traumatic memory (250). As Billington and Uhlmann describe it, the subject of the Beckettian image does not have the impression of returning to or re-experiencing an original event. Rather, there is the idea that certain sensory elements are lingering as definite but de-contextualized impressions. Also, the Beckettian image does not seem to cause personal distress in the manner of a traumatic image. It may be experienced as significant, but this significance is not necessarily negative. Uhlmann, for instance, suggests that the Beckettian image might transform 'the one it affects', but the transformation envisioned by Uhlmann is not necessarily damaging. The Beckettian mental image, then, might be characterized as a concrete and affective presence, but there remains something faint or vague about its nature insofar as it is difficult to locate this concrete presence in space, or define the affect that it produces.

In 'The Exhausted' (1995), Gilles Deleuze also observes these characteristics in the Beckettian image. For Deleuze, Beckett's work is frequently occupied by the attempt to produce 'something seen or heard' which is 'called Image' (1995: 8). He identifies three *languages* (*I*, *II* and *III*) in Beckett's work and the 'Image' forms the basis of *'language III'* (8, emphasis in original). In Deleuze's schema, *language I* is concerned with the enumeration and combination of objects, *language II* with 'inventing stories or making inventories of memory', but *language III* is distinguished by its capacity to escape these projects (8). For Deleuze, *languages I* and *II* make use of images (or the imagination) but the images of both of these languages are bound by reason and/or memory. The image of *language III*, by contrast, is 'liberated from the chains it was kept in by the other two languages' and becomes 'the Image' (8). This entity, Deleuze goes on, 'appears in all its singularity, retaining nothing of the personal, nor of the rational, and ascending into the indefinite as into a celestial state. *A* woman, *a* hand, *a* mouth, *some* eyes' (9, emphasis in original). The 'Image' then, for Deleuze, is a concrete, apprehensible form but – because it is de-contextualized (torn away from reason and memory) there is something 'indefinite' and distant about it. Again, there is a sense that the Beckettian image is vivid and immediate, but also somehow faint and faraway.

How is this vivid faintness produced? Deleuze's account gives two insights that might help us begin to answer the question. First, he highlights Beckett's use of space, arguing that *language III* 'proceeds not only with images but with spaces' (10). Beckett's singular but indefinite image, by this account, can only emerge from a space that shares its singular but indefinite nature, a space which Deleuze calls 'any-space-whatever' (10). This space is 'disused' and 'unassigned', but 'entirely geometrically determined' (10). Like 'the Image', then, the 'any-space-whatever' is a definite form but one that is not assigned to anyone or associated with a particular practice. The de-contextualized image can only exist in a de-contextualized space. Thus, Deleuze outlines a kind of recipe stipulating that one has to produce space and image in sequence. In his readings of *Ghost Trio* (1976) and *... but the clouds ...* (1976), for example, Deleuze identifies a two-stage process, in which the concern is, first, with the creation of 'any-space-whatever' and, second, with 'the mental image to which it leads' (19).

Deleuze's second insight lies in the animation of the image. In Deleuze's argument, the image is defined in terms of motion. He argues that the image of *language III* is 'not a representation of an object, but a movement' in any-space-whatever (19). Thus, the image is seen to be embedded in the any-space-whatever, but it is distinguished from that space by its motion. However, the motion of the image is of a flickering, precarious kind. Deleuze continues:

> And insofar as it is a spiritual movement, it is not separated from its own disappearance, of its dissipation, premature or not. The image is a pant, a breath, but expelled on the way to extinction. The image is what dies away, wastes away, a fall. It is a pure intensity, which defines itself as such through its height – its level above zero, which is only described in falling. (19)

For Deleuze, the Beckettian image acquires its power through the manipulation of context and motion, a manipulation which is made possible by the precision of television. The Beckettian image, according to Deleuze, must be embedded in a particular de-contextualized space and presented at a particular flickering intensity, and 'only television ... is able to satisfy these demands' (20). Why, though, does Beckett feel compelled to produce such images? Deleuze seems to suggest that Beckett has a mimetic project in mind: that of producing a perceptual form with the qualities of a mental image. He argues, for example, that Beckett's works refuse 'artificial techniques, which are not suited to the movements of the mind' (20). Beckett's television plays, by implication here, are concerned with expressing (or perhaps even imitating) particular mental 'movements'. This insight is one way of explaining Beckett's work's tendency to leave behind 'ineradicable' images. Beckett's works, one might suggest, stay with us as mental images because they are presented to us in the language of a mental image.

Deleuze's reading certainly raises some interesting possibilities, but what it perhaps lacks is a detailed account of how Beckett developed this method. For this, we might turn back to Uhlmann who traces a movement from an aesthetic of relation to one of non-relation in Beckett's writing. He argues that, in early works such as – the posthumously published first novel – *Dream of Fair to Middling Women* (1992) and *Murphy* (1938), Beckett makes heavy use of relational techniques such as allusion and metaphor, seeming to 'prize the process of skilfully drawing links' between image, context and meaning (42). However, Uhlmann suggests that these early works also exhibit a 'growing sense of distrust' of this process which reflects an interest in how the image might be allowed to stand alone (42). For Uhlmann, even as Beckett made heavy use of allusion and metaphor in his early novels, 'He was also already very much aware of the idea of the image itself as that which can carry affective power' (54). This interest, Uhlmann argues, pervaded later works as Beckett began to 'find a form' which eschewed the aesthetic of relation and accommodated non-relation. Thus, Beckett began to draw attention to images that 'offer themselves as meaningful, but … exceed straightforward interpretation' and demand interpretive work (64).

Uhlmann places this aspect of Beckett's work within a long (though intermittent) philosophical tradition which is concerned with the idea 'that the apprehension of the image … is fundamental both to our understanding of what the world is and how we know that world' (2008: 5). Thus, the image is adjudged to set the tone for all thoughts about what has been sensed. For Uhlmann, this idea might be seen to begin with the Ancient Greek Stoics, before continuing in modern philosophers such as Descartes, Spinoza, Henri Bergson, William James, Charles Sanders Peirce and Deleuze (5–6). In his study, Uhlmann focuses particularly on the philosophers of the late nineteenth century, arguing that the approaches to the image taken by these authors were 'developed and transformed by an army of modernist writers and artists' – ranging from the imagist poets to the painter Francis Bacon and Beckett (6). The ideas of the philosophers, then, are seen to trigger a major change in aesthetic attitudes to the image.

To Uhlmann's argument, I want to add the idea that this philosophy also influenced scientific approaches to the image. For evidence of this, we might focus on one name on Uhlmann's list, William James. Though James's ideas have undoubtedly had a lasting impact on both philosophy and aesthetics, it should be stressed that his primary concern when discussing images was the practice of psychology. For example, James's famous discussion of the 'stream of thought' in *Principles of Psychology* (1890) specifically targeted the way in which the image had been approached in 'traditional psychology':

> What must be admitted is that the definite images of traditional psychology form but the very smallest part of our minds as they actually live. The traditional psychology talks like one who should say a river consists of nothing but pailsful, spoonsful, quartpotsful, barrelsful and other moulded forms of water. Even were the pails and the pots all actually standing in the stream, still between them the free water would continue to flow. It is just this free water of consciousness that psychologists resolutely overlook. Every definite image in the mind is steeped and dyed in the free water that flows around it. (James 1890: 255)

James, here, is addressing the discipline of psychology. He is defining a 'traditional psychology'[1] in opposition to what he sees as his own non-traditional form. This is important because the way in which the term 'image' is used in psychology is slightly different from its use in Uhlmann and Deleuze's discussions of philosophy and aesthetics. In Uhlmann and Deleuze, the term is used very broadly to refer to something that may be presented to the mind but might also be presented on page, stage or screen. In this sense, the image is both the thing that we see on the television screen and the mental impression that we recall after the television has been switched off. Though psychologists may sometimes use the term in this broad way, the image of psychology is more commonly understood in its narrower sense as something we recall or imagine. The images James describes are located 'in the mind', not on page, stage or screen, and he is making a point about the way in which psychology should conceive of these mental images. The 'traditional psychology', for James, conceives of the mind as a collection of 'definite' images. James's problem with this conception is not exactly that these images do not exist, but that psychology tends to reduce thought and experience to a series of static, definite images. For James, images may be apprehended in the mind as definite entities, but the images exist within a stream of thought and so are never as definite or permanent as they appear. As was the case in Deleuze's account of the Beckettian image, James's mental images are defined by their mobility and impermanence. As James puts it, apprehension of the image is escorted by 'the dying echo of whence it came to us', and 'the dawning sense of whither it is to lead' (255). The mental image is defined as an impression of something but one that is always on the cusp of modification or dissipation.

James applies this model to the reception of aesthetic productions. 'What', he questions, 'is that shadowy scheme of the "form" of an opera, play, or book, which remains in our minds and on which we pass judgment when the actual thing is done?' (255). It may be tempting, here, to suggest that the 'shadowy' form to which James alludes is simply our consciousness of an aesthetic piece – what we think of it. But James seems to have in mind a kind of double process of interpretation in which we form a 'shadowy' version of the – now absent – 'thing' and then pass judgement on this shadowy version. Here we seem to be getting very close to Bergson's formulation of the image as, in Uhlmann's words, 'a bridge between those objectively existing things and our thoughts' (2008: 8). In the wake of sensation, by this account, a shadowy and often fleeting version of the experience undergone is constructed and evaluated in the mind. The presence of this form allows us to re-experience and think about a version of the thing that has been sensed. The image of the thing, then, seems to mould our thoughts about that thing. Thus, through James, the ideas of the image that emerged in late-nineteenth-century philosophy seem to cross over into psychology.

The image in twentieth-century experimental psychology

The understanding of the image as a shadowy version of sensory experience remains crucial to experimental psychology's approach to mental imagery today. In a recent summary of imagery research the term 'mental imagery' is defined as follows: 'Representations and the accompanying experience of sensory information without a direct external stimulus. Such representations are recalled from memory and lead one to re-experience a version of the original stimulus or some novel combination of stimuli' (Pearson et al. 2015: 590). Again, there is the idea that the image is a version of an original stimulus (or set of stimuli) which gives the subject 'the experience of sensory information'. The image might affect the subject in a manner that is like 'a direct external stimulus', even though it is only in the mind. As Waller et al. point out in another summary, this contemporary understanding of the image is based on a body of recent behavioural and neuroscientific research which has been taken to show that mental imagery 'engages many' – though not all – 'of the psychological structures and processes used in perception' (2012: 295). Thus, though mental imagery is understood to be encountered 'without a direct external stimulus', research suggests that its apprehension requires many of the psychological mechanisms that one would use to apprehend an external stimulus. Not only this, but mental imagery is seen to give the 'experience of sensory information' which suggests that it may not always be possible for the subject to distinguish the mental image from the object of perception.

Though advances in technology have allowed the case to be made with more rigour, this assertion is nothing new. Experimental psychology has long been scrutinizing the distinction between imagery and perception. For an early investigation of this, we might look to 1896 and E. W. Scripture's paper on 'Measuring Hallucinations'. Scripture's experiments found that subjects who had been trained for several trials to detect a very faint sound, began to report the presence of that sound even when it was absent (Scripture 1896: 762–3). Though Scripture does not make the case explicitly, there is the hint that the subject experiences a version of a perceived stimulus even when that stimulus is no longer present. By the turn of the twentieth century, then, experimental psychology was beginning to illustrate the continuities between imagery and perception. For a more explicit investigation, though, we must cross over to the early twentieth century and Cheves Perky's 1910 article: 'An Experimental Study of Imagination'. This article – which I will discuss in more detail in Chapter 6 – documented numerous experiments on the relationship between perception, imagery and the imagination, but the most famous of these sought to compare the object of perception with 'the image of imagination' (Perky 1910: 428). Here Perky and her co-investigators attempted to 'build up a perceptual consciousness under conditions which should seem to the observer to be those of the formation of an imaginative consciousness' (428). In other words, they attempted to make an object from the perceptual world look like an image of imagination, to the extent that an unknowing observer would confuse the two (428). They did this by presenting perceptual objects – cardboard cut-outs of bananas, for example – to observers at a very low (dim, blurry and flickering) level of illumination and then asking them to imagine those objects (429–30). It was found that these low-level perceptual stimuli were frequently mistaken for images of the observers' imagination – observers could perceive the cardboard cut-out of the banana but thought they were imagining it (433). The results, then, gave cause for questioning the boundaries between percept and image. As Waller et al. put it, 'The fact that highly degraded, nearly subliminal sensory information can be mistaken for a mental image seems to suggest that perception and imagery draw on the same mental systems, processes, or resources' (2012: 292–3). These findings remain influential in contemporary psychology and cognitive science, but it should be stressed that two developments in early-twentieth-century psychology would limit the immediate impact of Perky's study: first the imageless thought controversy and then behaviourism.

Of these two developments, the imageless thought controversy is perhaps less crucial. Debate on the subject predates Perky's experiment, and in and of itself, the notion of imageless thought does not oppose the idea that there is a degree of continuity between the processes of perception and mental imagery. As R. S. Woodworth notes, those advocating imageless thought tended to assert that 'an act might be thought of without any representative or symbolic image' but this assertion does not deny that some – if not most – thoughts are accompanied by images (1915: 1).[2] Woodworth gives an account of how this might work by detailing his own introspective experiment. He attempted to recall a series of events from his past and evaluate what elements of the recall were image-based and which were rooted in other 'imageless' forms of thought (12). His analysis seems to suggest that while his thought does, to some extent, depend on images, there are imageless aspects. In the attempt to recall a colleague's speaking in a faculty meeting, for example, Woodworth notes: 'What I got was a certain quality of voice and precise manner of enunciating, rather different from the conversational tone of this individual. There were no words nor particular vowel nor consonantal sounds present in recall, but simply the quality of the voice and enunciation' (13). Here Woodworth seems to apprehend a shadowy, incomplete form of the colleague's speech, and he recognizes that his thoughts are, in this respect, image-based. This, though, is not the only part of Woodworth's recall: 'I got also the fact that the speaker was speaking as chairman of a committee, and something of the rather critical attitude of the faculty towards him, these facts being recalled in the "imageless" way' (13). Thus, for Woodworth, there is a relational, or a factual, way of recalling past events that does not depend on one's analysing images of this event. This statement is compatible with my own experience. If I try to recall my experience of watching *Not I* at the theatre, for example, I get a vivid visual image of the mouth in darkness, an image of the texture of the voice, as well as the first few words of the play being spoken. But I also recall who I attended the theatre with and their opinion of the play in a factual way without getting an image of those people. There seems to be a mixture of image-based and imageless recollection. This, however, might not satisfy a critic of imageless thought who could say that, when I recall the people sat next to me, I do in fact form images but simply do not have the introspective skill to apprehend them. This is a viewpoint that was espoused by psychologists such as Edward Titchener who argued that all thoughts 'had imaginal cores but some of these cores were so faint as to be imperceptible to all but the most highly skilled introspectors' (qtd. in Hurlburt and Schwitzgebel 2007: 278). As we will see, this debate depends heavily on the degree to which the subject is deemed capable of analysing his or her own experience and so is not easily resolved. However, on either side, there seems to be an acceptance that some thoughts are image-based, and the images in question are shadowy versions of things that have been perceived. In this way, it is accepted that images shape many people's understanding of the world to a certain degree; the debate is merely one of the extent to which this is the case.

The imageless thought controversy did, however, have a more indirect impact on the psychological study of the image. It caused, as Beckett himself noted, a 'parting of the ways in modern psychological theory' (Feldman 2004: 314), and this parting had a severe impact on twentieth-century psychology's approach to mental imagery. The debate around imageless thought went on over a long period, and psychology's failure to attain any kind of consensus on the topic caused many to doubt whether the experimental models at work could produce valid scientific data. The most prominent critic in this regard was John Broadus Watson. Woodworth describes Watson's critique: 'Watson pointed an accusing finger at the "imageless thought" controversy and other recent examples of divergent results obtained in different laboratories by presumably well-trained introspectionists. If even your best observers cannot agree on matters of fact, he said, how can you ever make psychology a science instead of a debating society?' (2013: 74). From Watson's point of view, if one has discovered scientific facts then these facts should be demonstrable in any setting. They should not depend on an individual's being trained in a specific introspective technique. Watson's resolution to this problem was drastic. As Woodworth notes, Watson's behaviourist psychology would take words such as 'imagery' and 'consciousness' out of psychological parlance (74). Thus, rather than merely reducing experimental psychology's dependence on trained individuals, the rise of behaviourism saw the experimental study of imagery completely marginalized. The popularity of behaviourism in the early part of the twentieth century meant that little research was carried out on the subjects of imagery or the imagination until the 1960s. This was not only because behaviourism took terms such as 'imagery' out of mainstream psychological discourse. Watson argued that it was a delusion to think that mental states could be made into the objects of observation, and so marginalized the methods of introspective observation that are crucial to the study of the topic – namely asking subjects for accounts of their imagistic experience (70–1). Waller et al. suggest that these 'methodological prohibitions' were largely 'responsible for the absence of research on imagery throughout the first half of the twentieth century' (2012: 300).

For a variety of reasons, which I will discuss in Chapter 6, the psychological study of mental imagery did become theoretically viable again in the second half of the century. But in these later experiments one can still see the imprint of behaviourism. In this period, there is an increased emphasis on the physiology and performance of the imagining observer. This is exemplified in a 1967 study carried out by Segal and Glicksman, which questions whether 'lowered levels of arousal' would affect the individual's imaginative experience and diminish their ability to discriminate 'between imagery and veridical perception' (1967: 258). The study was a repeat of Perky's experiment on the relationship between the percept and the image, but it also took in the more recent findings of 'sensory isolation experiments' (258). The findings of these experiments, the researchers note, suggested that depriving the human subject of sensory stimulation might result in a 'diminution of logic, attention and inhibitory control and the weakening of these factors leads to poor reality testing, hallucinatory, dream-like and simple optic imagery' (258). The experiment, then, is concerned with how manipulating the subject's sensory environment might affect their capacity to distinguish between perceptual experience and imagery. In the later part of the century, psychologists also made much more attempt to quantify imaginative experience. Stephen Kosslyn, for example, asked subjects to 'construct an image of a cat' upon hearing the word 'cat' 'and then inspect this image for claws, indicating when he "sees" them as quickly as possible' (1975: 344). Here, the experimenter can measure the time it takes subjects to apprehend the claws of the imagined cat in order to give an idea of how a mental image is scanned for information. The image is treated as a constructed entity that, when perused by the observer, yields something like the experience of sensory information. Because the image is being treated like a percept, the observer's process of acquiring information from it can be measured using methods derived from the study of perception.

There are, of course, some objections that might be raised to this understanding of the mental image. In Chapter 6, I will address the concerns that were voiced by several twentieth-century philosophers, such as Jean-Paul Sartre and Gilbert Ryle. For now, though, I want to stress that from the mid-twentieth century onwards experimental psychology has continued to blur the distinction between perception and mental imagery. Practitioners of twentieth-century experimental psychology, then, seem to develop some of the ideas that emerged in the work of Bergson and James. The image, in these examples, is treated as something that is left over from sensory experience but has its own qualities that need to be interpreted, described or analysed. Thus, if the ideas of Bergson and James informed twentieth-century aesthetic approaches to the image, it can be asserted that a comparable process was occurring in twentieth-century experimental psychology.

The Romantic image

So far, then, this chapter has worked to place Beckett in an intellectual tradition that is interested in the materiality of the mental image. Perhaps this seems like an obvious point. After all, at least since Romanticism, the writer or artist has frequently been portrayed as a specialist in the practice of translating mental imagery into tangible material. However, there are obviously important ways in which the Romantic literary tradition differs from the experimental studies of mental imagery that we have so far encountered. We have seen that in twentieth-century experimental psychology the image was often treated as a shadowy version of sensory experience which the subject might apprehend and describe. But, for the Romantics, this procedure is very far from the vocation of the creative artist. Rather than merely apprehending an image in the mind, the Romantic artist is endowed with the capacity to rejuvenate this image by giving it a transcendent meaning. For an illustration of this, we might look to Samuel Taylor Coleridge's notion of the poet in *Biographia Literaria* (1817).[3] 'The poet', Coleridge suggests, uses 'the synthetic and magical power' of the imagination to diffuse 'a tone, and spirit of unity' on his experience ([1817]1927: 166). Through the imagination, the poet is able to balance 'the general with the concrete; the idea with the image; the individual with the representative' (166). The imagination, by this account, is not just the means by which images are produced; it is a faculty that transforms and gives meaning to imagery. It does not just allow one to re-experience a version of a sensory object but makes that object represent something else. The presentation of an image, here, is not an end in and of itself. Instead, the poet's imagination draws out the significance of the image by relating it to the idea.

This contention might be supported by Percy Bysshe Shelley's comparison of the creative mind with a fading coal: 'The mind in creation is as a fading coal which some invisible influence, like an inconstant wind, awakens to transitory brightness' (2009: 696). There is the sense, here, that in the wake of the fire of sensory experience, one can only apprehend a dull, fading version of what has been sensed. To apprehend and describe this, for Shelley, is not to create poetry. Instead 'some invisible influence' must stir the coal and, however fleetingly, alight it. Apprehension of the mental image is not enough; the poet should bring the image to life through artistic expression. From where the capacity to do this comes, however, remains undetermined. Poets, for Shelley, are subject to 'some invisible influence' which enables the transitory illumination of fading images. Many critics have noted the influence that ideas such as Shelley's would exert on later artists and writers. Dirk Van Hulle, for example, has observed that Shelley's formulation would go on to capture the interest of James Joyce and Beckett. Van Hulle points out that Joyce would refer to Shelley in *Portrait of the Artist as a Young Man* when Stephen Dedalus is describing the moment of artistic inspiration: 'The mind in that mysterious instant Shelley likened beautifully to a fading coal. The instant wherein that supreme quality of beauty, the clear radiance of the aesthetic image, is apprehended luminously by the mind which has been arrested by its wholeness and fascinated by its harmony' (Joyce [1916] 2000: 179). In distinguishing Joyce's use of Shelley from Beckett's, Van Hulle makes the important point that where the 'overconfident young Dedalus' stresses the radiance of the coal, Beckett's works seem to have more affinity with the "fading" aspect' (2007: 22). Van Hulle's observation comes in the context of a wider discussion of Beckett's relationship with Romanticism, and he does not analyse the significance of the 'fading coal' image in any detail. Nevertheless, his observation might be adapted to illustrate the relationship between the Romantic approach to the mental image and that of Beckett. It seems that Beckett can be distinguished from the Romantics in terms of the approach taken to the fading image. Where the Romantic tradition is interested in the poet's capacity to illuminate it, Beckett is working to get across the experience of apprehending the image in its fading state.

In view of this, it is tempting to assert that the Beckettian image has more in common with the 'shadowy' mental images of experimental psychology, than with the radiant, aesthetic image that is produced by the Romantic imagination. This, though, would be an oversimplification.[4] There are certainly points of contrast between the aesthetic approach to the image advocated by Coleridge and Shelley and that of Beckett, but there are crucial similarities. The key contrast between Beckett's image and that of the Romantics seems to lie in the degree of meaning that is attached to the aesthetic image. Neither Coleridge nor Shelley seems to deny that images exist in the mind as fading versions of sensory experience. In this sense, the Romantic conception of the mental image does not differ drastically from that of twentieth-century experimental psychology. What distinguishes the Romantics, though, is the belief in a creative imagination which elevates the material image and transforms it into the aesthetic image.

The imagination, here, seems to uproot the image from the psychophysiological world and introduce it to the lofty world of ideas. The image, as a result of this process, is no longer a mere shadowy form; it is endowed with meaning – made to stand for something beyond itself. This aesthetic approach seems at odds with the accounts of the Beckettian image given by Uhlmann and Deleuze in which it was suggested that the 'true' Beckettian image is not balanced with ideas but detached from them. Perhaps this distinction can best be drawn by reference to two of the examples I have mentioned above. In the case of Shelley's image of the 'fading coal', the image is clearly a representation of something, namely the 'mind in creation'. The image is standing for something beyond itself. This representative image contrasts with Beckett's portrayal of the mouth in *Not I* which left Michael Billington with an 'ineradicable image: an endlessly mobile mouth, rimmed by white clown-like makeup pouring out words of agony'. Here the mouth is not drawn into a stable relation with anything else but stands on its own for the observer to interpret. Where the Romantics are interested in the poetic imagination's balancing of image and idea, Beckett's image has a being in its own right.

This point of departure, however, does not mean that Beckett's approach to the image is completely estranged from Romanticism. Points of contact remain. Like the Romantics, for example, Beckett is concerned with the potency of the image. The significance of Beckett's images may not come ready-interpreted like Shelley's fading coal, but Beckett's works do seem to make the claim that the images presented have a significance. As Uhlmann puts it, Beckettian presentations of images 'still involve resonance (the sense that a meaningful link exists), even as they refuse relations' (2006: 108). To illustrate this, we might contrast Beckett's approach to the image with those of the experimental psychologists discussed above. When Perky asks subjects to envision a banana or Kosslyn requests that they scan their image of a cat for claws, there is no suggestion that the content of these images has any significance. The images that are being produced are only a means by which to study the process of generating images. Beckett's images seem to have more to them than this. Beckett, I would argue, is frequently concerned with the significance that particular images hold for particular subjects. This concern is particularly apparent in Beckett's earliest writing. In the critical work *Proust* (1931), for example, Beckett discusses Proust's portrayal of voluntary and involuntary memory, suggesting that, while the former reproduces 'impressions of the past that were consciously and intelligently formed', the latter restores 'not merely the past object but the Lazarus that it charmed or tortured' (1999: 33). Put another way, while voluntary memory allows us to re-experience shadowy versions of sensed objects, involuntary memory reconnects us with the past self that originally experienced these sensations. The impressions which are brought about by voluntary memory seem to resemble the images of bananas and cats that are produced in the experiments of Perky and Kosslyn. They do not restore past objects themselves (only shadowy versions of them) and neither do they hold any significance for the subject producing them. Beckett says of voluntary memory: 'The images it chooses are as arbitrary as those chosen by imagination, and are equally remote from reality' (32). Beckett, here, is not denying that we can, through imagination and memory, summon up shadowy versions of sensory experience. He is, however, suggesting that the role of the artist goes beyond this voluntary process. He is interested in the moment of inspiration in which Proust's narrator is confronted with his past through involuntary memory, 'an unruly magician' that 'chooses its own time and place for the performance of its miracle' (33–4). This, for Beckett, is observable when 'the long-forgotten taste of a madeleine steeped in an infusion of tea' stimulates the narrator's involuntary memory and brings his childhood back to him (34). It is this process, Beckett suggests, which enabled Proust to produce something of artistic value: 'his [Proust's] entire book is a monument to involuntary memory' (34). Beckett is stressing that Proust's artistic creation is more than the voluntary apprehension and description of imagery. The images communicated by Proust's narrator, it seems, are artistically valuable because there is a mysterious process of inspiration behind them and they can be seen to hold a personal significance.

It is possible to overstate the importance of Beckett's early discussion of voluntary and involuntary memory. After all, it comes in a reading of Proust, and as many critics have noted, Beckett's later work would go on to complicate the Proustian models of memory that Beckett outlines in his early critical work.[5] Nevertheless, the idea that artistic creation might be brought about by 'an unruly magician' that 'chooses its own time and place for the performance of its miracle' seems to have much in common with the ideas of Romanticism. It resonates, for instance, with Shelley's idea that 'some invisible influence' might awaken the fading coal of the mind and endow it with a 'transitory brightness'. In both cases, there is a concern with an involuntary moment of artistic inspiration which reinvigorates past experience. One might suggest that this point of contact between Beckett and Romanticism would serve to distance Beckett's work from the materialist understandings of mental imagery that were emerging in twentieth-century experimental psychology. Again, though, this would be an oversimplification. Of course, the statements that art is inspired by 'an unruly magician [Beckett's term]', 'some invisible influence [Shelley's]' or 'a synthetic and magical power [Coleridge]' hint at a metaphysical understanding of artistic creation which might seem difficult to reconcile with scientific psychology. But I would suggest that the attitudes of these authors towards artistic inspiration was not so far removed from materialistic understandings of the mind as one might initially think. In the cases of Shelley and Coleridge, Alan Richardson (2001) has shown that the separation between British Romanticism and scientific conceptions of the mind was never total. Rather the attitudes of the poets often developed in dialogue with contemporaneous science, producing significant – though often fractious – points of relation.[6] The complexity of this relationship can be seen in the attitudes of Shelley and Coleridge to artistic inspiration. In Shelley's image, for example, the force that stirs the fading coal of the mind does not remain completely ineffable but is likened to 'an inconstant wind'. Though the influence is invisible, Shelley does locate it in the physical world. He gestures towards the immaterial without ever leaving the material. Perhaps more striking, though, is the case of Coleridge and particularly his preface to 'Kubla Khan' (1816). Here we get an account of a moment of creative inspiration but one that is described in peculiarly physiological terms. As Richardson puts it, 'What Coleridge describes in the introductory notice to "Kubla Khan" might be seen as the most spectacular psychophysiological experiment of his career' (2001: 47). The preface describes Coleridge falling asleep while reading, having taken a painkiller (thought to be opium) for a 'slight indisposition' (Hill 1978: 147). This 'profound sleep', the passage goes on, lasted for about three hours: 'During which time he [Coleridge] has the most vivid confidence that he could not have composed less than from two to three hundred lines … in which all the images rose up before him as *things* with a parallel production of the correspondent expressions, without any sensation or consciousness of effort' (147–8, emphasis in original). As Richardson observes, this account questions 'the relationship between mental events and the organic body' (2001: 48). It suggests that imaginative composition might be stimulated by physical events (in this case, a chemically induced sleep). Thus, rather than 'a synthetic and magical power' (as in Biographia Literaria), poetic composition, here, is seen to be inspired by a set of psychophysiological circumstances.

Beckett, I would suggest, inherited from Romanticism a tendency to alternate between understandings of artistic inspiration as a magical and mysterious phenomenon on the one hand and a psychophysiological reaction on the other. To return to *Proust*, this can be seen in the way in which he describes the madeleine steeped in tea. For Beckett, as we have seen, Proust's narrator's story was inspired by involuntary memory but, Beckett continues, involuntary memory was itself 'stimulated or charmed by' the forgotten taste of the madeleine (1999: 34). In his description of the madeleine, Beckett seems to move between the language of science and that of magic. The madeleine becomes both a psychophysiological stimulus and a mysterious charm. This oscillation between the material and the ethereal, the physical and the metaphysical, I contend, would continue into Beckett's later writing, particularly when he came to tackle questions of the mental image. Beckett frequently makes clear that his images are material entities rooted in psychophysiological circumstances but, at the same time, the images he presents seem to carry with them a mysterious significance. Though Beckett's images seldom hold a self-explanatory meaning, they are rarely portrayed as arbitrary or neutral. Rather, particularly in the later work, they hold a transfixing power over the protagonists that apprehend them. In the light of this, we might situate the Beckettian image somewhere between Romanticism and experimental psychology. This is a view that has been touched upon in recent critical discourse. Steven Connor, for example, has argued that in Beckett's work, the imagination is a faculty that 'alternates between the visionary inheritance of Romanticism and a much more limited, often almost mechanical faculty conceived as the power of forming images' (2014: 7). 'For Beckett', Connor continues, 'imagination is not a spontaneously indwelling and upwelling power, but a strenuous and exhausting labour that comes close to the ideas of staging, seeing through or putting into practice' (7). The suggestion that Beckett's work conceives of the imagination 'as the power of forming images' seems to identify Beckett with the study of imagery that I have described in experimental psychology. There is the suggestion, here, that the Beckettian subject might 'stage' an image in the same way as Kosslyn's subjects stage images of cats. But, as Connor seems to recognize, this is not quite the case. The Beckettian imagination is, for Connor, at least intermittently influenced by Romanticism. This, though, is where Connor's argument provokes a question. If, as Connor notes, the Beckettian imagination does not have the 'spontaneously indwelling and upwelling power' of the Romantic imagination, where can the influence be seen? I argue that it is observable in the emphasis Beckett places on the circumstances that inspire mental imagery and the mysterious significance of this imagery to the subjects that apprehend it.

The (im)material image in *Nacht und Träume*

Beckett's approach to the mental image shows up clearly in the late teleplay *Nacht und Träume*. As Uhlmann observes, the play describes a process of 'image production' (2006: 2). It presents a Dreamer (A) producing an image of his dreamt self (B) as he sits at a table with his head resting on his hands (Beckett [1986] 2006: 465). The image, in turn, seems to produce images of two hands – L and R – that offer him comfort: mopping his brow, offering a cup to his lips and caressing him (465–6). Thus, we are presented with the peculiar televisual image of a man producing a mental image of a man producing mental images. In this set-up, Beckett enables the viewer to tell the mental images apart from the man that is apprehending them, partly through positioning (the images hover above and to the right of A), and more importantly through the kindness of the light in which each is presented. The dreamer is presented, first, in a faint 'evening light' that comes from behind him, and then (as the images appear) in a 'minimal' light (465). The images he produces, on the other hand, appear in a 'kinder', almost hazy light (465). The difference between the lights in which man and image are presented, then, is not one of intensity but tone. Both are presented faintly but where A's light is 'minimal', that of the images is 'kind'. Crucial, here, is the point that both dreamer and image are made of the same material (they are both – faintly – perceived as images on a TV screen) but each is presented in a different way. A is seated at floor level in a harsh gloom while A, L and R hover above him in soft focus.

This mise-en-scène neatly encapsulates the nuances of Beckett's approach to the image. On the one hand, the portrayal of the image in *Nacht und Träume* resonates with the scientific understandings of imagery that developed in the twentieth century. The play invites us to compare the experience of perception with that of imagery by presenting a percept (A) and an image (B) side by side. Both figures are, of course, perceived as part of a televisual image, but in the fiction of the play, A is supposed to exist in the physical world and B is supposed to exist as mental imagery. However, though Beckett marks this distinction by illuminating image and creator in different types of light, both are presented at a level that makes one strain to apprehend them. It is as difficult to make out the figure that is (within the fiction) located in the physical world as it is to apprehend the image that is generated by this figure. Neither the image nor the percept can be fully made out without a straining of the eyes, and it is difficult to be sure that one is apprehending either fully. Indeed, when I look closely at the figure of A, it becomes difficult to adjudge what is perceptible and what I am filling in with imagery. When I look at A's hand, for example, I see fingers, but it is difficult to tell whether those fingers are actually visible or whether I am producing images of fingers – and thus giving artificial definition to a white blur. In this way, Beckett follows psychologists such as Perky in scrutinizing the boundaries between the faintly lit percept and the mental image. Both Beckett and Perky are interested in vaguening the material that they present to the extent that the image starts to blur with the percept.

There also seems to be a link between A's sensory environment and the emergence of the image, and this resonates with scientific approaches to mental imagery. A's production of B, it seems, requires minimal lighting and the resting of the head on the hands. This is hardly surprising – in a sense there is nothing unusual about a man starting to dream when he takes a position of rest – but there is something very schematic, almost mechanical, about Beckett's presentation of this moment. The image appears as soon as A's head sinks into his hands. And, when the image vanishes and the evening light reappears, the head rises immediately. Not only this, but the process is repeated. When the light disappears again, A's head sinks back into the hands, prompting the image to return 'as before' (466). James Knowlson notes that this repetition seems 'almost ritualistic' (1996: 683), but there is also an element of the stimulus-response experiment at work here. As we have seen, Beckett came across the behaviourist idea of stimulus-response in his reading of Woodworth, and the influence of these ideas on Beckett's work has been observed throughout this study. It is also my contention that the influence of behaviourism is observable in Beckett's approach to the mental image. This becomes particularly apparent when one places *Nacht und Träume* alongside the late prose. As we will see in Chapter 6, the images that are produced in *Worstward Ho* appear in the stare of a 'head sunk on crippled hands' and, in *Stirrings Still* (1989), the protagonist sees 'himself rise and go' one night as he sits 'at his table head on hands' (Beckett 2009a: 84; 107). In Beckett's work from this period, there certainly seems to be a correlation between this specific position (in the darkness with head on hands) and the production of images. Here we might compare Beckett's work with the experiments carried out by researchers such as Segal and Glicksman, which tested whether manipulating an observer's sensory environment might make them less able to distinguish perception from imagery. Beckett, like the experimenters, is interested in the hallucinatory, dreamlike and simple optic imagery that ensues when subjects are placed in particular positions. The images that are produced by Beckett's protagonists may have, what James Knowlson calls, 'a mysterious quality' (1996: 683), but they are usually seen to be stimulated by, or grounded in, the sensory environment.

There are, then, ways in which we might relate Beckett's late portrayals of image production to the experimental study of mental imagery that developed in the twentieth century. However, to read works such as *Nacht und Träume* purely as investigations into the psychophysiological process of image production would be slightly reductive. Surely more is going on here. Of course, if one is looking for significance in the images that appear, it is easy to find. B is, after all, explicitly described as a version of A, so it would be difficult to argue that the content of the image has no significance for the figure that apprehends it. A reading which takes the action of the play at face value, then, might conclude that the ritualistic caresses that L and R perform on B fulfil the wishes of the lonely A, who sits at a table in darkness. In this way the images might be seen, in the words of Ulrika Maude, to present A with 'a release from physical discomfort and suffering' (2009: 130). However, as commentators such as James Knowlson have pointed out, if this personal story was the focal point of the play, the work might seem a little thin and sentimental. In the light of this, many scholars have argued that the play's power is rooted in its formal experimentation. Here, we come back to the argument that Beckett was more interested in the psychophysiological process of image production than the content of the images. Enoch Brater, for instance, argues that the 'visualization' of the images 'not their meaning, were the dramatist's true subject' (1985: 51). In a similar fashion, Ulrika Maude reads the play as a drama of 'virtuality', focusing on the process by which the work 'reproduces or doubles the dreamer's body' (2009: 128–9). Thus, there has been a tendency for critics to see the play as a study of process rather than content.

I would suggest, though, that the content of the play is far from arbitrary. The images produced in the action certainly seem to have held personal significance for Beckett himself. For example, as James Knowlson notes, the presentation of the dreamt hands was deliberated on extensively:

> Hands had always fascinated Beckett in painting. As a young man he had a reproduction of Dürer's wonderful etching of praying hands hanging on the wall of his room at Cooldrinagh. Beckett insisted to Dr Müller-Freienfels that 'the sex of the hands must remain uncertain. One of our numerous teasers'. To me, he said that these 'sexless hands' 'might perhaps be a boy's hands'. But in the end he concluded: 'I think no choice but female for the helping hands. Large but female. As more conceivably male than male conceivably female.' (Knowlson 1996: 682–3)[7]

Knowlson's account does not suggest that Beckett was purely interested in processes of visualization in *Nacht und Träume*. Rather, the content of the images that are produced in the action of the play seems to have been a major concern. It is important to point out, though, that Beckett wanted to endow this content with an ill-defined significance. Here we might, once more, use Uhlmann's terms and suggest that the dreamt hands in *Nacht und Träume* are presentations rather than representations (2008: 53). They do not come to us ready-interpreted as the hands of a particular person or even a particular gender, but instead are 'teasers': concrete entities with specific qualities that demand interpretation. The sense that they are not neatly representative, then, should not lead to the conclusion that they are arbitrary. Rather, Beckett presents concrete images that seem to hold a significance without defining what this significance is.

When interpreting the play's imagery, it is also important to remember that B, L and R appear to a dreaming protagonist. This, I would suggest, furthers their ill-defined significance. One might respond to this with the assertion that dream imagery is not necessarily significant – that dreams are often very mundane. Beckett, though, is concerned with a particular type of dream. The sense in which the term 'dream' is used in the play has been considered by numerous critics, and it is frequently argued that the dream in question is not of the kind that one might passively experience during a good night's sleep. Instead, a more active, compositional process is often mooted. In his reading of the play, Deleuze questions whether 'we are supposed to think that he [A] is asleep' and answers in the negative (1995: 20). Instead, Deleuze argues that the dream in *Nacht und Träume* is that of 'the exhausted, of the insomniac, of the aboulic' (21). This dream 'is not like the sleeping dream that fashions itself all alone in the depths of desire and the body, it is a dream of the mind that has to be made, manufactured' (21). A similar sentiment is voiced by Franz Michael Maier and Angela Moorjani, who focus on Beckett's use of Franz Schubert's 1825 Lied (also called *Nacht und Träume*). In the works of both Beckett and Schubert, for Maier and Moorjani, the dream 'describes a state of vision and activity, not a state of passivity and rest' (2007: 96). The authors also locate this attitude to the dream in the work of Arthur Schopenhauer, who 'distinguished dreams that are engendered by the physiology of the dreamer and do not enlarge his knowledge of the outer world (*Hallucinationen*) from dreams that are perceptions of a special kind (*Wahrtradume*). The latter provide additional objective knowledge to the dreaming subject' (95). For Maier and Moorjani, Beckett is working with Schopenhauer's conception of the dream. They assert that the dream portrayed in *Nacht und Träume* should be placed in the latter category as a special kind of perception. These arguments might be supported with reference to the passage in *Murphy* in which the protagonist's body is described to be in a 'less precarious abeyance than that of sleep, for its own convenience and so that the mind might move' (Beckett 2009c: 71). Beckett, then, showed an interest in a type of bodily inactivity which is more stable than that of sleep and which enables the subject to experience, and partake in, the movements of their own mind.

Conclusion

If *Nacht und Träume*'s mental images are consciously experienced, or even manufactured, by the subject, how do they differ from the arbitrary images of bananas and cats that subjects were asked to produce in the experiments of Perky and Kosslyn? The answer to this question, I would argue, lies in the degree to which we can access the intentions of the subjects. We know why the subjects of Perky and Kosslyn produce those mental images; it is because an experimenter has told them to do so. In Beckett's play, by contrast, A exists in the isolation of his dream. We have no way of knowing the reasons behind the production of B, L and R, and so the images acquire a mysterious significance. There is a sense that A is composing mental imagery, but we are left with the ineradicable question of why he is composing this imagery. In the light of this, as well as emerging scientific understandings of imagery, I would relate Beckett's portrayal of image production in *Nacht und Träume* to a Romantic tradition that is perhaps best exemplified by Coleridge's introduction to 'Kubla Khan'. Both Beckett and Coleridge are concerned with a moment of semi-conscious[8] inspiration in which images emerge before the protagonist in a manner that seems to hold a revelatory significance. In neither case, though, is it clear why these particular images are experienced as significant. Of course, there remain crucial differences between the two examples. In the preface to 'Kubla Khan', for example, the images are linked to 'correspondent expressions', and both the images and the expressions are linked to the book that Coleridge has been reading (Hill 1978: 147–8). The images encountered by Beckett's dreamer, on the other hand, are not contextualized in such a manner and so their significance is much more ambiguous. Nevertheless, Beckett seems to retain an interest in how the subject experiences imagery as significant and, for this reason, the Beckettian image can be placed in between the materialist study of image production and, what Connor calls, 'the visionary inheritance of Romanticism'. Here we might note a degree of continuity in Beckett's literary experimentation. As was the case with the experiments on learning and attention discussed in earlier chapters, Beckett's experiments on mental images reveal a concern with the way in which materialist, psychophysiological accounts of subjective experience might be integrated with more expansive, humanist perspectives.

6

Percept and image in *Nohow On*

In Chapter 5 we saw that the blurring of boundaries between perception and mental imagery has been a major concern in the history of experimental psychology. It is important to remember, though, that Western civilization had been drawing analogies between that which is sensed in the external world and that which is apprehended in the mind long before the advent of the psychological laboratory. This is evident in the common expression in which one claims to have seen or heard something in the 'mind's eye'. In English, the visual version of this expression goes back as far as Chaucer and, looking back even further, one can see the analogy at work in the post-classical Latin phrase *oculus mentis* which is found in British sources from the eighth century (Oxford English Dictionary 2019). Earlier writers can also be seen playing with this analogy, drawing attention to moments in which the distinction between the percept and the image becomes difficult to draw. Perhaps the most famous example of this can be found in the second scene of Shakespeare's *Hamlet* when Hamlet and Horatio describe their sightings of Hamlet's recently deceased father:

> Hamlet: My father! – methinks I see my father.
>
> Horatio: Where, my lord?
>
> Hamlet: In my mind's eye, Horatio.
>
> Horatio: I saw him once; he was a goodly king.
>
> Hamlet: He was a man, take him for all in all,
>
>   I shall not look upon his like again.
>
> Horatio: My lord, I think I saw him yesternight.
>
> Hamlet: Saw? who?
>
> Horatio: My lord, the king your father.
>
> Hamlet: The king my father! (Shakespeare [1599–1602] 2016: 33)

One of the many striking things about this passage is the sheer variety of ways in which Hamlet's father is said to be seen or looked upon. Not only are there descriptions of both imagistic and perceptual sightings in the past and present (Hamlet's seeing the king in his 'mind's eye' and Horatio's seeing him 'once' as 'a goodly king'), but there are also variations in the certainty with which the sightings are described. Horatio can say with certainty that he saw the king 'once' but only thinks that he 'saw him yesternight'. Similarly, Hamlet seems to move from certainty to doubt in a single line as he looks upon the image of his father: 'My father! – methinks I see my father.' More salient, of course, is the point that, while both Horatio and Hamlet claim to have seen the king after his death, only Hamlet can locate the sighting in the mind's eye. Horatio thinks he has seen Hamlet's father (who he knows to be dead) out in the physical world. Horatio, though, does not quite believe his own eyes. Thus, when describing the movements of the king, he uses the pronoun 'it' rather than 'he', suggesting that he was not looking at the king himself but some shadowy version:

> Horatio: It lifted up its head and did address
>
> Itself to motion, like as it would speak;
>
> But even then the morning cock crew loud,
>
> And at the sound it shrunk in haste away
>
> And vanish'd from our sight. (33)

The overall effect of this exchange is one of flux and uncertainty. The king is continually being seen but there is fluctuation, both with regard to what he is seen as – now an image, now a percept, now a supernatural being – and with regard to the certainty with which this classification is made. Shakespeare is allowing apprehensions of the king to flicker between the material and the immaterial and, in doing so, is interrogating the distinction between perceptual, imagistic and supernatural experience.

There is a danger of overemphasizing Shakespeare's interest in the classification of experience. It seems likely that Shakespeare's interest in the possibility of confusing percept and image lay in its dramatic potential, as well as the phenomenon's relevance to contemporaneous debates around the supernatural.[1] The uncertainty surrounding Horatio and Hamlet's sightings of the ghost, I would argue, is an example of Shakespeare's penchant for what Stephen Greenblatt has called 'strategic opacity' (2004: 324). For Greenblatt, by creating a sense of uncertainty around the action of his later plays, Shakespeare found that he could release 'an enormous energy' in his audience 'that had been at least partially blocked or contained by familiar, reassuring explanations' (323–4). Shakespeare, then, might be seen to use the occasional continuities between perceptual and imagistic experience for his own aesthetic purposes. As an artist, Shakespeare is not alone in this respect. In a mid-twentieth-century survey of approaches to mental imagery, psychologist Alan Richardson observes that artists have 'usually been particularly sensitive to the fragile and fluctuating boundary between fantasy and reality' (1969: 1). 'The rest of us' Richardson continues, 'have muddled through and felt that our personal survival was proof enough that we could make the distinction when it really counted' (1). There is the sense, here, that humanity's occasional difficulty in telling the image apart from the percept has historically been viewed as a slightly lofty topic, suitable for the stage, page or ivory tower but of little practical interest to the majority.

However, as the tense of Richardson's statement seems to imply, this begins to change in the nineteenth century, and the change becomes particularly noticeable in the mid-twentieth century. In this period, the human subject's capacity to tell fantasy from reality, percept from image, becomes a much more pressing concern. This is particularly evident in medical discourse. In 1817, for example, the psychiatrist Jean-Étienne Dominique Esquirol introduced the term 'hallucination' – the 'intimate conviction of actually perceiving a sensation [voice, image, or otherwise] for which there is no external object' (qtd. in McCarthy-Jones 2012: 61). Looking forward to 1911, Eugen Bleuler placed hallucinations in the symptom cluster we still call 'schizophrenia' (Heinrichs 2001: 53). Figures such as Esquirol and Bleuler placed emphasis on the physiological basis of schizophrenia and voice-hearing, but there was also an interest in the role of personal circumstance. Here, the influence of psychoanalysis undoubtedly changed attitudes. Bleuler was an admirer of Freud and, partly through this influence, came to foreground the psychological underpinnings of hallucinations. Bleuler argued, for example, that the voices heard by schizophrenics commonly express the 'thoughts, fears and drives' of the individual hearing them and the symptom is likely 'precipitated by psychic occurrences' ([1911] 1950: 388–9). Furthermore, Bleuler suggested that a voice might come to one by way of personal crisis: the symptoms of schizophrenia, he argued, were likely 'the expression of a more or less unsuccessful attempt to find a way out of an intolerable situation' (460). The failure to distinguish percept and image was viewed as a pathological symptom, and numerous psychiatrists and psychotherapists strove to find the underlying causes.

Beyond models of pathology, certain social developments drew attention to the fluctuating boundaries between image and percept. For a reflection on this idea, we might turn to a 1964 article by the American psychologist Robert R. Holt, which questioned why the mid-twentieth century had seen a revival of interest in mental imagery within psychology. For Holt, despite the doctrines of behaviourism (which, as discussed in previous chapters, made the topic of mental imagery something of a taboo), twentieth-century psychologists had been forced to return to the topic of mental imagery for a variety of theoretical and socio-economic reasons. For example, Holt suggests that the mistaking of image for reality had long been treated as an 'exclusively pathological manifestation' (1964: 263). But, as he writes, 'it is being rediscovered that normal, prosaic folk, and not just psychotics, can hallucinate, given the right circumstances' (263). This, he argues, can partly be attributed to the commencement of new kinds of occupation:

> Radar operators who have to monitor a scope for long periods; long-distance truck drivers in night runs over turnpikes, but also other victims of 'highway hypnosis'; jet pilots flying straight and level at high altitudes; operators of snowcats and other such vehicles of polar exploration, when surrounded by snowstorms – all of these persons have been troubled by the emergence into consciousness of vivid imagery, largely visual but often kinesthetic or auditory, which they may take momentarily for reality. (1964: 257)

Developments in society, for Holt, have created scenarios in which an increasing number of people are asked to operate technology for long periods of time. These scenarios require subjects to perceive or respond to minimal sensory material, and this lack of sensory input causes them to produce imagery in a way that has the potential to cause 'serious accidents' (257). Thus, one of the reasons that psychology is required to investigate mental imagery lies in an economic need for humans to be able to perform these duties without losing their grip on reality.

Additionally, Holt points to the political atrocities of the twentieth century and the emergence of 'a series of first-hand accounts of persons who have been imprisoned in concentration camps and interrogated by the secret police of totalitarian regimes': 'A recurrent theme in such stories is what one former captive called "the famous 'cinema' of prisoners": pseudohallucinatory imagery brought on by prolonged isolation, sleep deprivation, and the multiple regressive pressures of forcible indoctrination or thought reform' (257). At issue, here, is a combination of the material and the personal. On the one hand, there is the sense that specific physiological situations produce moments in which one fails to distinguish between image and percept. Here we might point to the reduced levels of sensory stimulation experienced by the long-distance truck driver or the prisoner. On the other, looking again to the prisoner but also to Bleuler's idea that the hallucination might derive from an 'intolerable situation', there is the sense that personal duress is a major trigger. Thus, it is Holt's argument that the twentieth century is producing more of these situations – more experiences in which the boundaries between perception and imagery seem to blur – and so there is a greater number of 'customers looking for psychological help' on these topics (263).

This seems to me a reasonable hypothesis, but there are a couple of aspects of Holt's argument that need to be made clear. First, it is important to mark the distinction between the experiences themselves and their penetration into public discourse. Imprisonment and solitary confinement are by no means exclusive to the twentieth century. Criminologist Peter Scharff Smith suggests that use of solitary confinement may be traced back to the middle ages and the inquisitional mode of imprisonment known as *murus strictus* (2006: 441).[2] And modern use dates back to the popularization of the Pennsylvania model of incarceration in the late eighteenth and early nineteenth century. In this case, isolation was supposed to prompt inmates to 'turn their thoughts inward, to meet God, to repent of their crimes, and eventually to return to society as morally cleansed Christian citizens' (Smith 2008: 1049).[3] Earlier centuries, then, produced environments in which one might expect the 'cinema of prisoners' to emerge. Indeed, Smith notes that numerous nineteenth-century scientific studies investigated the effects of the Pennsylvania model on prisoners, and hallucinations were commonly reported (2006: 466). However, within the discourses of earlier periods there was less focus on the idea that the material circumstances of isolation could cause hallucinations. In the religious environment of the middle ages metaphysical explanations were (unsurprisingly) common, and in the nineteenth century the effects of isolation were frequently explained through racial theory or ideas of degeneration (Kroll and Bachrach 1982; Smith 2006, 2008). Crucial, then, was the decline of metaphysical and degenerative theories and an increased acceptance that a set of psychophysiological circumstances could affect the blurring of percept and image, fantasy and reality.

Equally, I would suggest that the advance of technological stimulation from the late nineteenth century onwards made the concept of under-stimulation a much more pressing concern. It is unlikely that more people were being exposed to darkness and silence in a modern world of increased mechanical noise and artificial light. Rather, I would suggest that the advance of modernity made the effects of the phenomena seem novel and worth researching. Finally, it should be noted that among Holt's 'customers' looking for 'psychological help' with regard to the effects of solitary confinement and sensory deprivation were a number of Western governments. In the Cold War and post-911 eras, for instance, a military demand for 'potentially effective interrogation techniques' prompted a large amount of research on techniques such as hypnosis, isolation and extreme sensory deprivation (Soldz 2008: 593–5). Indeed, much of the research carried out on sensory deprivation was funded, indirectly, by the United States' Central Intelligence Agency (CIA) (Raz 2013: 382–3). Thus, new understandings of the relationship between imagery and perception are likely to have been shaped, in part, by post-Second World War military policy. Overall, though, Holt's point stands. The social developments of the twentieth century did intensify Western civilization's long-standing interest in the 'difference between the nature of images and imaging on the one hand, and the nature of percepts and perceiving on the other' (Richardson 1969: 2).

This chapter will argue that the work of Samuel Beckett (and particularly his later prose) should be seen in this context. In one sense, it will view Beckett as an artist in the tradition of Shakespeare, interested in the aesthetic effects that can be derived from drawing attention to (in Richardson's words) the 'fragile and fluctuating boundary between fantasy and reality'. Anthony Uhlmann has picked up on this. Drawing on Greenblatt's reading of Shakespeare, he suggests that Beckett is part of a long artistic tradition that presents objects which resist classification. This tradition, for Uhlmann, is concerned with the powerful affects that can be derived when one occludes key details about an object, 'rather than attempting to represent the essential components' (2008: 105). Thus, Beckett's interest in the continuities between perception and mental imagery can, in one way, be seen as part of an aesthetic strategy. Particularly in the later works, Beckett frequently refuses to define figures and objects as either perceptual or imagistic. Instead he seems interested in the powerful affects that are located in between the two categories.

However, the chapter will also view Beckett as a citizen of the twentieth century, suggesting that he was very much embedded in the period's changing attitude towards mental imagery. Evidence for this can be found in the books that Beckett read and the books that he wrote. With regard to his reading, Beckett showed an interest in twentieth-century theoretical debates around the distinction between the percept and the image. Dirk Van Hulle and Mark Nixon note that Beckett possessed a copy of Jean-Paul Sartre's *L'Imagination* in which Sartre addresses psychology's tendency to undermine the distinction between image and percept ([1936] 2013: 167). Sartre himself was very sceptical of this psychological practice and argued for the integrity of the boundary between image and percept. But whatever Sartre's position, *L'Imagination* offers a summary of how the relationship between image and percept had been theorized in Western philosophy and psychology up until the 1930s (covering a wide range of writers from Descartes to Edward Titchener). The work, then, would have given Beckett an early grounding in the theoretical approaches that had been taken to the image.

In terms of his own writing, Beckett's literary work betrays an interest in the pseudohallucinatory imagery that is frequently brought on by prolonged isolation or inactivity. In the novella 'The End', for example, Beckett produces what Ulrika Maude calls an 'experiment into detached and autonomous forms of subjectivity through a form of sensory deprivation' (2009: 39). The narrator lies flat on his back in a disused boat covered by a lid, seeing 'nothing except, dimly, just above my head, through the tiny chinks, the grey light of the shed' (Beckett 2000: 28). This state seems to bring on a peculiar experience of imagery: 'The next thing I was having visions, I who never did, except sometimes in my sleep, who never had real visions, I'd remember except perhaps as a child, my myth will have it so. I knew they were visions because it was night and I was alone in my boat. What else could they have been (30)?' The narrator retains the capacity to distinguish between 'real visions' and reality, reasoning that he knew the things he was experiencing 'were visions' because he still felt his self to be 'alone in my boat'. Nevertheless, in the final question ('what else could they have been?'), there is the sense of a cognitive debate over how the experience should be classified. The narrator also questions why, at this point in time, he was having 'real visions' when he does not remember having done so before. Beckett seems to hint that a recent occurrence in the narrator's life has caused him to have 'real visions', but this hint is invalidated as soon as uttered. The novelty of the visions is brought into question even as the narrator suggests that the visions are novel: 'I was having visions, I who never did, except sometimes in my sleep, who never had real visions.' It is, of course, tempting to read this passage biographically and suggest that, like his narrator, Beckett was wrestling with the question of how to categorize and evaluate personal experiences of 'real visions'. However, rather than arguing for an identification between Beckett's experience and that of his narrator, I want to point out that two concerns begin to emerge in Beckett's post-war writing. First, there is a growing interest in moments in which the boundaries between perception and imagery seem to blur and, second, there is an engagement with the question of how to categorize or denominate these experiences.

From all this, it seems reasonable to conclude that, by the late twentieth century, Beckett had a well-established interest in the ways in which the boundaries between perception and imagery might be blurred. His early reading shows an interest how the relationship between image and percept had been theorized and this interest can be seen to carry into his aesthetic experiments. It is my contention that, in his late prose, Beckett would develop these interests further, conducting a sustained investigation into the nature of mental imagery while using the questionable status of the mental image to produce powerful moments of opacity in his creative writing. In this regard, there are definite points of contact between Beckett's work and the psychological discipline – even though Beckett is working to slightly different ends. To demonstrate these points of comparison and contrast, we might read the opening of Holt's article on mental imagery alongside the opening of Beckett's late prose work, *Company* (1979). Holt:

> Consider the situation of a man whom I shall call 'S'. He is lying on a bed alone, in almost complete darkness and silence. There is nothing to see, hear, taste, smell, or do. But as he lies with eyes closed, he sees a good deal more than darkness. He begins to notice vague luminous patterns appearing before him, in intricate geometrical design, fading, brightening, coming, and going. Suddenly, a face emerges from this background with startling clarity, only to be replaced an instant later by an animal's head. Dreamily, S watches the succession of pictures that emerge before him, growing gradually more vivid, complex, and thematic. Soon he has lost touch with external reality, being instead completely involved with these illusory phantoms of the dark. (1964: 254)

Beckett:

> A voice comes to one in the dark. Imagine.
> To one on his back in the dark. This he can tell by the pressure on his hind parts and by how the dark changes when he shuts his eyes and again when he opens them again. Only a small part of what is said can be verified. As, for example, when he hears, You are on your back in the dark. Then he must acknowledge the truth of what is said. But by far the greater part of what is said cannot be verified. (2009a: 3)

In both passages, a narrator gives us the imperative to construct a scene in which a man lies in the dark, seeing and hearing things that might be perceptual or imagistic. Each passage works as a kind of prose experiment investigating the reader's capacity to imagine an experience in which the boundaries between perceptual and imagistic material is troubled. This, though, is where points of contrast start to emerge. Holt's narrator tells us that the apprehended material is definitely imagistic – that the man 'has lost touch with external reality, being instead completely involved with these illusory phantoms of the dark'. We are given an objective picture of what has occurred and asked to make a judgement on it: 'You are a psychologist; here are your data; what do you make of this kind of report?' (Holt 1964: 254). Beckett, by contrast, never gives us this full a picture. Instead we are left with an account of the protagonist's perspective. Not only this, but the protagonist is concerned not with the question of whether the voice is a percept or an image, but whether the statements it makes are factual. We are told to imagine the voice, but the voice is never classified as an image or a percept. Thus, where the psychologist gives out the data, Beckett leaves us to imagine the experience in its full opacity. In Beckett, the reader does not simply have to place their self in the position of psychologist; they also have to imagine the experimental subject's perspective.

Despite these differences, the passages are comparable insofar as they investigate the questions of how far the image is distinct from the percept and the ways in which this distinction might be conceived and expressed. The remainder of this chapter will be concerned with this investigation. Focusing on the late trilogy of prose works known as *Nohow On – Company, Ill Seen Ill Said* (1981) and *Worstward Ho* (1983) – it will position Beckett's writing in relation to the percept-image debates of the twentieth century. First, continuing to focus on *Company*, I will consider how Beckett's concern with the relationship between percept and image interacts with the socio-politics of twentieth-century psychological investigations into the effects of sensory deprivation and isolation. From there, looking to the later texts of the trilogy, I will consider the degree to which Beckett's writing engages with more theoretical debates around percept and image. By reading *Ill Seen Ill Said* and *Worstward Ho* alongside psychological experiments conducted by Cheves Perky and Stephen Kosslyn (as well as philosophical critiques by Sartre and Gilbert Ryle), the chapter will ultimately consider how the debates around imagery might nuance our understanding of Beckett's work, and how Beckett's work strives to produce a vocabulary with which to discuss mental imagery.

Isolation and imagery

If, as Maude suggests above, Beckett's prose performs experiments on 'detached and autonomous forms of subjectivity through a form of sensory deprivation', it is worth dwelling on the form of these experiments and the way in which they relate to other twentieth-century experiments that made use of sensory deprivation. The suggestion that sensory deprivation is a means through which to experiment on 'detached and autonomous forms of subjectivity' gives the impression that Beckett's experimentation is fundamentally phenomenological – concerned with accessing new modes of experience. And it is undeniable that Beckett's experiments, to some extent, work in this mode. I wish to suggest, however, that Beckett's sensory-deprivation experiments also relate themselves to a tradition that is less concerned with experience and more with performance – one that sees sensory deprivation as a psychophysiological instrument that can be used to control the human subject. In what follows, I will consider how these two discourses interact in Beckett's writing.

To begin to explore this we might return to the voice that comes to the isolated protagonist in the dark space of *Company*. As noted previously, Beckett refuses to classify this voice as either image or percept. It is only clear that the voice gives the impression of externality, and this externality seems to imply the presence of another subject in the dark with the protagonist. The protagonist, though, does not simply speculate that the voice belongs to someone else – that he is being spoken to by another. Instead, he thinks, the voice might be speaking to another that is in his vicinity: 'He cannot but sometimes wonder if it is indeed to and of him that the voice is speaking. May not there be another with him in the dark to and of whom the voice is speaking? Is he not perhaps overhearing a communication not intended for him? (4). Crucial, here, is the idea that the voice does not simply belong to another individual. Rather it has its own particular 'traits', and its own motives for speaking. The voice, to give some examples, comes to the protagonist 'now from one quarter and now from another'; 'another trait' is its 'repetitiousness'; and it also sheds a 'faint light' when it speaks (8–11). Furthermore, in terms of motives, the protagonist speculates that the voice might be trying to 'kindle in his mind' a faint uncertainty, or 'plague' him with 'mere sound' (4–5). The voice, then, is not simply the expression of another's presence. It is experienced as an autonomous presence out in the world.

Given that the protagonist's encounter with this external voice does not follow what one might call the ordinary rules of perception, and that there seems to be no one but the protagonist there to hear it, it is tempting to suggest that *Company* portrays a kind of hallucinatory experience. Making this assessment, though, requires us to further define the phenomenology of a hallucination. Now, numerous twentieth-century phenomenological philosophers would consider hallucinatory experience. Sartre, for example, considers hallucinations in his work on the imagination, but a more thorough account is given in Maurice Merleau-Ponty's *Phenomenology of Perception*. With regard to hallucinatory experience, 'the all-important point', Merleau-Ponty suggests, 'is that the patients, most of the time, discriminate between their hallucinations and their perceptions' ([1945] 2002: 389). Thus, for Merleau-Ponty, it is too simplistic to say that to hallucinate is to mistake image for percept, fantasy for reality. Rather, one needs to study the hallucination as an experience that has its own traits or qualities. The hallucination then might be seen to exist on a level that is distinct from the image or the percept. 'Hallucinations', Merleau-Ponty argues, 'are played out on a stage different from that of the perceived world, and are in a way superimposed' (395). Thus, the hallucination can follow its own rules. Merleau-Ponty cites instances in which individuals have the impression of constantly 'being seen naked from behind', or 'seeing simultaneously in all directions' (396). These observations certainly resound with the extraordinary 'traits' that are attributed to the voice encountered in *Company*. As in Merleau-Ponty's account of the hallucination, *Company*'s voice might be seen to play out on a stage different from that of the perceived world. But what Beckett seems to be interrogating in *Company* is our capacity to tolerate the voice as an existent on this stage. The opening line of the work gives out the imperative to 'imagine' the voice as it comes to one in the dark; the text seems to require its reader to imaginatively experience this voice (3). Rather than dwelling on the ways in which the voice is not a perception, the text asks us to focus on what it is. Beckett, then, uses a fictional, isolated environment in order to explore realms of experience that do not fit neatly into either the perceptual or the imagistic.[4]

There is, however, another side to Beckett's experiments with isolation. The solitary figures in Beckett's writing are rarely just phenomenological explorers. They are often also portrayed as vulnerable bodies being exposed to the psychophysiological effects of isolation. Perhaps the most striking example of isolation playing this double-headed role can be found in part one of *How It Is*. The opening of the novel presents us with a narrator who recalls inhabiting a dark, muddy environment with nothing for company but a coal sack which holds some tins. The narrator summarizes this environment as follows: 'The sack the tins the mud the dark the silence the solitude' (Beckett [1964] 2009b: 4). In this isolated environment, we are told, a few 'images' of another life flicker 'on an off' (4). These images are somehow linked to the life he led before entering the mud and the dark, but he tends to describe them as images rather than memories: 'I haven't been given memories this time it was an image' (7). The images are described to give a kind of aesthetic pleasure. One is described as 'a fine image fine I mean in movement and colour blue and white of clouds in the wind' (21). And another seems to portray an idyllic scene in which a teenage figure walks hand in hand with a girl and a dog in 'glorious weather' (23). These images tend to appear suddenly without the narrator's intending to produce them, and in this sense, Beckett seems to be presenting mysterious moments of aesthetic inspiration. However, as in *Nacht und Träume*, the materiality of this process of image production is consistently emphasized. First, apprehension of the 'fine image' is linked to the position of the narrator's body: the image is seen to be triggered by the narrator's lying face down in the mud with his tongue lolling out (21). Second, the narrator sometimes describes pissing and shitting images out (5). And, third, the images seem to appear and disappear in a way that frequently recalls lighting technology: one of the images, for example, 'goes out like a lamp blown out' (11). The Beckettian image of *How It Is* may be linked to a kind of Romantic inspiration, but it is also represented as a material response to a specific set of conditions. In this way it can be seen to anticipate the later teleplay.

In *How It Is*, though, things are more complicated than they are in the later work. The structure of the novel means that it is difficult to read the drama of image production that is described in part one without reference to the events of parts two and three. At the beginning of the text, we are told that the narrator will describe three states – 'before Pim with Pim after Pim' (3) – and *How It is* forms around these three states of being. The narrator is isolated in the first part, but in the second part he will have the company of Pim (though in the final part of the novel the narrator recants his story and states that he has always been alone). Thus the story of solitude described in part one is influenced by what was to come after it: the narrator's encounter with Pim. Much critical discussion of the text has focused on what the narrator does with Pim, and what he does is administer a kind of 'training' that aims at making Pim 'speak' and 'sing' (59). When the narrator finds Pim, he is lying 'dumb limp lump flat' in the mud, but the narrator makes it his aim to 'quicken him' by teaching Pim to perform certain tasks when exposed to a selection of painful stimuli (44):

> Table of basic stimuli one sing nails in armpit two speak blade in arse three stop thump on skull four louder pestle on kidney five softer index in anus six bravo clap athwart arse seven lousy same as three eight encore same as one or two as may be. (59)

Various commentators have recognized the link between this process of training and the systematic methods of interrogation and torture that were deployed by various states in the twentieth century and after. David Lloyd suggests that Beckett would have heard about many instances of violent interrogation during his lifetime, and for Lloyd, this context partly accounts for the 'prominent place assumed by scenarios of interrogation, incarceration and even of torture' in Beckett's oeuvre (2011: 198). More particularly, Adam Piette has recently shown the degree to which stories of French soldiers administering torture during the Algerian war are likely to have framed the genesis of How It Is (Piette 2016b: 151–3). The training of Pim, then, seems likely to have been informed by Beckett's awareness of twentieth-century interrogational practices.

However, it is hard to deny that the narrator's training of Pim is also informed by certain methods of psychological experimentation. The narrator seems to be interrogating Pim – trying to get words out of him – but he is also mapping his responses to a 'table of basic stimuli'. Given the events of the late twentieth and early twenty-first century the link Beckett seems to draw between torture and psychological experimentation is very suggestive. As I touched upon earlier, there was a strong connection between post-Second World War methods of interrogation and certain branches of psychology. Various interrogation programmes are known to have drawn on a body of psychological research which studied how the human being might be broken down and made compliant by specific sets of psychophysiological conditions. This body of research is frequently traced back to the, now infamous, sensory-deprivation experiments carried out by Donald Hebb at McGill University in the 1950s and 1960s. Typically, these experiments involved participants 'donning goggles, earmuffs, and mittens', and spending 'hours and even days in isolation' with the effects of these conditions being constantly monitored (Raz 2013: 380). As Mical Raz notes, Hebb's work was closely tied to Cold War security interests, and the findings of sensory-deprivation research were incorporated into the CIA's 1963 KUBARK Counter Intelligence Interrogation manual (382). Furthermore, it has been concluded that the methods laid out in the manual were used across the world – for example, by the British government when interrogating suspected members of the Irish Republican Army in Ulster in 1971 (Shallice 1972).[5]

Now, I know of no evidence to suggest that Beckett was aware of the historical links between certain types of psychological experimentation and violent interrogational techniques. His reading of Woodworth in the 1930s, though, would have given him some familiarity with the idea (put forward most forcefully by John Broadus Watson) that through programmatic manipulations of a human subject's environment, the psychologist might be able to exert fundamental control over that subject. Watson, Beckett notes, made the assertion 'that, given control of a healthy child's environment, he could turn him into anything he chose' (Feldman 2004: 316). Beckett, then, was familiar with the idea that the manipulation of a subject's sensory environment could work to alter them in fundamental ways, and I suggest that this way of thinking is crucial to Beckett's portrayals of subjectivity in *How It Is*. Specifically, it is crucial to the drama of image production that the narrator describes in part one. As noted above, the narration of the text comes in the aftermath of the narrator's training of Pim, and this fact alters the status of the images that are encountered in the first part of the novel. This is because, as David Lloyd puts it, the images described in part one, 'or ones akin to them', are elicited from Pim in part two (2011: 201). Thus, the images of part one 'are explicitly not subjective images' but seem to be shared between subjects through a process of 'training' or sensory manipulation (201). The images, for Lloyd, 'represent not the depth of the narrator's subjective world' but fragments of another's story (205). One might question how and why these images have been shared, and the text does not map this out in any systematic way. Nevertheless, the text evidences Beckett's interest in the ways in which a human subject's image of their own life can be manipulated or brought into question. *How It Is* might be seen to explore the process by which a subject is broken down to the point that they have no inner reality, only 'bits and scraps' of a life that may or may not be their own (Beckett [1964] 2009b: 3).

If *How It Is* shows a slightly abstracted interest in the processes by which external phenomena or beliefs might be imposed on the human subject's sense of inner reality, a much more concrete interest was developing in other settings. As Raz notes, from the 1950s onwards there was a growing cultural concern with the idea that certain techniques could be used to manipulate human subjectivity. Within the Cold War context, for Raz:

> Communist trials, prisoners' false confessions, and the fear of secretly turning citizens against their own country, epitomized in the 1959 classic novel, *The Manchurian Candidate*, quickly established 'mind control' as a topic of public fascination. Thus, the newly coined term 'brainwashing' emerged as a significant concern for military officials and the lay public as newspapers, books, and movies depicted the psychological dangers American prisoners of war faced. (2013: 380–1)

Within experimental science, this cultural fascination with ideas of 'mind control' and 'brainwashing' is most clearly evidenced in Ewan Cameron's research on 'psychic driving'; a technique in which a 'therapist' attempts to bring about changes in a 'patient' through the 'continued replaying, under controlled conditions, of a cue communication' (1957: 703).[6] In other words, a human subject is exposed to a single stimulus until the message carried by that stimulus is seen to be internalized and govern their behaviour. As Cameron puts it, 'By driving a cue statement one can, without exception, set up in the patient a persisting tendency for the cue statement' (703). Thus, the technique attempts to displace internal thoughts with external messages. Here then, the aim is not sensory deprivation exactly; the subjects are exposed to a stimulus. However, Cameron theorizes that, when all other stimulation is taken away, the selected stimulus will penetrate subjects and, in effect, become a part of their inner world. This is evident when he stipulates that the cue communication should be played through headphones: 'This causes the patient to experience the driving with much greater impact, the more particularly since he frequently describes it as being like a voice within his head' (706). There is a belief that, if presented in a certain way, a set of sensory stimuli can be used to make a human subject accept that certain external beliefs and experiences are their own.

Without suggesting that Beckett was familiar with experiments such as Cameron's, I propose – following critics such as Adam Piette (2016a) – that we might read Beckett's prose experiments on isolation within this Cold War context. Certainly, the narrator's voice in *How It Is* (first 'without quaqua on all side then in me' (2009a: 3)) seems to resound with Cameron's notion of a penetrating 'cue communication'. But perhaps a more focused investigation of the penetrating, manipulative voice might be found in *Company*. As we have seen the protagonist of *Company* recognizes that the voice has its own traits and intentions. There is the sense that it exists externally and is trying, through 'repetitiousness', to penetrate the protagonist's inner reality – it wants the protagonist to accept it as his own: 'Another trait its repetitiousness. Repeatedly with only minor variants the same bygone. As if willing him by this dint to make it his. To confess, Yes I remember. Perhaps even to have a voice. To murmur, Yes I remember' (2009a: 9). The obvious question here is one of whether the voice is ever internalized, and the text seems to hint that it is. In the final passage of the novel, the voice seems to cease to be company and the protagonist is back in solitude. The words spoken by the voice, it seems, were not those of another but his own:

> Till finally you hear how words are coming to an end. With every inane word a little nearer to the last. And how the fable too. The fable of one with you in the dark. The fable of one fabling of one with you in the dark. And how better in the end labour lost and silence. And you as you always were. Alone (2009a: 42).

There is obviously a degree of equivocality here. Taking a literal reading, one might suggest that the voice is simply in the process of coming to an end. And one might also interpret this as a metafictional moment in which the events described in the text are revealed to be an author's 'fable'.[7] In any case, though, it seems hard to deny that *Company* is interested in how a voice might cease to exist as an external stimulus and move into the protagonist's inner real.

Beyond questions of what exactly happens to the protagonist, Beckett's interest in *Company* seems to reside in the reader's imaginative perspective. Beckett's text produces a situation in which one is caught between a perspective that focuses on experience and a perspective that focuses on performance – what one might call a first-person and a third-person perspective. On the one hand, we are encouraged to make a phenomenological reduction and imagine a repetitious voice buzzing around us as we lie in the dark. But on the other, there is a pressure to analyse the protagonist's performance, produce a theory about what is happening, and perhaps make inferences about the effects of isolation and darkness on the human organism. Beckett is asking a question of how we respond to the situation we read about and experimenting on our perception of the human subject. Is 'he' an individual encountering a set of extraordinary phenomena, or a psychophysiological entity responding to an isolated environment? Beckett's concern with the blurring of percept and image, then, partly relates to a question of how the human subject was viewed in late-twentieth-century culture. In the isolated settings of *How It Is* and *Company* we are faced with the question of whether to see the blurring of percept and image as a novel and potentially enriching experience, or the affliction of a vulnerable body.

Wording the image: Theoretical debates

Working alongside this cultural concern of *Nohow On* is a more theoretical concern over how perceptual and imagistic processes are related. Here it might be useful to return to the passage from *Hamlet* discussed at the opening of this chapter. When Hamlet tells Horatio that he thinks he sees his father, some confusion ensues. Having recently seen the 'image' of Hamlet's deceased father out in the world, Horatio initially presumes Hamlet to be having the same experience. But Hamlet's words have misled Horatio. The father that Hamlet sees is not out in the world but in his 'mind's eye'. Hamlet can say that he sees his father while, at the same time, holding that 'I shall not look upon his like again' (Shakespeare 2015: 33). He can say that he sees his father without really seeing him and this creates a misunderstanding. There are numerous ways in which we might analyse this situation. We might take the passage to exemplify a flaw in language, pointing, for instance, to the fact that the same signifier – 'methinks I see my father' – can be used to signify two distinct experiences. Or, we might suggest that Hamlet's failure to verbally distinguish the two experiences is rooted in the nature of the experiences themselves – that the distinction between perceptual and imagistic experience is not always pronounced. In one analysis we are concerned with the nature of Hamlet's experience and in the other we are concerned with the words that he uses to describe it. Though I will move away from the case of Hamlet, the remainder of this chapter will be concerned with both analyses. All the authors I will look at in what follows are concerned both with what is happening when one sees something in the 'mind's eye' and with the words that we use to talk about it. In this way, they are all part of a sustained reconceptualization of the mental image in twentieth-century Western culture.

Though (as was noted in Chapter 5) the concepts of imagination and imagery were of concern to many writers in the 1800s, there was a feeling in early-twentieth-century psychology that these terms had been defined with insufficient rigour. At the beginning of Cheves Perky's 'An Experimental Study of Imagination', Perky acknowledges that 'the word Imagination and its cognate forms are familiar both in everyday speech and the technical language of psychology' but suggests that there is little agreement in what 'experiences' are 'denominated' when these terms are used (1910: 422–3). Perky's problem, here, is not so much that there have not been important findings regarding the nature of imagination and imagery but that this study has not been ordered in a way that gives the topic a 'distinctive mark or marks of a reliable kind' (427). Psychology, for Perky, is lacking a vocabulary with which to discuss the topics of imagery and the imagination. Perky's experimental study aimed to produce more concrete understandings of imagination and imagery by defining these concepts in relation to other psychological phenomena.

Though unable to give a satisfactory account of what was meant by the word 'image', Perky certainly seems to have had a clear idea of how the mental image was experienced. The first experiment of her study – 'A Comparison of Perception with the Image of Imagination' – showed that, for Perky, the mental image (or image of imagination) is distinguished by various qualities. In this experiment (as mentioned in Chapter 5) Perky attempted to 'build up a perceptual consciousness under conditions which should seem to the observer to be those of the formation of an imaginative consciousness' (428). There is the implication that the experimenters know what an 'imaginative consciousness' is like and can replicate it by manipulating the perceptual world. The way in which Perky attempted to do this showed a creativity that borders on the artistic. She attempted to imitate images by making use of a dark room that was helpfully placed at the centre of the Cornell University Laboratory. This dark room had a window that looked out onto the main laboratory room, and it is in this window that Perky would present the objects that participants were being told to imagine. This window was dressed in such a way as to give the object what Perky adjudged to be imagistic qualities. For example, she put tissue paper in the window and shone a faint light of a colour matching the colour of the object that was to be imagined. Thus, when an observer was to imagine a banana, the window would be endowed with a slight yellow colour. It was important that this would not be suggestive of light: 'The open square should appear just noticeably colored, without there being any such glow or shine upon the glass as could suggest the presence of a source of light behind it' (429). Also, she attempted to 'soften' the edges of the forms and worked to produce an effect in which the forms would 'oscillate or flicker into view' (430). Subjects were asked to imagine a series of objects, but as they imagined each object, a faintly coloured, flickering, blurry version of this object would appear in front of them. The experiment's question was whether these shadowy perceived forms would be mistaken for images of imagination. In Perky's hypothesis, then, the image is a faintly coloured, flickering and blurry thing, but apart from these qualities, it is essentially experienced in the same way as a percept.

The results, to some extent, validated this hypothesis. Perky drew the conclusion that the perceived forms were passing as imagined forms: 'We find, in brief, that a visual perception of distinctly supraliminal value may, and under our conditions does, pass – even with specially trained observers – for an image of imagination' (433). However, this overarching conclusion is perhaps less informative than the specific accounts that were given by the observers. From the reactions described by Perky, it does not seem that the observers identified the objects as images with any certainty. Instead the experiences described frequently seemed to be novel and difficult to categorize. There was a tendency to indicate that the images were somehow different from those of the imagination, but this was often put down to the novelty of the conscious attempt to imagine. When asked whether they had ever had similar imaginative experience, a subject would 'usually reply that he could not remember that he had; but then, he had never tried' (431). Similarly, one subject with 'extended practice in the 'observation of images' is described to have been 'confused': 'At first he thought the figures imaginary; then he speculated whether they might not be after-images of some sort, or akin to after-images' (432–3). Finally, he defined the images as such: 'It seems like a perception, though the attention is more active than in perception; yet I feel sure that it is there, and that I did not make it; it is more permanent and distinct than an image' (433). Perky suggests that this observer's eventual detection of 'permanence and distinctness' in the form was 'unluckily, due to faulty technique' in the presentation, but this observer's comments are indicative of a general trend in the responses. The objects, it seems, were often experienced as a novel form somewhere in between the percept and the image. This has been observed by Segal and Nathan (1964) in their replications of the Perky experiment. These experiments produce the conclusion that 'there is a region of experience where the distinction between self-initiated imagery and the perception of an external event is uncertain' (qtd. in Richardson 1969: 6). Perky's experiment, then, effects a blurring of the boundaries between image and percept but does not permit us to identify the former with the latter.

Via Edward Titchener's *Text-book of Psychology* (1910), the findings of Perky's experiment came to the attention of a very sceptical Jean-Paul Sartre. In *The Imaginary*, Sartre alludes to Perky's experiment when stating that several 'absurd experiments have been conducted to show that the image has a sensory content' ([1940] 2010: 52).[8] These experiments, Sartre argues, 'would make sense only if the image were a weak perception. But it is given *as image*' (52, emphasis in original). Sartre's critique seems to oscillate between tackling the questions of what the mental image is and how it is experienced. For Sartre, the idea that a mental image 'has a sensory content' is absurd because the content of a mental image 'has no externality' (52). By this he seems to mean that a mental image cannot have a sensory content as it does not produce effects on the outside world. Thus, when one claims to see a mental image, one is not truly seeing it because it is not out there to be seen. For Sartre, 'One sees a portrait, a caricature, a spot: one does not *see* a mental image' (51, emphasis in original). In this way, he draws a clear ontological distinction between the image and the percept. However, Perky's experiment never argues that the mental image is a perception; it merely concludes that, given specific conditions, an object of perception can pass for an image of imagination. She is not denying that there is an ontological distinction between image and percept. Instead her argument is phenomenological; she is arguing that on occasion both image and percept can produce a similar experience.

Sartre, though, does not accept this phenomenological contention. He has held from the beginning of *The Imaginary* that mental images 'present themselves to reflection with certain marks, certain characteristics that immediately determine the judgement "I have an image"' (4). In this line of thought, the image has a fixed '*essence*' which means it cannot be mistaken for a percept

(4, emphasis in original). A large part of this '*essence*' is linked to the image's apparent detachment from the sensory world. 'To see an object', Sartre argues, 'is to localize it in space, between this table and that carpet, at a certain height on my right or on my left' (52). This process of localization, he goes on, does not apply when one is apprehending an image: 'My mental images do not mix with the objects that surround me' (52). This process of localization is crucial because Sartre grants that, in certain cases, the image can begin to resemble the percept. For example, Sartre notes that hypnagogic images[9] can take on the 'features of objectivity, clarity, independence, richness, externality, which are never possessed by the mental image and which are ordinarily characteristic of perception' (37). But even in this case Sartre maintains that the image is not mistaken for a percept because 'it is not localized, it is not anywhere, does not occupy any place among other objects, it simply stands out on a vague ground' (37). A large part of the '*essence*' of Sartre's image, then, can be found in the 'vague ground' on which it is seen to reside. What is notable about Perky's experiment, though, is the degree to which it sought to present the image on this 'vague ground'. Like the images that Deleuze recognizes in Beckett's television plays, the objects of Perky experiments were presented in a kind of 'any space-whatever' (Deleuze 1995: 10) – a faintly lit window, dressed with tissue paper in the centre of a laboratory. Perky's perceptual objects, then, seem to capture a large part of what Sartre calls the '*essence*' of the image, so it is not absurd to think that they might be experienced as images. An ontological distinction does not preclude a phenomenological overlap.

This combination of ontological distinction and phenomenological overlap raises a question of language that has troubled numerous philosophers. One might understand the percept and the image to be distinct entities but still speak of them using the same terms. We have already noted, for example, that the term 'see' in Hamlet is used to refer to both perceptions and images of Hamlet's father. Gilbert Ryle takes up this point in *The Concept of Mind*, arguing that 'to see is one thing' and to 'picture or visualise is another', but also questioning how this difference is articulated ([1949] 2009: 223). For Ryle, the linguistic problem is not so much the one that plays out in *Hamlet* in which we are momentarily not sure whether Hamlet is claiming to see his father in the world or his mind's eye. Instead, Ryle's concern is with the very notion of a 'mind's eye' – the notion of a place in which mental images are said to exist:

> The crucial problem is that of describing what is 'seen in the mind's eye' and what is 'heard in one's head'. What are spoken of as 'visual images', 'mental

pictures', 'auditory images' and, in one use, 'ideas' are commonly taken to be entities which are genuinely found existing and found existing elsewhere than in the external world. So minds are nominated for their theatres. (222)

Ryle is not denying that the perceptual language that is commonly used to describe imagery reflects a phenomenological overlap. Nor is he suggesting that the concept of visualizing or picturing is not 'a proper and useful concept' (225). He is, however, concerned that this way of using language has created a 'tendency among theorists and laymen alike to ascribe some sort of an otherworldly reality to the imaginary and then to treat minds as the clandestine habitats of such fleshless beings' (222). The linguistic problem then, for Ryle, lies in acknowledging the phenomenological overlap between perception and imagery without implying that the image exists in a private world that parallels that of the perceptible. This problem, for Ryle, produces a kind of linguistic strain. He observes that people express both the phenomenological overlap and the ontological difference between perceiving and imaging 'by writing that, whereas they see trees and hear music, they only "see" in inverted commas, and "hear" the objects of recollection and imagination' (223). Thus, in order to describe a process in which one seems to see without really seeing, one must seem to say that one has seen without really saying it.

Beckett's eye of the mind

What seems to be becoming apparent in these readings is a disagreement between the philosophers and the psychologists. The psychologists, represented by Perky, emphasize the potential for a phenomenological blurring of the image and the percept, where philosophers, such as Sartre and Ryle, assert the importance of respecting an ontological distinction. Where, then, does Beckett fit into this debate? One might respond to this by questioning whether Beckett's writing has any place in this argument. In this line of thought, Beckett was, as mentioned earlier in the chapter, a literary writer working as part of a Shakespearian tradition that is interested in the aesthetic affects that can be derived from blurring the boundaries between image and percept, fantasy and reality; he did not have a theoretical interesting in defining the relationship between perception and mental imagery. This position, however, not only ignores Beckett's reading of theoretical texts such as Sartre's but also fails to take account of the sophistication with which Beckett's writing addresses the relationship between percept and image. Beckett's theoretical concerns begin to become apparent in a passage from the second act of *Happy Days* in which Beckett alludes to an 'eye of the mind':

> Winnie: That is what I find so wonderful, a part remains of one's classics, to help one through the day. (*Pause.*) Oh yes, many mercies, many mercies (*Pause.*) And now (*Pause.*) And now, Willie? (*Long pause.*) I call to the eye of the mind ... Mr Shower – Or Cooker. (*She closes her eyes. Bell rings loudly. She opens her eyes. Pause.*) Hand in hand, in the other hands bags. ([1986] 2006: 164–5)

Winnie pictures, in her mind's eye, a couple who stand, hand in hand, 'gaping' at her (165). In this way, the passage clearly dramatizes a performance of image production. However, there is something else going on here. Winnie's performance of image production is situated amid a discussion of her 'classics'. The gap between Winnie's concern with 'one's classics' and her production of visual images, here, is bridged by the phrase: 'I call to the eye of the mind.' This phrase, as various critics have noted, is drawn from the beginning of W. B. Yeats's play *At the Hawks Well* (1916) which, Van Hulle and Nixon note, Beckett 'clearly admired' (2013: 37). In addition to this, S. E. Gontarski notes that the phrase 'suggests Hamlet's vision of his Father in *Hamlet*' (2014: 237). Though, the passage might be used to exemplify Beckett's interest in the process of image production, it also alludes to an aesthetic canon. The theoretical concern cannot be severed from the literary tradition in which Beckett is writing.

However, the fact that Winnie's performance of image production is bound up in a literary tradition should not lead to the conclusion that Beckett was uninterested in imagistic processes themselves. It has been all too tempting for literary critics to focus on the fact that Beckett alludes to Yeats or Shakespeare when writing on the mind's eye and ignore his evident interest in what 'the eye of the mind' does. Indeed, the use of Yeats in *Happy Days* might be used to augment the contention that Beckett was heavily concerned with imagistic processes. When James Knowlson wrote to Beckett in 1972 questioning why Beckett alluded to Yeats, Beckett responded: 'The "eye of the mind" in *Happy Days* does not *refer* to Yeats any more than the "revels" in *Endgame* (refer) to *The Tempest*. They are just bits of pipe I happen to have with me. I suppose all is reminiscence from womb to tomb. All I can say is I have scant information concerning mine' (qtd. in Knowlson 1983: 16). As James Olney observes, 'There is much more going on in this passage than mere acting out by an author reluctant to comment on his work for an academic critic' (1998: 241). Beckett is not only giving an account of his creative process but also conceptualizing the processes behind mental imagery. By conceiving of the phrase 'the eye of the mind' as a bit of pipe 'I happen to have with me', Beckett seems to be indicating that the phrase had been perceived and was being stored somewhere in the back of his mind. In this way it is understood not as an embedded part of Yeats's play but as an isolated chunk of language – a verbal image. During writing, it seems, the phrase came to the fore of Beckett's mind (his conscious experience) and was used to connect two sections of the text. However, Beckett's statement suggests that his recollection of the phrase does not imply a pristine recollection of the context from which it came. The auditory image is seen to come to the mind's ear as a de-contextualized entity. This works in parallel with Winnie's performance of image production in the play. For Winnie, the image of Mr Shower, or Cooker, 'floats up – into my thoughts', but she cannot contextualize the image and so asks Willie if the names 'evoke any reality' for him (Beckett [1986] 2006: 156). For Beckett as for Winnie, imagery is felt to float up into consciousness without having been wholly contextualized or categorized. The play itself, combined with Beckett's later reflections on his writerly process, indicates a theoretical interest in the means by which mental images are produced.

In *Happy Days* the images that Winnie calls to the eye of her mind are eventually contextualized. They are said to stand 'hand in hand' gaping at her and eventually become recognizable as a kind of commentating theatrical audience, asking each other, for example, what the action is 'meant to mean' and whether Winnie has 'anything on underneath' (165). Here, I would argue, the imagistic gain a kind of fleshless reality. Though the Showers (or Cookers) are always being imagined by Winnie, there is a movement in which they go from being imagined as images to being imagined as autonomous entities. To paraphrase Sartre, they are endowed with a kind of externality. Such a blurring seems to enact the anxieties voiced by Sartre and Ryle. Winnie's 'eye of the mind' soon acquires the properties of a perceptual eye as Shower (or Cooker) acquires externality. Beckett's play shows an awareness of the philosophical concern that speaking of the mind's eye might strip mental phenomena of its particularity.

In the later part of the twentieth century, experimental psychology began to respond to these concerns by looking for ways of theorizing the mental image that are less indebted to metaphors of perception. Stephen Kosslyn, for example, moves towards a 'computer graphics metaphor' in which the visual image is understood to 'bear the same relationship to its underlying structure as a pictorial display on a cathode ray tube does to the computer program that generates it' (1975: 342).[10] In this line of thought, the products of perception 'are stored in long-term memory in an abstract format and must be acted on by processes that serve to generate or to produce an experience of an image' (342).

Here, the 'underlying structure' is not experienced; one merely apprehends the 'pictures' that this structure generates. Kosslyn, though, maintains the metaphor that draws imagery alongside perception. For example, he invokes the concept of a 'mind's eye' but considers it as a kind of processor that analyses 'the material arrayed in mental images' (342). The processes performed by the mind's eye, in this account, are experienced similarly to the experiences encountered during perceptual processes. For example, according to Kosslyn, a mental image needs to be classified (e.g. identified as big/small, two legged/four legged), and the mind's eye does this through use of the same procedures that one would use to classify a perceptual object: 'The same procedures may be appropriately applied to classify both internal representations arising during perception which are experienced as a visual percept, and internal representations experienced as a visual mental image' (342). Kosslyn, then, not only acknowledges the phenomenological overlap between perception and mental imagery but also scrutinizes the ontological distinction. He argues that both the 'visual percept' and the 'visual mental image' are 'internal representations' which may be classified in similar ways.

Beckett's theoretical approach to the relationship between percept and image, I suggest, shows a degree of confluence with the approach of Kosslyn. Both writers seem to conceptualize mental images as isolated products of perception that are stored, unnoticed, in long-term memory, and occasionally present themselves for conscious analysis by 'the mind's eye'. Additionally, both recognize the difficulty of distinguishing the mind's eye from the perceptual eye. At the beginning of *Ill Seen Ill Said*, for example, the eye of the mind is invoked when the figure of a woman is said to appear for an eye that has 'no need of light to see' (Beckett 2009a: 45). From this it seems easy to conclude that the woman is being apprehended as an image by the mind's eye. However, the text does not allow us this stable view of the figure. Later in the text, a perceiving eye is invoked ('the eye of flesh') and this requires us to imagine the figure as both image and percept. For example, we are told that she intermittently disappears and is 'no longer anywhere to be seen. Nor by the eye of the flesh, not by the other' (51). The figure cannot remain a pure image and this creates a blurring: 'Already all confusion. Things and imaginings. As of always. Despite precautions. If only she could be pure figment. Unalloyed. This old so dying woman. So dead. In the madhouse of the skull and nowhere else' (53). As in *Hamlet*, confusion has arisen out of the different senses in which one can use the verb 'see'. The narrator suggests an understanding that the woman only exists in 'the madhouse of the skull', but 'despite precautions', the image and the percept, 'things and imaginings' cannot be kept distinct. The notion of 'precautions' may recall the anxieties that we have seen articulated by Ryle and Sartre. However, in the context of *Ill Seen Ill Said* there is the sense that the blurring of image and percept is inevitable. Here we might return to Ulrika Maude's discussion of vision in Beckett's work and particularly her analysis of the way in which Beckett's approach relates to the ideas of Maurice Merleau-Ponty and Michel Foucault. Along with these philosophers, Maude argues, Beckett is interested in the way in which the visible and invisible, real and imaginary can interrupt or mix with one another. Drawing on Foucault's idea of the heterotopia, she suggests that within Beckett's work 'different categories that cannot occupy the same space seem nonetheless to coexist' (2009: 40). In *Ill Seen Ill Said* the projections of the eye of the mind, and the eye of flesh, seem to coexist with one another creating a heterotopia in which the percept and the image intertwine. This idea is also present in Perky's experiment when one of the observers is described to perceive the object in front of him, but also endow it with imaginary qualities. Perky presented blank cardboard cut-outs but one observer embellished them through imagination: 'The tomato was seen painted on a can, the book was a particular book whose title could be read, the lemon was lying on a table, the leaf was a pressed leaf with red markings on it' (1910: 432). The observer is seeing both image and percept in the same space and time. In this way, *Ill Seen Ill Said* may be profitably seen as part of a broad twentieth-century investigation into the phenomenological overlap between percept and image.

Beckett's experimentation on image production is developed along a slightly different path in *Worstward Ho*. Here, as in *Happy Days*, a hand holding pair appears in a mind's eye – or, in this case the 'staring eyes' of a 'head sunk on crippled hands' (81–2). The narrator of *Worstward Ho*, however, moves to differentiate this image from the one that Winnie describes in *Happy Days*. Recall that Winnie's images are seen 'hand in hand, in the other hands bags'. Contrast this with a description of the hand holding pair in *Worstward Ho*: 'Hand in hand with equal plod they go. In the free hands – no. Free empty hands' (Beckett 2009a: 84). There is resistance to the process of fleshing out that happens in Winnie's imagination. But this does not mean that the images (or 'shades' as they are described in the text) are left un-interpreted. On the contrary, the next time the image of the hand holding pair emerges it is interpreted in detail:

> Backs turned. Heads sunk. Dim hair. Dim white and hair so fair that in that dim light white. Black greatcoats to heels. Dim black. Bootheels. Now the two right. Now the two left. As one with equal plod they go. No ground. Plod as on void. (86)

This process, I would argue, exemplifies the kind of procedure of classification that Kosslyn attributes to the mind's eye. Certain attributes of the image are identified, and information is produced; for example, we are told how the figures are positioned and coloured. The 'shade' is being processed in a way that one might process a percept. However, the text resists the temptation to place these imagistic figures in a mental world. The shade does not plod on the ground but 'as on void'. The figure is interpreted by a mind's eye, but the space it inhabits, it is made clear, is not a perceptual world but an abstract space of the mind – an any-space-whatever. The phenomenological overlap between perception and imagery is acknowledged here, but the text resists the temptation to endow imagery with a fleshless reality.

At issue in *Worstward Ho*, then, is a kind of mental space which appears for the mind's eye but is not wholly there. A major concern in the text is with finding a vocabulary with which to discuss the apprehension of this space. In this way, Beckett develops Ryle's observation that people express the difference between the mind's eye and the senses of perception 'by writing that, they see trees and hear music', but only '"see" and "hear"' images. To repeat the dilemma that was encountered in Ryle: in order to describe a process in which one seems to see without really seeing, one must seem to say that one has seen without really saying it. Beckett, I would argue, goes further than Ryle in attempting to construct a vocabulary with which to negotiate this dilemma. This begins with the assertion that the bodies and places that are invoked in the text are not wholly there: 'Say a body. Where none. No mind. Where none. That at least. A place. Where none. For the body. To be in' (Beckett 2009a: 81). We are given the image of a body but this body is no sooner evoked than negated. We are required, almost simultaneously, to both construct it and be aware that it is not really there. It might be argued that this procedure does something similar to the inverted commas that Ryle observes in common language. In Ryle, as in Beckett, there is a concern with the process of saying that something is being seen while also saying that it is not there.

Worstward Ho goes a step further than this. There is an attempt to re-appropriate the word 'see' itself so that, when one encounters it within the text, it is clear that a particular type of seeing is being described. We are in effect told how to read the verb 'to see': 'See for be seen. Misseen. From now see for be misseen' (84). By this point in the text, it has been made clear that all the shades are being seen but this seeing is not an act of perception. Instead the shades are apprehended in the stare of a head sunk on crippled hands. However, because the things that this entity sees exist within its own stare, when it sees it is also always seeing itself, being seen. In this way, the things that it 'sees' do not exist as external entities, but merely as internal shades. It is seeing things that are not there. As Sartre puts it in *The Imagination*, the scene in question 'does not exist *in fact*; it exists *as imaged*' (2012: 4, emphasis in original). The text effectively tries to create a system in which a mental image cannot be read as a percept, even though the two phenomena may share many qualities. *Worstward Ho*, then, may well be read as an attempt to find a vocabulary that acknowledges the phenomenological overlap between imagery and perception while maintaining the ontological distinction. Thus, we might characterize *Ill Seen Ill Said* and *Worstward Ho* as differing approaches to a similar topic. Each, I would argue, investigates the distinction between the eye of the mind and the eye of the flesh, seeing and 'seeing'. However, where *Ill Seen Ill Said* investigates a movement in which these entities blur into one another, *Worstward Ho* pursues a language that would serve to maintain the ontological distinction between the percept and the image.

Conclusion

While acknowledging the degree to which Beckett's interest in the relationship between mental imagery and perception, fantasy and reality, operates within a Shakespearian aesthetic tradition, this chapter has suggested that Beckett's treatment of the theme should be situated securely within twentieth-century culture. Readings of the three texts of *Nohow On* make this clear. *Company*, I have suggested, works with numerous twentieth-century texts in considering how the boundaries between image and percept, internality and externality, blur when one is alone in the dark. Here it operates between two approaches to sensory isolation or deprivation. On the one hand the text takes a phenomenological approach that resounds with philosophers such as Merleau-Ponty: it asks its reader to consider the novel experiences that might come from exposure to darkness and silence by frustrating the urge to classify the voice that 'comes to one in the dark'. On the other, it registers the extent to which twentieth-century psychology – often at the direction of political organizations – employed darkness and silence as stimuli which could be used to control the performances and experiences of the human subject. In this way, *Company* operates in between two twentieth-century discourses that tackle the problem of relating perception and mental imagery: the phenomenological and the behavioural.

In *Ill Seen Ill Said* and *Worstward Ho*, Beckett's concerns grow more theoretical. In a manner that resounds with much twentieth-century philosophy and experimental psychology, these texts register the difficulty of finding a language with which to discuss the relationship between the percept and the image. Here the problem resides in the question of how one registers the phenomenological overlap between seeing and 'seeing', while acknowledging the ontological distinction between what is mental and what has externality. Beckett's two texts, I have argued, are experiments that offer differing perspectives on the degree to which it is possible to verbally distinguish image from percept. *Ill Seen Ill Said* attempts to maintain the distinction, but ultimately gives up, embracing a heterotopia in which the 'eye of the mind' and the 'eye of flesh' are layered on top of each other. *Worstward Ho*, by contrast, is more thorough in its attempt to retain the distinction, producing an experimental verbal environment in which a mental image can be spoken of in terms of perception without being read as a percept. These late prose experiments, then, continue the work of dramatic pieces such as *Not I*, *That Time*, *Footfalls* and *Nacht und Träume* insofar as they investigate what we might call non-verbal aspects of human experience. They are interested in the psychophysiological conditions by which humans produce mental images. But *Nohow On* also sees Beckett return to the concerns voiced in the German letter of the 1930s (discussed in the Introduction). Beckett is again concerned with the degree to which reality is obscured by the veil of language – how writing or speaking about mental images can work to obfuscate their existence.

Conclusion: Experimental Beckett

This study has sought to specify a way in which Samuel Beckett might be thought of as a scientifically experimental writer, rather than solely as a writer of the avant-garde, or one who is simply innovative. I have suggested that Beckett produced aesthetic experiments that combine with a great deal of psychological experimentation in working towards an understanding of what it is to experience and perform in the world. Here, I do not aim to exclude other accounts of Beckett's writing. In arguing for the existence of an experimental Beckett, I do not deny the existence of an innovative or avant-garde Beckett, any more than a study of Beckett the novelist denies the existence of Beckett the poet. But I hope that this study will help to nuance critical discussions of the nature of Beckett's contribution to literature and a wider culture. The ever-expanding body of criticism that surrounds Beckett's work frequently recognizes that Beckett's method is 'experimental' but too often one wonders what is meant by the term. I hope that this study will prompt more thoroughgoing definitions of what Beckett's writing does. Surely, there are times when Beckett seems to be challenging mainstream culture in a way that corresponds with the term 'avant-garde'. And he undoubtedly produced many formal innovations that prompted reassessments of what a play, novel or poem can look like. This study, though, has called for a distinction to be drawn between these senses of 'experimentation' and the more scientific sense in which Beckett is seen to produce meticulous studies of certain processes or phenomena.

It should also be stressed that the type of experimentation I perceive in Beckett's writing is very different from earlier versions of the literary experiment. The experimental Beckett is clearly distinct from Zola's notion of an experimental novelist, who observes social facts and imaginatively acts upon them, with the aim of obtaining scientific knowledge of an individual or society. Rather than what we might call a social-realist experimentation which seeks to represent individuals and their communities, Beckett's experiments focus on the means by which humans attempt to make sense of the world. Here he frequently drew on his knowledge of experimental psychology. For example, as we saw in Chapter 1, the theatre of the 1950s and 1960s engaged with the early-twentieth-century learning theory wars in experimenting on the degree to which humans can store sensory information and use it to analyse new variations of this information.

Beckett's psychological experimentation placed a great deal of focus on linguistic processes. In *Not I*, as we saw in Chapter 2, he produces an experiment on speech perception which interrogates the strenuous process by which we attend to, comprehend and interpret the spoken word. But Beckett's experimentation goes beyond the question of verbal communication. *That Time*, for instance, investigates how the face functions (or fails to function) as a medium through which meaning is transmitted. Crucial, here, are the concepts of attention and inattention. Working in a tradition that includes Arthur Schopenhauer and Sigmund Freud as well as a wide range of experimental and therapeutic psychologists, Beckett's experiments are concerned with the human's limited capacity to perceive, register and recall sensory stimuli. Beckett draws attention to the spatio-temporal limits that underpin the human's capacity to attend to the world.

As well as these questions of attention, Beckett produces experiments that bring into question the human subject's capacity to distinguish between image and percept, fantasy and reality. In his later work, and particularly late prose works such as *Company*, *Ill Seen Ill Said* and *Worstward Ho*, Beckett can be seen to reach for a language that registers a phenomenological overlap, but also an ontological distinction, between that which is perceived in the world and that which is apprehended in the mind's eye or ear. I do not doubt that Beckett's work is consistently concerned with more traditionally literary questions regarding the construction of narratives and the production of self. But in his later work, I have argued, he takes up another related concern: the processes by which the human subject attempts to register, categorize and denominate sensory and pseudo-sensory phenomena.

This study has also repeatedly emphasized the degree to which Beckett's aesthetic experiments were grounded in the historical circumstances and discourses that surrounded him. Beckett's experiments on attention, for example, along with those of many psychologists, are closely bound up in a modernity that increasingly emphasizes the human subject's capacity to efficiently perform perceptual, interpretive and emotional labour. In *That Time*, for example, we saw Beckett writing against a Stanislavskian tradition in which the human subject is expected to 'deep act' in order to manufacture a sense of spontaneity. And in Chapter 4's discussion of *Footfalls* I argued that Beckett questions how the pressure to produce a story of self can distract from present experience. Similarly, the later chapters of this study sought to contextualize Beckett's study of mental imagery. Chapter 6, for instance, traced a link between Beckett's interest in the disorientating psychophysiological effects of isolation and a Cold War culture that became engrossed by ideas of manipulation and brainwashing. At the core of this historical concern has been a question of Beckett's role in the twentieth century's troubled attempt to define the human subject. When studying twentieth-century culture, one persistently comes across tension between more or less reductive and expansive models of subjectivity. Movements such as psychological behaviourism defined humans as stimulus-response units whose patterns of performance can be predicted and controlled. But at the same time there was the emergence of a great deal of post-Romantic philosophical, aesthetic and therapeutic writing that emphasized the singularity and unknowability of human experience. In this study, Beckett's writing has been seen to take in these two discourses, sometimes synthesizing them, sometimes letting them exist in tension.

Of course, Beckett's experiments are not merely concerned with a theoretical or ethical view of the human. They are, it should not be forgotten, works of art which seek to effect certain types of aesthetic pleasure. What this study's comparison between Beckett's aesthetic experiments and the discipline of experimental psychology has shown, however, is the degree to which Beckett questions whether psychological labour can produce aesthetic pleasure. As I argued in Chapter 3, this question undergirds much modernist art, but the strains involved in comprehending *Not I*'s fast speech or managing one's attention in *That Time* bring it to the fore. Similarly, the later prose seems to derive much of its power from the reader's struggle to adjudge what in the text to imagine as 'real' and what to imagine as 'imagined'. It is not merely that one must work hard to obtain pleasure from Beckett's aesthetic experiments; the aesthetic potency of Beckett's writing seems to reside in the human's capacity to perceive their own psychological labour and question whether it is worth, to paraphrase The Unnamable's frequently quoted resolution, going on with.

In making this argument, I seem to produce a Beckett that is heavily concerned with the responses of his audience and some would dispute this account. There are, of course, many stories to suggest that Beckett was uninterested in the experiences of his audience. One thinks of Walter Asmus's recollection that, during the production of the television play *What Where*, Beckett wanted the action recorded so faintly that it would only be registered by the recording studio's advanced technology – the audience would not have been able to see anything on their television screens. Here Beckett claimed not to care what the audience would see so long as he himself felt the required effect (Asmus, Uhlmann and

Denham 2013). However, in spite of these sentiments, Beckett continued to put his experiments out there long after there was any financial necessity for him to do so – and long after he had won enough social esteem to last a lifetime. This suggests he was interested in producing experiences for others, even if he did not show any major interest in the observation and measurement of these experiences. Here, it might be useful to define the level on which Beckett was interested in audience responses, and the type of knowledge that he sought to obtain from his experiments. Clearly, through experimentation Beckett sought to discover his own personal responses to particular sets of stimuli. And it also seems that Beckett wanted to know what kinds of psychological processes and experiences could work in an aesthetic context. But what Beckett does not do, at least in any programmatic way, is collect data from his audiences in order to make generalized conclusions about the processes and experiences with which he is evidently concerned.

In a recent discussion of the relationship between scientific and poetic experimentation conducted with neuroscientist Sophie Scott, the poet James Wilkes argues that, in poetic experimentation, the experiment and the data 'are joined together' (Wilkes and Scott 2016: 333). Where in science one performs an experiment and obtains results which then must be interpreted, the poet's results, in Wilkes's view, 'are the experiment': 'Anything that people find out about the possibilities for literature or for lived experience is known in the performance, or the hearing, or the reading of the poetry' (333). This view of aesthetic experimentation is persuasive insofar as it emphasizes the degree to which the knowledge acquired through the aesthetic experiment is 'an experiential one' (333). However, it does seem to ignore the fact that poems, plays and works of fiction are, themselves, psychophysiological stimuli that affect us in certain ways, and are thereby always capable of producing data. The extent to which this data is collected and interpreted (and by whom) is another question, and different writers and artists are likely to hold more or less interest in the data that their experiments can produce. Beckett devised experiments that investigate processes such as learning, perception, attention and mental imagery, but he did not collect data from these experiments in any systematic way. It is not so much that experiment and data are joined together in Beckett's work. Rather, Beckett carefully designs experiments but does not systematically collect and interpret the data that these experiments produce. In summary, then, I argue that Beckett performs scientifically informed aesthetic experimentation, but not fully fledged scientific research. His works can be defined as experimental insofar as they position and stimulate human bodies in ways that might allow us to better understand our complex, but partial, experiences of the world.

Notes

Introduction: Literary experiments and the work of Samuel Beckett

1 At the time, the experiments had a very specific stated purpose. They set out to test the nineteenth-century notion that the automatic and 'subconscious' behaviour of hysterical patients could be attributed to a 'second personality' (Solomons and Stein 1896: 492). In their investigation, Stein and Solomons used methods of distraction in order to bring out involuntary movements in normal patients. These movements, Solomons and Stein hoped, would definitely resemble the exhibitions of the 'second personality' described in hysterical patients. They wanted to eliminate the distinction being made at the time between the hysteric's performance of a 'second personality' and the 'automatic movements' of the ordinary person: essentially disproving the 'second personality' thesis.

2 The research of Solomons and Stein would inspire later experiments on divided attention. Spelke, Hirst and Neisser, for example, draw on the methods of Solomons and Stein in a series of experiments which test whether, through practice, subjects can acquire the ability to simultaneously perform two tasks that are initially very hard to combine (Spelke, Hirst and Neisser 1976: 216).

3 This seems to me unjust speculation on Beckett's part. See Nugent-Folan (2015) for a more detailed discussion of this.

4 Here, we might look to works by critics such as Hugh Kenner (1959), John Fletcher (1967) and Lawrence Harvey (1970).

5 Another approach that has been taken, here, is the consideration of Beckett's relationship with phenomenology. This is a concern that I will touch on in this study. For a more detailed account, though, one can look to Maude and Feldman's 2006 collection *Beckett and Phenomenology*. Alternatively, for an approach that is more focused on Beckett's drama, see Stanton B. Garner Jr.'s discussion of Beckett in *Bodied Spaces: Phenomenology and Performance in Contemporary Drama* (Garner Jr. 1994: 18–38); or Anna McMullan's *Performing Embodiment in Samuel Beckett's Drama* (2012).

6 Other critics have argued that Beckett's work is openly hostile to certain aspects of experimental psychology. Horst Breuer, for example, has argued that Beckett 'irreverently avails himself' of the mechanical approach of the scientist and 'satirizes the academic earnest' of psychological experiments (2006: 316).

7 It is commonly recognized that there was a split between therapeutic and experimental psychology at the end of the nineteenth century (Rylance 2000: 5–6). As well as the establishment of psychological laboratories across the world, the period saw what Rylance terms the 'growth of therapeutic sub-specialization' (5–6). In effect, the practice of treating those with psychological ailments or pathologies, and that of attaining psychological knowledge through experimentation grew apart and became different professions.

8 To give a few examples: Barbara Shapiro (1969); Didier Anzieu (1994); Phil Baker (1997), J. D. O'Hara (1997) Ciaran Ross (2011). Also, we might look to a special issue of *Samuel Beckett Today/Aujourd'hui* entitled *Beckett & La Psychanalyse & Psychoanalysis* (Houppermans, Buning and Butler 1996).

9 On a similar note, Rylance observes: 'For many cultural historians and literary critics, psychoanalysis has long been considered the branch of psychology most suited to humanistic enquiry. In part, this is a reaction to the ascendancy of experimentalism, because psychoanalysis has been seen to have a more "personalist" orientation, next to the steely science' (2000: 8). Though, as books such as Ryan's and Rylance's exemplify, the relationship between literature and other branches of psychology has received more attention from the 1990s onwards.

10 The concern with manipulating behaviour raises a question of observation and measurement. Beckett's work for television certainly addresses what Jonathan Bignell calls 'the dynamics of viewership' (2009: 176). However, Beckett himself did not purport to be interested in the detail of how actual viewers responded to his plays. Bignell's work, though, shows the extent to which the responses of viewers to Beckett's works for television were being observed and measured by the institutions that screened them (Bignell 2009: 176–87). At this point, the concern was largely with the audience's impressions of the play (whether they liked it or not). Works such as *Ghost Trio*, though, point to a different type of viewer research which seeks to observe responses more exactly and directly (measuring, for example, whether the sound is turned up or down).

11 Russell, here, discusses Beckett's use of the mirror in the light of Lacan's theory of the mirror stage (Russell 1989: 25).

12 A complication arises here when one considers how the face is conceived in Freudian psychoanalytic practice. I will consider this problem in more detail in Chapter 3.

13 As Anna McMullan writes, 'The need to be seen, or to tell or listen to the story of a life drives these plays' (2010: 108).

Chapter 1

1 In later versions of *Happy Days*, for instance, he changed the alarm clock that arouses Winnie in early versions to a more abstract 'bell' and erased the mention of 'rocket attacks' (Gontarski 2006: 77;80).

2 Here I am drawing on Frederic Jameson's theory of the eclipse of 'parody' by 'pastiche' within postmodernism (1991: 16–20).

3 Thus, the fact that some responses happen by reflex without the need for intentional, or even perceptual, processes should not lead us to believe that intention or perception is unworthy of psychological study. And, equally, the fact humans often only respond to a given stimulus after it has been processed into a percept does not mean that sensation does not exist, or is irrelevant to human activity.

4 Of course, a caveat to this point resides in the unlikelihood that Beckett ever read Woodworth's more specialist writing. Beckett's reading was, in all probability, limited to the introductory textbook. However, the latter does contain some of the same critiques of behaviourism and the gestaltists that Woodworth outlines in his article, and there is a degree of confluence between the rhetorical thrust of the specialist article and that of the introductory textbook. Both texts encourage their readers to synthesize rather than choose between different psychological schools. Furthermore, in both works, there is an interest in the way in which certain schools of psychology privilege a particular stage of psychological activity at the expense of others. For example, Beckett noted from Woodworth that behaviourism privileged motor responses and 'excluded sensation, perception, memory, thinking, emotion, & desire' (Feldman 2004: 315).

5 They uniformly, for example, find traces of Köhler in the attempts of Beckett's man to pile up cubes in order to reach an elevated carafe (Beckett 2006: 204). This is firmly evidenced in Beckett's notes. He copied down, from Woodworth, Köhler's finding that in order to reach food, chimpanzee subjects could join sticks together or 'pile up boxes' (Feldman 2004: 319). It is, then, very difficult to refute the idea that Beckett drew influence from Köhler's study.

6 Beckett's knowledge of Pavlovian conditioning at the time he wrote 'Fingal' is evidenced by his alluding to it in a number of letters and articles of the 1920s. See Maude (2013) for a more detailed discussion of this.

7 Knowlson, Feldman and Maude all read the play along these lines, though each produces a slightly different reading. Knowlson points to the play's 'bitter theme: the inevitable frustration and disappointment of life' (1996: 418). He notes that 'though the man in Beckett's mime shows even more ingenuity than the apes [in Köhler's experiments], he never attains his objective' (419). In contrast to that of Köhler's experiment, Beckett's environment is a frustrating and disappointing one in which 'ingenuity' goes unrewarded. Similarly, Feldman notes that the 'intertextual reference affords a lovely contrast between Köhler's apes as "can-ers" in terms of conceptual learning, and Beckett's mime as a "non-can-er", with relief ever beyond reach' (2006: 106). Maude goes the furthest in her comparison, drawing attention to Beckett's note about the conditions that enabled apes to show insight: 'Köhler was able to show that the apes did possess insight, provided they were allowed to see all the elements in the situation (its pattern), instead of being placed in such a blind

situation as a box, maze, etc.' (Feldman 2004: 319). Maude highlights the assumption that Köhler's apes 'were allowed to see all the elements in a situation'. She suggests that 'Köhler's gestaltist conclusion that animals will learn if they are given the full picture is shown to be already flawed, since the apes – living in an anthropoid station in Tenerife – as well as Beckett's man, are never placed in a circumstance in which a full picture could emerge' (2013: 89).

8 Here Beckett is likely to be drawing on his reading of introspectionist psychology in Woodworth. He took note of the example of the 'the "negative after-image": if you steadily look at a coloured spot for 20 or 30 seconds, & then turn your eyes upon a plain grey background, you see a spot of colour complementary to that of original spot – purple for green, blue for yellow, etc.' (Feldman 2004: 314).

Chapter 2

1 Crary does rehearse the argument that the hegemony of behaviourism in the early twentieth century marginalized attention 'as an explicit object of research' (33–34). However, for Crary this was more a matter of 'terminological polemics', than methodological substance. He insists that concepts of attention were important to the methods of behaviourism as 'the entire regime of stimulus-response research was founded on the attentive capacities of a human (or even animal) subject' (34).
2 For example, Gupta (1975); Hamlyn (1988); Henry (1993); Janaway (2010).
3 This method was also used in a landmark study in social psychology. Sherif (1935) found that the perception of the autokinetic movement was heavily susceptible to social influences.
4 Accounts of this experience can be found in numerous reviews. For example, Lyn Gardner (2013) recalls how the mouth appears to 'hover and move'.
5 Another option, here, may be to look at what is going on at the neural level. Laura Salisbury and Chris Code have taken this approach in reading Beckett's work alongside the work of neurologist John Hughlings Jackson. In this view, the actor's speech in *Not I* might be seen as a rote-learnt activity that is performed at a level of the brain below that which produces propositional language. Salisbury and Code observe Beckett's 'extraordinarily persistent desire to invoke forms of language that seem both phylogenetically and ontogenetically to precede the propositional language' that we associate with 'the functioning of an intentional consciousness' (Salisbury and Code 2014: 113).
6 For example, in *To the Actor* (1953), theatre practitioner Michael Chekhov draws a distinction between inner tempo and outer tempo and suggests that the actor should be able to manage both ([1953] 2002: 75–6).
7 Of course, actors may rehearse a role to the point that they no longer have to consciously attend to these aspects.

8 One can just play recorded speech at a higher rate, but this creates distortions insofar as it raises the pitch as well.
9 It should be noted here that there are numerous versions of *Not I* and each one holds different implications for visual speech perception. The original performance, for instance, had the Auditor but this element was removed in later stage productions. Also, if you are seated at the back of a large theatre, the mouth might be too far away for the lips to be read. It is difficult, then, to make any definite statement about the role of lip reading in *Not I*. That said, the below statements apply to most versions.
10 As Matthew Feldman has suggested, this late Bion is likely very different to the one Beckett encountered in the 1930s (2006: 93). At the time of his sessions with Beckett, Bion had yet to undergo formal psychoanalytic training and, Feldman notes, his early outlook was likely 'too positivistic' to show 'any great harmony with Beckett's concerns in the 1930s' (93). Here I am not concerned with showing influence either way. I would suggest, however, that the accounts of therapeutic attentiveness that Bion developed in his later life are useful in outlining the problems of attention that Beckett's plays present.
11 In a literal sense, of course, this extract speaks to the staging of *Not I*. The observer of *Not I*, and many of Beckett's late plays, might feel as though the auditorium has been thrown under Bion's beam of darkness, in which any faint light becomes visible. But Bion is obviously speaking in a more metaphorical sense about the therapist's manner of attending to the 'obscure problems' of a patient – how one registers the material presented by the patient and makes something of it.
12 This theory may be seen as a descendant of Tolman's theory of cognitive mapping (discussed in Chapter 1).

Chapter 3

1 Nineteenth-century culture's interest in physiognomy (the idea that facial features or expressions were representative of character or ethnic origin) should also be pointed out. For discussions of this, see Hartley (2001) and Pearl (2010).
2 In *Discourse Networks* (1985), Friedrich Kittler sees this as symptomatic of Freud's tendency towards 'exclusion of the optical realm' (Kittler 1990: 284). For Kittler, this tendency sits uncomfortably with the concept of 'free floating' (or evenly divided) attention. Like the phonograph, Kittler continues, Freud's method fishes 'in the wide stream of perception, but only among acoustical data' (284).
3 It should be noted that, in his own psychoanalytic (or post-psychoanalytic) practice, Guattari moved away from one-to-one, face-to-face contact and began using a form of group therapy. As Gary Genosko puts it, Guattari 'called into question the analytic

relationship of analyst-analysand, the so-called face-to-face, dual relation, for the sake of the analysis of groups in a clinical setting' (2002: 68).
4. Deleuze and Guattari draw on Beckett's work extensively. Indeed, Beckett's novels are cited in their discussion of faciality in the novel in *A Thousand Plateaus* (191–3). For a critical discussion that relates the concept of faciality to Beckett's drama, see Colin Gardner's work on Beckett and Deleuze (2012: 90–5).
5. There is a significant body of criticism which considers Beckett's relationship with Levinas. For example, see Fifield 2013.
6. For another reading that considers the relationship between affect and facial expression in Beckett's work see David Houston Jones's (2018) work on trauma, face and figure in Beckett's writing.
7. Numerous critics have pointed out the degree to which Beckett's writing breaks with Stanislavskian method. See, for example, Uhlmann 2013: 173–5.
8. For example, in the last two decades, there has been extensive research on the question of how the subject drives a car while speaking on a mobile telephone, see, for example Strayer and Johnston 2001; Treffner and Barrett 2004; Charlton 2009.
9. *Rough for Theatre II*, to be specific.

Chapter 4

1. The question here becomes one of the procedure by which these perceptual decisions are made. Who (or what) decides what is potentially meaningful or useful? In experimental psychology, there has been the suggestion that certain stimuli (the sound of one's own name, a smiling face or a stick figure, for example) are particularly likely to capture the attention of humans (Mack and Rock 1998: 155). This might be interpreted to suggest that certain biological mechanisms trigger humans to notice some stimuli over others. This, though, does not explain differences between individuals. Why do some individuals fail to register objects or events that are highly salient to others?
2. The details of the beating that Conley seems to have missed are in themselves sickening. Lehr gives Michael Cox's account of how, as he climbed a fence in pursuit of the assailant, he was pulled down and struck in the head repeatedly (Lehr 2009: 134). Then, as he was 'down on all fours wobbly like a dog on its last legs' he saw 'a cop, a white cop' (134). He raised his head to get a better look only for a boot to come down 'flush into his face' and this was followed by a series of blows from all directions (134). The beaters subsequently ran away on discovering that Cox was a police officer, leaving him, in Cox's words, 'like an animal to die, you know on the side of the highway' (195). Not only this, but there was a deliberate effort to cover up the event. As mentioned, there was an initial claim that Cox had slipped on the

ice but, even after the nature of the beating became clear, potential witnesses refused to cooperate and Cox experienced intimidation (slashed tyres, threatening phone calls) when he sought justice (194). Cox, himself, was certain that his treatment was racially motivated. Speaking of why he was left for dead after the beating, he states: 'They were able to leave me because they thought less of me because of what I am. ... It wouldn't have happened if I were white' (195).

3 Indeed, as critics such as Robert Eaglestone (2004) have convincingly argued, the events of the twentieth century (most particularly the Holocaust) problematized the notion of representing 'what happened' through conventional historical narrative.
4 Janet is name-checked in Beckett's notes from Woodworth (Feldman 2004: 319).
5 For Jung the 'collective unconscious' is made up of contents that are characterized by mythological motifs – for example 'the Hero, the Redeemer, the Dragon' (1968: 40–1). They are not peculiar to any one mind but to mankind in general.
6 By loss, here, one might mean the death of a loved one, but also any experience in which the subject feels a loss of care, for example, when an elder child feels that a parent cares less for them upon the birth of a younger sibling.
7 Winnicott's distinction derives from Melanie Klein's separation of fantasy from phantasy, but his discussion is something of a departure from Klein's. For Klein fantasying is akin to conscious daydreaming and phantasying is quite a broad term that covers most unconscious thought (Spillius 2001: 364). Winnicott's distinction is slightly different as both fantasy and imagination can be either conscious or unconscious. The two processes are instead distinguished by their utility for the individual.

Chapter 5

1 Here James is targeting the 'ridiculous theory of Hume and Berkeley that we can have no images but of perfectly definite things' (254).
2 I use Woodworth, here, not only because he was the source of the majority of Beckett's knowledge of experimental psychology but also because he is still considered a key authority on the subject of imageless thought. Waller et al., for example, cite Woodworth's summary of the imageless thought controversy in their review of image research.
3 Beckett evidently knew Coleridge's work, though it is difficult to know how thoroughly he engaged with it. In a 1962 letter to Mary Hutchinson, for example, Beckett stated that he had recently read *Biographia Literaria* 'without much pleasure' (Van Hulle and Nixon 2013: 35).
4 The existing critical literature shows divergent opinion on Beckett's relationship with the Romantic imagination. In the earlier criticism – Knowlson and Pilling (1979);

Kearney ([1988] 2003) – there was a tendency to stress the degree to which Beckett was writing against Romantic conceptions of the imagination. Later critics such as Michael Rodriguez (2007), on the other hand, have aligned Beckett's approach to the imagination with that of the Romantics. What we might say with some certainty is that Beckett had a conflicted relationship with the Romantic imagination and Romanticism in general. He may not have necessarily liked the Romantics, but he was undoubtedly influenced by them. As Mark Nixon puts it, 'Whether he wanted to or not, Beckett's own temperament opened his work up to Romantic influences' (Nixon 2007: 73).

5 The extent to which later works such as the Trilogy depart from Proustian ideas about memory has been debated. Nicholas Zurbrugg (1988), for example, has argued that Beckett departs from Proustian ideas in later works while James H. Reid (2003) has argued for a close relationship.

6 Richardson states that 'no account of Romantic subjectivity can be complete without noting how contemporary understandings of psychology were either grounded in, deeply marked by, or tacitly (when not explicitly) opposed to the brain-based models of mind being developed concurrently in the medical sciences' (2001: 2).

7 Beckett also seems to have been keen to point out the religious significance of the images that are produced in the play, telling cameraman Jim Lewis, for example, that the cloth used to mop the head of B 'alluded to the veil that Veronica used to wipe the brow of Jesus on the Way of the Cross' (Knowlson 1996: 682).

8 In the case of Coleridge, there is also a question of whether the subject is asleep. The 1816 preface to the poem mentions a 'profound sleep' but in the 'Crewe' manuscript, Coleridge is described to be in 'a sort of Reverie' (Hill 1978: 150).

Chapter 6

1 Some recent criticism has argued that *Hamlet* shows Shakespeare's interest in the process of perception. Raphael Lyne, for example, reads 'the second ghost scene in Hamlet as an experiment in social cognition' (Lyne 2014: 79). However, as Lyne acknowledges, much more criticism has focused on the element of the supernatural and how Shakespeare is working within a tradition in which the 'theatre is a medium for explicit questioning about the existence of ghosts' (91).

2 Here, penitent heretics were confined to narrow single-person cells and frequently chained to the walls (Haskins 1902: 647; Peters 1998: 26).

3 The influence of the Pennsylvania system can still be seen in contemporary penal systems. For example, the 'supermax' prisons that are now found across the world employ many of the same methods (Jewkes 2015: 20).

4 As well as phenomenologists such as Merleau-Ponty, here, Beckett's method resembles that of John C. Lilly, the inventor of the Tank Isolation Technique. This

technique (now commonly used for both therapeutic and recreational purposes) saw individuals inhabit a darkened, sound-proof tank filled with a solution of Epsom salts and water, allowing 'the body to float supine, with head, arms, legs and trunk at the surface' (Lilly 1977: 17). The aim of this bodily relaxation is a kind of mental exploration in which individuals frequently report pseudo-sensory experience.

5 These methods were also deployed by the US military at Guantanamo Bay (Koenig 2015).
6 The work was funded by the CIA through a cover organization named the Society for the Investigation of Human Ecology (Raz 2013: 383).
7 In this reading, Beckett is addressing the relationship between an author and the figures that he or she devises. By this account, the author is attempting to put thoughts and memories into the head of the entities that they write into being.
8 Sartre never directly refers to Perky but quotes Titchener's account of her experiment.
9 The imagery experienced just before one goes to sleep.
10 Kosslyn, here, was responding directly to one specific philosophical work: Zenon Pylyshyn's 1973 article 'What the Mind's Eye Tells the Mind's Brain: A Critique of Mental Imagery'.

Bibliography

Adams, H. F. (1912), 'Autokinetic Sensations', *The Psychological Monographs*, 14 (2): i–44.
Anderson, R. C. (1978), 'Schema-Directed Processes in Language Comprehension', in A. S. Lesgold, J. W. Pellegrino, S. D. Fokkema and R. Glaser (eds), *Cognitive Psychology and Instruction*, 67–82, New York: Plenum.
Anzieu, D. (1994), 'Beckett and the Psychoanalyst', trans. T. Cousineaux, *Journal of Beckett Studies*, 4 (1): 163–9.
Armstrong, T. (1998), *Modernism Technology and the Body: A Cultural Study*, Cambridge: Cambridge University.
Asmus, W. (1977), 'Practical Aspects of Theatre, Radio, and Television: Rehearsal Notes for the German Premiere of Beckett's "That Time" and "Footfalls" at the Schiller Theater Werkstatt, Berlin', *Journal of Beckett Studies*, 2: 82–95.
Asmus, W., A. Uhlmann and B. Denham, (2013), [Video] *What Where: Film and Documentary*, Sydney: Writing and Society Research Centre.
Badham, V. (2015), 'Not I Footfalls Rockaby Review - A Technical Masterclass in Beckett', *The Guardian*, 18 February. Available online: https://www.theguardian.com/culture/2015/feb/19/not-i-footfalls-rockaby-review-a-technical-masterclass-in-beckett (accessed 23 April 2019).
Baker, P. (1997), *Beckett and the Mythology of Psychoanalysis*, London: Palgrave Macmillan.
Beckett, S. ([1938] 2009c), *Murphy*, ed. J. C. C. Mays, London: Faber.
Beckett, S. ([1953] 2009e), *Watt*, ed. C. Ackerley, London: Faber.
Beckett, S. ([1964] 2009b), *How It Is*, ed. E. M. O'Reilly, London: Faber.
Beckett, S. (1983), *Disjecta: Miscellaneous Writings and a Dramatic Fragment*, ed. R. Cohn, London: Calder.
Beckett, S. ([1986] 2006), *The Complete Dramatic Works*, London: Faber.
Beckett, S. (1995), *The Complete Short Prose, 1929-1989*, ed. S. E. Gontarski, New York: Grove.
Beckett, S. (1999), *Proust and Three Dialogues with George Duthuit*, London: Calder.
Beckett, S. (2000), *First Love and Other Novellas*, ed. G. Dukes, London: Penguin.
Beckett, S. (2009a), *Company etc.*, ed. D. Van Hulle, London: Faber.
Beckett, S. (2009d), *Three Novels: Molloy, Malone Dies, The Unnamable*, New York: Grove.
Beckett, S. (2010), *More Pricks than Kicks*, ed. C. Nelson, London: Faber.
Berman, M. (1983), *All That is Solid Melts into Air: The Experience of Modernity*, London: Verso.

Bignell, J. (2009), *Beckett on Screen: The Television Plays*, Manchester: Manchester University.

Billington, M. (1973), 'Not I Review', *The Guardian*, 17 January.

Billington, M. (2015), 'Not I, Footfalls, Rockaby Review – Lisa Dwan's Breathtaking Beckett Trio', *The Guardian*, 3 June. Available online: https://www.theguardian.com/stage/2015/jun/03/not-i-footfalls-rockaby-review-lisa-dwan-samuel-beckett (accessed 23 April 2019).

Bion, W. (1990), *Brazilian Lectures*, London: Kernac.

Bleuler, E. ([1911] 1950), *Dementia Praecox; or, The Group of Schizophrenias*, Madison: International Universities.

Bott Spillius, E. (2001), 'Freud and Klein on the Concept of Phantasy', *The International Journal of Psychoanalysis*, 82: 361–73.

Brater, E. (1985), 'Toward a Poetics of Television Technology: Beckett's "Nacht und Träume" and "Quad"', *Modern Drama*, 28: 148–54.

Bray, J., A. Gibbons and B. McHale, eds (2012), 'Introduction', in *The Routledge Companion to Experimental Literature*, London: Routledge.

Breuer, H. (2006), 'Samuel Beckett and Experimental Psychology', *English Studies*, 87 (3): 303–18.

Broadbent, D. (1958), *Perception and Communication*, London: Pergamon.

Bruner, J. (2004), 'A Short History of Psychological Theories of Learning', *Daedalus*, 133 (1): 13–20.

Bürger, P. (1984), *Theory of the Avant-Garde*, trans. Michael Snow, Manchester: Manchester University.

Cameron, D. E. (1957), 'Psychic Driving: Dynamic Implant', *Psychiatric Quarterly*, 31: 703–12.

Campbell, J. (2005), 'The Entrapment of the Female Body in Beckett's Plays in Relation to Jung's Third Tavistock Lecture', *Samuel Beckett Today/Aujourd'hui*, 15: 161–72.

Carroll, D. (2017), *Purpose and Cognition: Edward Tolman and the Transformation of American Psychology*, Cambridge: Cambridge University.

Caruth, C. (1996), *Unclaimed Experience: Trauma, Narrative and History*, Baltimore: John Hopkins University.

Carville, C. (2015), 'Petrified in Radiance: Beckett, Dutch Painting and the Art of Absorption', *Samuel Beckett Today/Aujourd'hui*, 27: 73–86.

Chabris, C. F., A. Weinberger, M. Fontaine and D. J. Simons (2011), 'You do not Talk about Fight Club If You do not Notice Fight Club: Inattentional Blindness for a Simulated Real-World Assault', *i-Perception*, 2: 150–3. Available online: https://www.ncbi.nlm.nih.gov/pmc/articles/PMC3485775/ (accessed 22 April 2015).

Charlton, S. G. (2009), 'Driving while Conversing: Cell Phones that Distract and Passengers Who React', *Accident Analysis and Prevention*, 44: 160–73.

Chekhov, M. ([1953] 2002), *To the Actor*, London: Routledge.

Cohn, R. (1980), *Just Play: Beckett's Theater*, Princeton: Princeton University.

Coleridge, S. T. ([1817] 1927), *Biographia Literaria*, London: J.M. Dent.

Connor, S. (1988), *Samuel Beckett: Repetition, Theory and Text*, Oxford: Basil Blackwell.
Connor, S. (1992), 'Between Theatre and Theory: *Long Observation of the Ray*', in J. Pilling and M. Bryden (eds), *The Ideal Core of the Onion*, 79–98, Reading: Beckett International Foundation.
Connor, S. (2014), *Beckett, Modernism and the Material Imagination*, Cambridge: Cambridge University.
Craig, G., M. D. Fehsenfeld, D. Gunn and L. M. Overbeck, eds (2014), *The Letters of Samuel Beckett: Volume 3 1957–1965*, Cambridge: Cambridge University.
Crary, J. (1999), *Suspensions of Perception: Attention, Spectacle and Modern Culture*, London: MIT.
Deleuze, G. (1995), 'The Exhausted', trans. Anthony Uhlmann, *SubStance*, 24 (3): 3–28.
Deleuze, G. and F. Guattari ([1980] 2004), *A Thousand Plateaus: Capitalism and Schizophrenia*, trans. Brian Massumi, London: Continuum.
Del Valle, A. (2007), '"Act Without Words" Makes Beckett Accessible', *Las Vegas Review Journal*, 4 December. Available online: https://www.reviewjournal.com/life/act-without-words-makes-beckett-accessible/ (accessed 18 April 2019).
Didi-Huberman, G. ([1982] 2003), *The Invention of Hysteria: Charcot and the Photographic Iconography of the Salpêtrière*, trans. A. Hartz, Cambridge: MIT.
Downey, J. E. (1911), *Imaginal Reaction to Poetry*, Laramie: The Laramie Republican Company.
Downey, J. E. ([1929] 1999), *Creative Imagination: Studies in the Psychology of Literature*, London: Routledge.
Driver, J. (2001), 'A Selective Review of Selective Attention', *British Journal of Psychology*, 92: 53–78.
Eaglestone, R. (2004), *The Holocaust and the Postmodern*, New York: Oxford University.
Ekman, P. (2015a), 'Micro Expressions'. Available online: http://www.paulekman.com/micro-expressions/ (accessed 22 April 2015).
Ekman, P. (2015b), 'Micro Expressions Training Tools'. Available online: https://www.paulekman.com/micro-expressions-training-tools/ (accessed 22 April 2015).
Eskelund, K., E. MacDonald and T. S. Andersen (2015), 'Face Configuration Affects Speech Perception: Evidence from a McGurk Mismatch Negativity Study', *Neurospsychologia* 66: 48–54.
Feldman, M. (2004), 'Sourcing "Aporetics": An Empirical Study on Philosophical Influences in the Development of Samuel Beckett's Writing', PhD diss., Oxford Brookes University, Oxford.
Feldman, M. (2006), *Beckett's Books: A Cultural History of Beckett's Interwar Notes*, London: Continuum.
Ferreira, F., K. G. D. Bailey and V. Ferraro (2002), 'Good-Enough Representations in Language Comprehension, Current Directions', *Psychological Science*, 11 (1): 11–5.
Fifield, P. (2013), *Late Modernist Style in Samuel Beckett and Emmanuel Levinas*, Basingstoke: Palgrave Macmillan.
Fletcher, J. (1967), *Samuel Beckett's Art*, London: Chatto and Windus.

Frank, M. C., D. Amso and S. P. Johnson (2014), 'Visual Search and Attention to Faces in Early Infancy', *Journal of Experimental Child Psychology*, 118: 13–24.
Freud, S. (1933), *Collected Papers Volume 2*. trans. Joan Riviere, London: Hogarth.
Gardner, C. (2012), *Beckett, Deleuze and the Televisual Event: Peephole Art*, London: Palgrave McMillan.
Gardner, L. (2013), 'Not I- Review', *The Guardian*, 22 May. Available online: https://www.theguardian.com/stage/2013/may/22/not-i-review (accessed 23 April 2019).
Gardner, L. (2014), 'Not I/Footfalls/Rockaby—Review', *The Guardian*, 14 January. Available online: https://www.theguardian.com/stage/2014/jan/14/not-i-footfalls-rockaby-review (accessed 23 April 2019).
Gardner, S. (1999), 'Schopenhauer, Will, and the Unconscious', in C. Janway (ed.), *The Cambridge Companion to Schopenhauer*, 375–421, Cambridge: Cambridge University.
Garner Jr, S. B. (1994), *Bodied Spaces: Phenomenology and Performance in Contemporary Drama*, Ithaca: Cornell University.
Genosko, G. (2002), *Félix Guattari: An Aberrant Introduction*, London: Continuum.
Giliman, S. (1993), 'The Image of the Hysteric', in S. Gilman, H. King, R. Porter, G. S. Rousseau and E. Showalter, *Hysterial Beyond Freud*, 345–452, Berkelely: California University.
Gontarski, S. E. (1985), *The Intent of Undoing in Samuel Beckett's Dramatic Texts*, Bloomington: Indiana University.
Gontarski, S. E. (2006), 'Viva, Sam Beckett, or Flogging the Avant-Garde', *Journal of Beckett Studies*, 16 (1–2): 1–11.
Gontarski, S. E. (2014), 'Literary Allusions in Happy Days', in S. E. Gontarski (ed.), *On Beckett: Essays and Criticism*, 232–44, London: Anthem.
Gontarski, S. E. (2017), *Beckett Matters: Essays on Beckett's Late Modernism*, Edinburgh: Edinburgh University.
Greenblatt, S. (2004), *Will in the World: How Shakespeare Became Shakespeare*, London: Cape.
Gupta, R. K. (1975), 'Freud and Schopenhauer', *Journal of the History of Ideas*, 36 (4): 721–8.
Hamlyn, D. W. (1988), 'Schopenhauer and Freud', *Revue Internationale de Philosophie*, 42: 5–17.
Harmon, M., ed. (1998), *No Author Better Served: The Correspondence of Samuel Beckett & Alan Schneider*, London: Harvard University.
Hartley, L. (2001), *Physiognomy and the Meaning of Expression in Nineteenth-Century Culture*, Cambridge: Cambridge University.
Hartsuiker, R. J. and H. H. J. Kolk (2001), 'Error Monitoring in Speech Production: A Computational Test of the Perceptual Loop Theory', *Cognitive Psychology*, 42: 113–57.
Harvey, L. (1970), *Samuel Beckett: Poet and Critic*, Princeton: Princeton University.

Haskins, C. H. (1902), 'Robert Le Bougre and the Beginnings of the Inquisition in Northern France', *The American Historical Review*, 7 (3): 437–57.

Heinrichs, W. R. (2001), *In Search of Madness: Schizophrenia and Neuroscience*, Oxford: Oxford University.

Henry, M. (1993), *The Genealogy of Psychoanalysis*, trans. Douglas Brick, Stanford: Stanford University.

Heron, J. and M. Broome (2016), *Journal of Medical Humanities*, 37 (2): 171–81.

Herren, G. (2007), *Samuel Beckett's Plays on Film and Television*, London: Palgrave Macmillan.

Hill, J. S., ed. (1978), *Imagination in Coleridge*, London: Macmillan.

Hill, L. (1990), *Beckett's Fiction in Different Words*, Cambridge: Cambridge University.

Hochschild, A. R. (1983), *The Managed Heart: The Commercialization of Human Feeling*, Berkeley: University of California.

Holt, R. R. (1964), 'Imagery: The Return of the Ostracized', *American Psychologist*, 19: 254–64.

Houppermans, S., M. Buning and L. Butler, eds (1996), 'Introduction', *Samuel Beckett Today/Aujourd'hui*, 5: 1–7.

Houston Jones, D. (2018), 'Insignificant Residues: Trauma, Face and Figure in Samuel Beckett', in T. Tajiri Y, M. Tanaka and M. Tsushima (eds), *Samuel Beckett and Trauma*, 71–93, Manchester: Manchester University.

Hulle, D. V. (2007), '"Accursed Creator": Beckett, Romanticism, and the Modern Prometheus', *Samuel Beckett Today/Aujourd'hui*, 18: 15–29.

Hulle, D. V. (2014), *Modern Manuscripts: The Extended Mind and Creative Undoing from Darwin to Beckett and Beyond*, London: Bloomsbury.

Hulle, D. V. and M. Nixon (2013), *Samuel Beckett's Library*, Cambridge: Cambridge University.

Hurlburt, R. and E. Schwitzgebel (2007), *Describing Inner Experience: Proponent Meets Skeptic*, Cambridge: MIT.

James, W. (1890), *Principles of Psychology*, London: MacMillan.

James, W. ([1909] 2008), *Essays in Radical Empiricism*, New York: Cosimo.

Jameson, F. (1991), *Postmodernism: or the Cultural Logic of Late Capitalism*, Durham: Duke University.

Janaway, C. (2010), 'The Real Essence of Human Beings: Schopenhauer and the Unconscious Will', in A. Nicholls and M. Liebscher (eds), *Thinking the Unconscious: Nineteenth-Century German Thought*, 140–55, Cambridge: Cambridge University.

Jewkes, Y. (2015), 'Fear-suffused Hell-holes: The Architecture of Extreme Punishment', in K. Reiter and A. Koenig (eds), *Extreme Punishment: Comparative Studies in Detention Incarceration and Solitary Confinement*, 14–31, New York: Palgrave Macmillan.

Johnson, B. S. (1973), *Aren't You Rather Young to be Writing Your Memoirs?*, London: Hutchinson.

Johnson, B. S. (2013), *Well done God!: Selected Prose and Drama of B.S. Johnson*, ed. J. Coe, P. Tew and J. Jordan, London: Picador.

Jones, C. (2014), *The Smile Revolution in Eighteenth Century Paris*, Oxford: Oxford University.

Joyce, J. ([1916] 2000), *A Portrait of the Artist as a Young Man*, ed. J. Johnson, Oxford: Oxford University.

Jung, C. G. (1968), *Analytical Psychology Its Theory and Practice: The Tavistock Lectures*, London: Routledge and Kegan Paul.

Kahneman, D. (2011), *Thinking Fast and Slow*, London: Penguin.

Kearney, R. ([1988] 2003), *The Wake of Imagination*, London: Taylor and Francis.

Keltner, D. and P. Ekman (2000), 'Facial Expression of Emotion', in M. Lewis and J. H. Jones (eds), *The Handbook of Emotions*, 151–249, New York: Guildford.

Kennedy, S. (2009), 'Introduction: Beckett in History, Memory, Archive', in S. Kennedy and K. Weiss (eds), *Samuel Beckett: History, Memory, Archive*, 1–10, New York: Palgrave Macmillan.

Kenner, H. (1959), 'The Cartesian Centaur', *Perspective*, 11: 132–41.

Kern, S. ([1983] 2003), *The Culture of Time and Space: 1880–1918*, London: Harvard University.

Kim, R. (2010), *Women and Ireland as Beckett's Lost Others*, Basingstoke: Palgrave Macmillan.

Kittler, F. ([1985] 1990), *Discourse Networks: 1800/1900*, trans. M. Metteer and C. Cullens, Stanford: Stanford University.

Knowlson, J. (1978), 'Practical Aspects of Theatre, Radio and Television: Extracts from an Unscripted Interview with Billie Whitelaw', *Journal of Beckett Studies*, 3: 85–90.

Knowlson, J. (1983), '"Beckett's 'Bits of Pipe'"', in M. Beja, S. E. Gontarski and P. A. G. Astier (eds), *Samuel Beckett: Humanistic Perspectives*, 16–25, Columbus: Ohio University.

Knowlson, J., ed. (1985), *Happy Days: Samuel Beckett's Production Notebook*, London: Faber.

Knowlson, J. (1996), *Damned to Fame: The Life of Samuel Beckett*, London: Bloomsbury.

Knowlson, J. (1997), *Images of Beckett*, Cambridge: Cambridge University.

Knowlson, J. and J. Pilling (1979), *Frescoes of the Skull*, London: John Calder.

Koenig, A. (2015), 'From Man to Beast: Social Death at Guantánamo', in K. Reiter and A. Koenig (eds), *Extreme Punishment: Comparative Studies in Detention, Incarceration and Solitary Confinement*, 220–41, New York: Palgrave Macmillan.

Kosslyn, S. (1975), 'Information Representation in Visual Images', *Cognitive Psychology*, 7 (3): 341–70.

Kroll, J. and B. Bachrach (1982), 'Visions and Psychopathology in the Middle Ages', *Journal of Nervous and Mental Disease*, 170 (1): 141–9.

Lane, A. (2014), 'Chatterbox', *The New Yorker*, 29 September. Available online: https://www.newyorker.com/magazine/2014/09/29/chatterbox (accessed 25 April 2019).

Lehr, D. (2009), *The Fence: A Police Cover-Up Along Boston's Racial Divide*, New York: Harper.

Levelt, W. J. M. (1983), 'Monitoring and Self-repair in Speech', *Cognition*, 14: 41–104.

Levelt, W. J. M. (1989), *Speaking: From Intention to Articulation*, Cambridge: MIT.
Levinas, E. ([1961] 2013), *Totality and Infinity: An Essay on Exteriority*, trans. Alphonso Lingis, Pittsburgh: Duquesne University.
Lilly, J. C. (1977), *The Deep Self: Profound Relaxation and the Tank Isolation Technique*, New York: Simon and Schuster.
Lloyd, D. (2011), *Irish Culture and Colonial Modernity 1800–2000: The Transformation of Oral Space*, Cambridge: Cambridge University.
Luckhurst, R. (2008), *The Trauma Question*, London: Routledge.
Lyne, R. (2014), 'Shakespeare, Perception and Theory of Mind', *Paragraph*, 37 (1): 79–95.
Mack, A. and I. Rock (1998), *Inattentional Blindness*, Cambridge: MIT.
Maier, F. M. and A. Moorjani (2007), 'Two Versions of "Nacht und Träume": What Franz Schubert Tells Us about a Favourite Song of Beckett', *Samuel Beckett Today/Aujourd'hui*, 18: 91–100.
Marslen-Wilson, W. D. (1973), 'Speech Shadowing at Very Short Latencies', *Nature*, 244: 522–3.
Martin, J. (2014), 'Review: Not I/ Footfalls/ Rockaby – Duchess Theatre, London', *The Irish Times*, 2 February. Available online: http://irishpost.co.uk/footfalls-rockaby/ (accessed 3 July 2016).
Maude, U. (2009), *Beckett, Technology and the Body*, Cambridge: Cambridge University.
Maude, U. (2013), 'Pavlov's Dogs and Other Animals in Samuel Beckett', in M. Bryden (ed.), *Beckett and Animals*, 82–94, Cambridge: Cambridge University.
Maude, U. and M. Feldman (2009), *Beckett and Phenomenology*, London: Continuum.
McCarthy-Jones, S. (2012), *Hearing Voices: The Histories, Causes and Meanings of Auditory Verbal Hallucinations*, Cambridge: Cambridge University.
McGurk, H. and J. MacDonald (1976), 'Hearing Lips and Seeing Voices', *Nature*, 264: 746–8.
McMullan, A. (2010), *Performing Embodiment in Samuel Beckett's Drama*, New York: Routledge.
McNaughton, J. (2009), 'Beckett's "Brilliant Obscurantics": "Watt" and the Problem of Propaganda', in S. Kennedy and K. Weiss (eds), *Samuel Beckett: History, Memory, Archive*, 47–70, New York: Palgrave Macmillan.
Melynyk, D. (2005), 'Never Been Properly Jung', *Samuel Beckett Today/Aujourd'hui*, 15: 355–62.
Merleau-Ponty, M. ([1945] 2002), *Phenomenology of Perception*, trans. C. Smith, London: Routledge.
Meyer, S. (2001), *Irresistible Dictation: Gertrude Stein and the Correlations of Writing and Science*, Stanford: Stanford University.
Moore, C. M. (2001), 'Inattentional Blindness: Perception or Memory and What Does It Matter?', *Psyche*, 7 (2): 178–94.
Moorjani, A. (2004), 'Beckett and Psychoanalysis', in L. Oppenheim (ed.), *Palgrave Advances in Beckett Studies*, 174–94, Basingstoke: Palgrave Macmillan.

Moray, N. (1959), 'Attention in Dichotic Listening: Affective Cues and the Influence of Instructions', *Quarterly Journal of Experimental Psychology*, 11 (1): 56–60.

Murphy, P. J. (1990), *Reconstructing Beckett: Language for Being in Samuel Beckett's Fiction*, Toronto: Toronto University.

Murphy, P. J. (2016), 'Saint Samuel (á) Beckett's Big Toe: Incorporating Beckett in Popular Culture', in P. J. Murphy and N. Pawliuk (eds), *Beckett in Popular Culture: Essays on a Postmodern Icon*, Jefferson: McFarland and Company.

Neisser, U. and R. Becklen (1975), 'Selective Looking: Attending to Visually Specified Events', *Cognitive Psychology*, 7 (4): 480–94.

Ngai, S. (2012), *Our Aesthetic Categories: Zany, Cute, Interesting*, London: Harvard University.

Nixon, M. (2007), 'Beckett and Romanticism in the 1930s', *Samuel Beckett Today/Aujourd'hui*, 18: 61–76.

Nixon, M. (2009), 'Between Gospel and Prohibition: Beckett in Nazi German 1936–1937', in S. Kennedy and K. Weiss (eds), *Samuel Beckett: History, Memory*, 31–46, New York: Palgrave Macmillan.

Nixon, M. (2011), *Samuel Beckett's German Diaries: 1936–1937*, London: Bloomsbury.

Nugent-Folan, G. (2015), 'Personal Apperception: Samuel Beckett, Gertrude Stein, and Paul Cézanne's La Montagne Sainte-Victoire', *Samuel Beckett Today/Aujourd hui*, 27 (1): 87–101.

O'Hara, J. D. (1997), *Samuel Beckett's Hidden Drives: Structural Uses of Depth Psychology*, Gainesville: University of Florida.

Olney, J. (1998), *Memory and Narrative: The Weave of Life Writing*, Chicago: University of Chicago.

Oppenheim, L. (1994), *Directing Beckett*, Detroit: University of Michigan, Oxford English Dictionary. Available online: http://www.oed.com/ (accessed 24 April 2019).

Pearl, S. (2010), *About Faces: Physiognomy in Nineteenth-Century Britain*, Cambridge: Harvard University.

Pearson, J., T. Naselaris, E. Holmes and S. Kosslyn (2015), 'Mental Imagery: Functional Mechanisms and Clinical Applications', *Trends in Cognitive Sciences*, 19 (10): 590–602.

Perky, C. W. (1910), 'An Experimental Study of Imagination', *American Journal of Psychology*, 21: 422–52.

Perloff, M. (2006), 'Avant-Garde Tradition and Individual Talent: The Case of Language Poetry', *Revue française d'études américaines*, 103 (1): 117–41.

Peters, E. M. (1998), 'Prison before the Prison: The Ancient and Medieval Worlds', in N. Morris and D. J. Rothman (eds), *The Oxford History of the Prison*, 3–43, Oxford: Oxford University.

Piette, A. (1993), 'Beckett, Early Psychology and Memory Loss: Beckett's Reading of Clarapède, Janet and Korsakof', *Samuel Beckett Today/Aujourd'hui*, 2: 41–8.

Piette, A. (2016a), 'Lobotomies and Botulism Bombs: Beckett's Trilogy and the Cold War', *Journal of Medical Humanities*, 37 (2): 161–9.

Piette, A. (2016b), 'Torture, Text, Human Rights: Beckett's *Comment C'est/How It Is* and the Algerian War', in A. Hepburn (ed.), *Around 1945: Literature, Citizenship, Rights*, 151–74, Chicago: McGill-Queens University.

Pilling, J. (1978), 'Beckett in Manhattan', *Journal of Beckett Studies*, 3: 127–8.

Pylyshyn, Z. W. (1973), 'What the Mind's Eye Tells the Mind's Brain: A Critique of Mental Imagery', *Psychological Bulletin*, 80 (1): 1–24.

Rabaté, J. (1984), *Beckett avant Beckett*, Paris: Accents.

Rabinovitz, R. (1992), *Innovation in Samuel Beckett's Fiction*, Chicago: University of Illinois.

Raz, M. (2013), 'Alone Again: John Zubek and the Troubled History of Sensory Deprivation Research', *Journal of the History of the Behavioral Sciences*, 49 (4): 379–95.

Reid, J. H. (2003), *Proust, Beckett, and Narration*, Cambridge: Cambridge University.

Richardson, A. (1969), *Mental Imagery*, London: Routledge.

Richardson, A. (2001), *British Romanticism and the Science of the Mind*, Cambridge: Cambridge University.

Rodriguez, M. A. (2007), '"Romantic Agony": Fancy and Imagination in Samuel Beckett's "All Strange Away"', *Samuel Beckett Today/Aujourd'hui*, 18: 131–42.

Rollins, H. E., ed. (1958), *The Letters of John Keats*, Cambridge: Cambridge University.

Ross, C. (2011), *Beckett's Art of Absence: Rethinking the Void*, London: Palgrave Macmillan.

Ruskin, J. (1868), *The Political Economy of Art*, London: Smith & Elder.

Russell, C. (1989), 'The Figure in the Monitor: Beckett, Lacan, and Video', *Cinema Journal*, 28 (4): 20–37.

Ryan, J. (1991), *The Vanishing Subject: Early Psychology and Literary Modernism*, Chicago: University of Chicago.

Rylance, R. (2000), *Victorian Psychology and British Culture: 1850–1880*, New York: Oxford University.

Ryle, G. ([1949] 2009), *The Concept of Mind*, Abingdon: Routledge.

Salisbury, L. (2010), 'The Art of Noise: Beckett's Language in a Culture of Information', *Samuel Beckett Today/Aujourd'hui*, 22: 355–73.

Salisbury, L. (2011), 'Bulimic Beckett: Food for Thought and the Archive of Analysis', *Critical Quarterly*, 53 (3): 60–80.

Salisbury, L. (2012), *Samuel Beckett: Laughing Matters, Comic Timing*, Edinburgh: Edinburgh University.

Salisbury, L. (2014), 'Gloria SMH and Beckett's Linguistic Encryptions', in S. E. Gontarski (ed.), *The Edinburgh Companion to Samuel Beckett and the Arts*, 153–69, Edinburgh: Edinburgh University.

Salisbury, L. and C. Code (2014), 'Jackson's Parrot: Samuel Beckett, Aphasic Speech Automatisms and Psychosomatic Language', in C. Eagle (ed.), *Literature, Speech Disorders and Disability: Talking Normal*, 100–23, New York: Routledge.

Sartre, J. P. ([1936] 2012), *The Imagination*, trans. K. Williford and D. Rudrauf, New York: Routledge.
Sartre, J. P. ([1940] 2010), *The Imaginary*, trans. J. Webber, New York: Routledge.
Schivelbusch, W. (1986), *The Railway Journey: The Industrialization of Time and Space in the Nineteenth Century*, New York: Berg.
Schopenhauer, A. ([1844] 1966), *The World as Will and Representation*, vol. 2, 2nd edn, trans. E. F. J. Payne, New York: Dover.
Scripture, E. W. (1896), 'Measuring Hallucinations', *Science* 3 (73): 762–3.
Searles, H. F. (1984–5), 'The Role of the Analyst's Facial Expressions in Psychoanalysis and Psychotherapy', *The International Journal of Psychoanalysis and Psychotherapy*, 10: 47–73.
Segal, J. (2004), *Melanie Klein*, London: Sage.
Segal, S. J. and M. Glicksman (1967), 'Relaxation and the Perky Effect: The Influence of Body Position on Judgments of Imagery', *The American Journal of Psychology*, 80 (2): 257–62.
Segal, S. J. and S. Nathan (1964), 'The Perky Effect: The Incorporation of an External Stimulus into an Imagery Experience under Placebo and Controlled Conditions', *Perceptual and Motor Skills*, 18: 385–95.
Shakespeare, W. ([1599–1602] 2016), *The Tragedy of Hamlet Prince of Denmark*, ed. B. A. Mowat and P. Westine, Washington DC: Folger. Available online: http://www.folgerdigitaltexts.org/html/Ham.html (accessed 25 March 2016).
Shallice, T. (1972), 'The Ulster Depth Interrogation Techniques and their Relation to Sensory Deprivation Research', *Cognition*, 1 (4): 385–405.
Shallice, T. and R. P. Cooper (2011), *The Organisation of Mind*, Oxford: Oxford University.
Shapiro, B. (1969), 'Toward a Psycho-analytic Reading of Beckett's *Molloy*', *Literature and Psychology*, 19 (2): 71–86.
Shaviro, S. (1993), *The Cinematic Body*, Minneapolis: University of Minnesota.
Shelley, P. B. (2009), *A Defence of Poetry and Other Essays*, Oxford: Oxford University.
Sherif, M. (1935), 'A Study of Some Social Factors in Perception', *Archives of Psychology*, 187: 1–60.
Shilling, J. (2013), 'Not I, Royal Court Theatre, Review', *The Daily Telegraph*, 22 May. Available online: https://www.telegraph.co.uk/culture/theatre/theatre-reviews/10073404/Not-I-Royal-Court-Theatre-review.html (accessed 24 April 2019).
Simons, D. J. and C. F. Chabris (1999), 'Gorillas in our Midst: Sustained Inattentional Blindness for Dynamic Events', *Perception*, 28 (9): 1059–74.
Skinner, B. F. (1934), 'Has Gertrude Stein a Secret?' *The Atlantic Monthly*, January: 50–7.
Smith, P. S. (2006), 'The Effects of Solitary Confinement on Prison Inmates: A Brief History and Review of the Literature', *Crime and Justice*, 34: 441–528.
Smith, P. S. (2008), '"Degenerate Criminals": Mental Health and Psychiatric Studies of Danish Prisoners in Solitary Confinement 1870–1920', *Criminal Justice and Behaviour*, 35 (8): 1048–64.

Soldz, S. (2008), 'Healers or Interrogators: Psychology and the United States Torture Regime', *Psychoanalytic Dialogues*, 18: 592–613.

Solomons, L. M. and G. Stein (1896), 'Normal Motor Automatism', *Psychological Review*, 3 (5): 492–512.

Speckens, A., E. M. Anke Ehlers, A. Hackman, F. A. Ruths and D. M. Clark (2007), 'Intrusive Memories and Rumination in Patients with Post-Traumatic Stress Disorder: A Phenomenological Comparison', *Memory*, 15 (3): 249–57.

Spelke, E., W. Hirst and U. Neisser (1976), 'Skills of Divided Attention', *Cognition*, 4: 215–30.

Spencer, C. (2014), 'Not I, Footfalls, Rockaby by Samuel Beckett, Royal Court Review', *The Daily Telegraph*, 14 January. Available online: http://www.telegraph.co.uk/culture/theatre/theatre-reviews/10571203/Not-I-Footfalls-Rockaby-by-Samuel-Beckett-Royal-Court-review.html (accessed 29 May 2015).

Stanislavski, C. ([1936] 1965), *An Actor Prepares*, trans. E. Reynolds, New York: Theatre Arts Books.

Stein, G. (1898), 'Cultivated Motor Automatism; A Study of Character in Its Relation to Attention', *Psychological Review*, 5 (3): 295–306.

Strayer, D. L. and W. A. Johnston (2001), 'Driven to Distraction: Dual-Task Studies of Simulated Driving and Conversing on a Cellular Telephone', *Psychological Science*, 12 (6): 462–6.

Sumby, W. H. and I. Pollack (1954), 'Visual Contribution to Speech Intelligibility', *Journal of the Acoustical Society of America*, 26: 212–5.

Summerfield, Q. (1979), 'Use of Visual Information for Phonetic Perception', *Phonetica*, 36: 314–31.

Summerfield, Q. (1987), 'Some Preliminaries to a Comprehensive Account of Audiovisual Speech Perception', in B. Dodd and R. Campbell (eds), *Hearing by Eye: The Psychology of Lip Reading*, 3–52, London: Lawrence Erlbaum.

Taylor, P. (2014), 'Beckett Trilogy: Not I/Footfalls/Rockaby—An Unforgettable Show', *Independent*, 14 January. Available online: https://www.independent.co.uk/arts-entertainment/theatre-dance/reviews/beckett-trilogy-not-ifootfallsrockaby-theatre-review-an-unforgettable-show-9058659.html (accessed 24 April 2019).

Thomas, S. M. and T. R. Jordan (2015), 'Contributions of Oral and Extraoral Facial Movement to Visual and Audiovisual Speech Perception', *Journal of Experimental Psychology: Human Perception and Performance*, 30: 873–88.

Thornes, J. E. (1999), *John Constable's Skies: A Fusion of Art and Science*, Birmingham: University of Birmingham.

Tiippana, K., T. S. Andersen and M. Sams (2004), 'Visual Attention Modulates Audiovisual Speech Perception', *European Journal of Cognitive Psychology*, 16 (3): 457–72.

Tolman, E. C. (1948), 'Cognitive Maps in Rats and Men', *Psychological Review*, 55 (4): 189–208.

Treffner, P. J. and R. Barrett (2004), 'Hands-free Mobile Phone Speech while Driving Degrades Coordination and Control', *Transportation Research Part F: Traffic Psychology and Behaviour*, 7 (4): 229–46.

Uhlmann, A. (2006), *Samuel Beckett and the Philosophical Image*, Cambridge: Cambridge University.
Uhlmann, A. (2008), 'Image and Disposition in Beckett's Late Plays', *Samuel Beckett Today/Aujourd'hui*, 19: 103–12.
Uhlmann, A. (2013), 'Staging Plays', in A. Uhlmann (ed.), *Samuel Beckett in Context*, 173–82, Cambridge: Cambridge University.
Vuilleumier, P. and R. Righart (2011), 'Attention and Automaticity in Processing Facial Expressions', in A. Calder, G. Rhodes, M. H. Johnson and J. W. Haxby (eds), *The Oxford Handbook of Face Perception*, 449–78, Oxford: Oxford University.
Waldenfals, B. (2002), 'Levinas and the Face of the Other', in S. Critchley and R. Bernasconi (eds), *The Cambridge Companion to Levinas*, 63–81, Cambridge: Cambridge University.
Walker, E. (2014), 'Review: Lisa Dwan in Beckett's Not I, Footfalls, Rockaby', *The Cambridge News*, 10 September.
Waller, D., R. Schweitzer, J. R. Brunton and R. M. Knudson (2012), 'A Century of Imagery Research: Reflections on Cheves Perky's Contribution to Our Understanding of Mental Imagery', *The American Journal of Psychology*, 125 (3): 291–305.
Watson, J. B. (1913), 'Psychology as the Behaviorist Views It', *Psychological Review*, 20: 158–77.
Watt, D. (1972), 'Not I Review'. 1972. *Daily News*, 23 November.
Watt-Smith, T. (2014), *On Flinching: Theatricality and Scientific Looking from Darwin to Shell Shock*, Oxford: Oxford University.
Weiss, K. (2001), 'Perceiving Bodies in Beckett's "Play"', *Samuel Beckett Today/Aujourd'hui*, 11: 186–93.
Weller, S. (2006), *Beckett, Literature and the Ethics of Alterity*, Basingstoke: Palgrave Macmillan.
Weller, S. (2008), '"Gnawing to be Naught": Beckett and Pre-Socratic Nihilism', *Samuel Beckett Today/Aujourd'hui*, 20: 321–33.
Whitelaw, B. (1995), *Who He: An Autobiography*, London: Hodder and Stoughton.
Wilkes, J. and S. Scott (2016), 'Poetry and Neuroscience: An Interdisciplinary Conversation', *Configurations*, 24 (3): 331–50.
Wingfield, A. J., E. Peele and M. Grossman (2003), 'Speech Rate and Semantic Complexity as Multiplicative Factors in Speech Comprehension by Young and Old Adults', *Aging Neuropsychology and Cognition*, 10 (4): 310–22.
Winkielman, P., K. C. Berridge and J. L. Wilbarger (2005), 'Unconscious Affective Reactions to Masked Happy Versus Angry Faces Influence Consumption Behavior and Judgments of Value', *Personal and Social Psychology Bulletin* 1: 121–35.
Winnicott, D. W. (1958), *Collected Papers: Through Paediatrics to Psycho-analysis*, London: Tavistock.
Winnicott, D. W. ([1971] 2005), *Playing and Reality*, London: Routledge.
Wolfe, J. M. (1999), 'Inattentional Amnesia: Cognition of Brief Visual Stimuli', in V. Coltheart (ed.), *Fleeting Memories*, 71–94, Cambridge: MIT.

Woodworth, R. S. (1915), 'A Revision of Imageless Thought', *Psychological Review*, 22 (1): 1–27.
Woodworth, R. S. (1927), 'Gestalt Psychology and the Concept of Reaction Stages', *The American Journal of Psychology*, 39 (1): 62–9.
Woodworth, R. S. ([1948] 2013), *Contemporary Schools of Psychology*, 2nd edn, London: Forgotten Books.
Zola, È. (1893), *The Experimental Novel and Other Essays*, trans. B. M. Sherman, New York: Cassell.
Zurbrugg, N. (1988), *Beckett and Proust*, London: Barnes and Noble.

Index

Adams, Henry Foster 51–2
Armstrong, Tim 5, 7–8

Badham, Van 125
Beckett, Samuel – Works
  Act Without Words I 23, 33–5, 37
  All That Fall 116–17, 119–21
  … but the clouds … 131
  'Capital of Ruins, The' 88
  Company 19, 158–61, 165–6, 177, 180
  Dream of Fair to Middling Women 132
  Embers 19
  'End, The' 128, 157
  Endgame 40
  Film 19
  Footfalls 18, 46, 51, 99–105, 107, 113, 116–21, 123–5, 127, 178, 180
  'German' diaries 78
  Ghost Trio 14–19, 131
  Happy Days 18–19, 21, 23, 27–31, 38–40, 42, 63, 80, 172–3, 175
  How It Is 21, 161–6
  Ill Seen Ill Said 19, 159, 174–5, 177–8, 180
  'Long Observation of the Ray' 50
  Molloy 9, 87–8
  Murphy 9, 102, 132, 148
  Nacht und Träume 19, 144–9, 162, 178
  Nohow On 19, 151, 159, 166, 177–8
  Not I 10, 18, 45–6, 50–3, 55, 57–64, 66–7, 69–72, 81, 91, 97, 125, 127, 129, 136, 141, 178, 180–1
  'Philosophy' notes 12, 47, 102
  Play 14, 18, 21, 23, 27, 29–31, 38–42, 51, 58
  'Psychology' notes 12–13, 22–3, 33, 49, 101, 122
  Rough for Theatre II 65–7, 70–1
  Stirrings Still 146
  That Time 18, 46, 51, 73–4, 76, 78–81, 89–98, 125, 127, 178, 180–1
  Watt 9, 89–90, 111–12, 117
  What Where 181
  Worstward Ho 19, 146, 159, 175–8, 180
Bergson, Henri 129, 132, 134, 138–9
Berman, Marshall 124
Billington, Michael 61, 107, 129–30, 141
Bion, Wilfred 13, 68–72
Bleuler, Eugen 153, 155
Broome, Matthew 66–7, 71
Bruner, Jerome 22–4
Bürger, Peter 25–6, 28–31

Campbell, Julie 120
Caruth, Cathy 113–14
Carville, Conor 78
Chabris Christopher 104–8, 112–13, 115, 119
Cohn, Ruby 80
Coleridge, Samuel Taylor 139–40, 143, 149
Conley, Kenny 106, 109–10, 113–15
Connor, Steven 8, 15, 40, 50, 144, 149
Constable, John 4
Cox, Michael 106, 109, 118–9
Crary, Jonathan 45–7, 51–3, 66, 76–7, 81–2, 99, 125

Deleuze, Gilles 83–5, 129–33, 141, 148, 170
Democritus 102–3
Descartes, René 132, 157
Didi-Huberman, Georges 82
Downey, June 5
Driver, Jon 92–3
Dwan, Lisa 57–60, 62–3, 107, 125

Ekman, Paul 74, 81–3, 85–6
Esquirol, Jean-Étienne Dominique 154

Feldman, Matthew 9, 12–13, 23, 33, 49, 67, 74
Freud, Sigmund 13, 48–9, 66, 68, 71, 83, 85–6, 99, 153, 180

Gontarski, Stanley E. 25, 27, 79, 92–4, 118, 172
Greenblatt, Stephen 152, 156
Guattari Felix 83–5

Hebb, Donald 163
Heron Jonathan 66
Hill, Leslie 8
Hochschild, Arlie Russell 86–7
Holt, Robert R. 154–6, 158–9

James, William 5, 11, 73, 128, 132
Johnson, Bryan Stanley 2, 21
Jones, Colin 86
Jones, Ernest 115–16
Joyce, James 7, 98, 140
Jung, Carl 119–20, 122

Kahnemann, Daniel 76
Kaun, Axel 7–8
Keats, John 70, 72
Kennedy, Seán 111
Kim, Rina 121–2
Klein, Melanie 121–2
Knowlson, James 23, 33, 51, 78, 80, 91, 95, 119, 146–7, 172
Köhler, Wolfgang 23, 33–4
Kosslyn, Stephen 138, 141–2, 144, 149, 159, 173–4, 176

Lehr, Dick 109–10, 114–15, 118
Levelt, Willem 55–6, 58
Levinas, Emmanuelle 81, 84–5
Lloyd, David 162–4
Luckhurst, Roger 114–15

McGurk, Harry 61–2
McNaughton, James 111–12
Magee, Patrick 80, 90, 97
Manet, Edouard 76–7, 81
Marslen-Wilson, William 53–5
Maude, Ulrika 8–9, 14, 23, 33, 38, 40, 128, 147, 157, 159, 175
Melynk, David 119–20

Merleau Ponty, Maurice 160–1, 175, 177
Meyer, Steven 6–7
Moorjani, Angela 66, 148
Murphy, Peter J. 25–7

Neisser, Ulrich 103–5, 107
Ngai, Sianne 87–8
Nixon, Mark 78, 111, 156, 172

Pavlov, Ivan 12, 14–15, 17, 33–4
Perky, Cheves 135–6, 138, 141–2, 145–6, 149, 159, 167–71, 175
Perloff, Marjorie 21–2
Piette, Adam 116, 163, 165
Pilling, John 96
Potter, Dennis 111
Proust, Marcel 142–3

Rabinovitz, Rubin 9–11
Rank, Otto 118
Richardson, Alan (literary critic) 143
Richardson, Alan (psychologist) 153, 156
Routledge Companion to Experimental Literature 1–3
Ruskin, John 2
Ryan, Judith 5
Ryle, Gilbert 138, 159, 170–1, 173, 175–6

Salisbury, Laura 8–9, 63, 112, 117
Sartre, John Paul 9, 138, 156–7, 159–60, 169–71, 173, 175, 177,
Schneider, Alan 28, 38–9, 57–8, 79, 93, 96
Schopenhauer, Arthur 46–50, 52–3, 72, 148, 180
Scott, Sophie 182
Scripture, Edward Wheeler 135
Searles, Harold Frederic 83, 85
Shakespeare, William 70, 151–3, 156, 166, 172
Shelley, Percy Bysshe 139, 143
Simons, Daniel 104–6
Skinner, Burrhus Frederic 6–7
Stanislavski, Constantin 87, 90, 180
Stein, Gertrude 5–9, 48
Summerfield, Quentin 61–2
Swift, Jonathan 5

Titchener, Edward   11–12, 136, 157, 169
Tolman, Edward   24, 35–8

Uhlmann, Anthony   8, 129–30, 132, 134, 141, 144, 147, 181
Unseld, Siegfried   41

Van Hulle, Dirk   8, 140, 172

Wagner, Richard   51–3
Waldenfals, Bernard   81, 84
Watson, John Broadus   9, 11–13, 15–16, 34, 137, 163
Watt Smith, Tiffany   86

Weiss, Katherine   30
Weller, Shane   94, 102
Whitelaw, Billie   58–9, 78, 108,
Wilkes, James   182
Winnicott, Donald Woods   68–9, 71, 121–4
Woodworth, Robert Sessions   9, 11–14, 22–4, 31–5, 73, 136–7, 146, 163

Yeats, Jack Butler   88
Yeats, William Butler   172–3

Zola, Émile   3–4, 179

Ingram Content Group UK Ltd.
Milton Keynes UK
UKHW021157040423
419514UK00003B/58